The sociology of power

International Library of Sociology

Founded by Karl Mannheim
Editor: John Rex, University of Warwick

Arbor Scientiae
Arbor Vitae

A catalogue of the books available in the **International Library of Sociology** and other series of Social Science books published by Routledge & Kegan Paul will be found at the end of this volume.

The sociology of power

Roderick Martin
Trinity College, Oxford

Routledge & Kegan Paul
London, Henley and Boston

First published in 1977
by Routledge & Kegan Paul Ltd
39 Store Street,
London WC1E 7DD,
Broadway House,
Newtown Road,
Henley-on-Thames,
Oxon RG9 1EN and
9 Park Street,
Boston, Mass. 02108, USA
Set in Monotype Times New Roman
by Kelly, Selwyn & Co., Melksham, Wilts
and printed in Great Britain by
Unwin Bros., Ltd

ISBN 0 7100 8563 X

Contents

Preface

This book was originally conceived as an introduction to the sociology of politics, in the conventional mid-Atlantic mould. However, although the book retains some introductory features, it is no longer an introductory textbook; it does not attempt a comprehensive survey of the 'literature' of the sub-discipline of political sociology as conventionally defined in English-speaking universities.[1] This change in the character of the book stemmed partly from a desire to avoid overburdening the student market – if not mind – with a repetitive survey of the field, and partly from disquiet with conventional definitions of the subject.[2] The sub-discipline so confidently mapped out by Lipset and others in the early 1960s has disintegrated, with scholars attacking new substantive problems and adopting new theoretical approaches in a way not anticipated fifteen years ago.[3] A new general approach is now necessary, based upon a new conception of the subject. This redefinition should be based upon the analytical concepts of sociological theory not the conventions of craft custom and practice. This book represents such an attempt, reorienting political sociology around the concept of power. It is a study in the sociology of power relations – or, to use Weber's apposite term, domination. I have attempted to examine relations of domination and subordination under different systems of labour exploitation – slavery, feudalism and capitalism.

The basic concepts used in the study are not original, although I hope that the particular manner in which they are combined and applied is. The terms and concepts used are derived mainly from classical sociological theory, especially the writings of Marx and Weber, and, to a lesser degree, from contemporary social exchange theorists, especially R. Emerson and P. M. Blau. Following Marx, fundamental importance is attached to the system of labour exploitation, whilst the repeated emphasis upon the independent significance of actors' goals and expectations is Weberian. Much of the terminology used is adapted from social exchange theory, although used less rigorously than by formal social exchange theorists. Despite the aspirations of its exponents, exchange theory is incomplete in itself, and is more relevant for understanding interpersonal interaction within specific kinds of Western social institutions (like university social science departments in P. M. Blau's famous study *Exchange and Power in Social Life*) than for understanding fundamental universal social processes.[4] An adequate sociology of domination involves locating exchange theory within a more structural, Marxist framework.[5]

The general plan of the book is as follows. In the first two chapters I discuss critically the two major approaches current in contemporary sociological theory, systems theory and social action theory (although I recognize that conflating a number of different theoretical positions into two rival approaches obscures important distinctions). Social action theory is seen as more promising, if less ambitious, than systems theory. These two chapters attempt to locate the study of domination in the main tradition of contemporary sociological theorizing about political behaviour. Chapters 3 and 4 comprise a very general outline of the approach, together with a detailed discussion of problems of definition and measurement: chapter 3 draws heavily upon a paper I published in the *British Journal of Sociology* in 1971, 'The Concept of Power: a Critical Defence', and I am very grateful to the publishers, Messrs Routledge & Kegan Paul, for permission to quote from the paper. In chapters 5 through to 10 I follow the approach outlined in the preceding chapters in examining power relations under slavery, feudalism and capitalism as major systems of labour exploitation. Finally chapter 11 briefly summarizes the basic argument of the study and briefly locates the study within the framework of contemporary Marxism. Following this chapter are the Notes. As this reference section contains full documentation no formal bibliography was thought necessary.

The Sociology of Power is an approach to the study of power relations, not a formal theory of power: it does not comprise a linked set of general propositions to be tested by quantitative research. Such a theory would be premature at this stage, and only possible by ignoring important problems. However, I have drawn extensively upon historical and sociological evidence, and regard the approach as directly relevant to empirical sociological research, not simply an exercise in armchair theorizing. The evidence used here varies in quality and quantity, but this is inevitable in a catholic comparative historical study.

As many writers have commented, power is one of the most important, but also most problematic, concepts used in contemporary sociological theory: hence its interest.[6] I hope the present book will help to stimulate further the revival of interest in the concept which is already under way, and show that a truly political sociology must focus upon the concept of power.[7]

I am very grateful to Mr Alan Fox, of the Department of Social and Administrative Studies, University of Oxford, and Mr David Knights, of the Department of Management Science University of Manchester Institute of Science and Technology, for comments upon an earlier draft of the book. I am also very grateful to Mrs Antonia Cretney, of Trinity College, Oxford, for typing successive drafts of the book quickly and accurately.

1 Systems theory

The theoretical paradigm most frequently used in conventional research in political sociology is that of 'systems theory'.[1] Since its first application to the study of politics in the early 1950s systems theory has aroused enthusiasm amongst many, and exasperation amongst a few. According to some, the systems revolution is now over, and we are all systems theorists now: 'Few social scientists, no matter what their persuasion, question the validity of some type of system concept'; '[the concept of system] is indispensable [for political science]'.[2] Others believe that systems theory is the best way forward for political science, but requires defending against a minority of benighted traditional institutionalists.[3] Yet others believe that conventional systems theory provides a useful language for the storage and recall of data, but does not represent a contribution to knowledge, much less a theoretical breakthrough.[4] For a minority systems theory represents a massive waste of intellectual energy and a serious barrier to the proper understanding of politics: '[the concept of system] is an otiose and confusing [piece of jargon].'[5] In this chapter I want to present a brief outline of some systems theories, as a backcloth against which to present an alternative view, and show why systems theory, as conventionally interpreted, is seriously misleading when used as a model for the sociological analysis of politics.

The general concepts of 'systems thinking', derived from physics in the case of Herbert Spencer and his successors, and from biology in the case of L. J. Henderson and his followers, have been used in economics, anthropology and psychology, as well as in political science and sociology, and have been elaborated most fully, perhaps, in organizational theory.[6] The basic principle of systems theory is

1

simply that society is an interdependent whole, like a motorcar according to the physicists, like an organism according to the biologists, or like a species according to the more sophisticated biologists. Systems survive by exchanging inputs and outputs with their environment. Each system is divided into variable numbers of sub-systems, like the political sub-system, each integrated into the larger whole by a complex network of 'boundary-exchanges'. Each sub-system is itself composed of lower-order sub-systems. The conventional terms of cybernetics-system, environment, response, feedback, negative feedback – form the current array of concepts, although similar metaphors are at least a hundred years old.[7] David Easton has provided a representative summary of systems theory in his *A Framework for Political Analysis*:[8]

> in general, systems analysis . . . takes its departure from the notion of political life as a boundary-maintaining set of interactions imbedded in and surrounded by other social systems to the influence of which it is constantly exposed . . . an open system [like the political system is] one that must cope with the problems generated by its exposure to influences from these environmental systems.

Systems theorists agree on little more than this very general basic principle: the definition of the concept of 'system', the nature of the links between different parts of the system, and the explanation for system change, are all substantial sources of disagreement. As Peter Nettl commented, 'as things stand now the concept of system as such yields no automatic focus of meaning, no immediate signalling of any particular form of analysis or analogy, no diamond sharp tools for understanding and classifying societies or forms of political activity'.[9] Because of this heterogeneity I have summarized four individual systems theorists, each of whom has exercised a considerable influence upon political science and sociology – David Easton, Talcott Parsons, G. A. Almond, and Karl Deutsch – instead of presenting a misleading composite portrait.[10] These four represent three, or perhaps three and a half, different views: Easton and Deutsch have each developed their own individual approaches, whilst Almond draws upon Parsons's sociological theory and modifies it for use in political science.

David Easton was the first political scientist to adopt systems thinking explicitly, and his 1953 book *The Political System* remains one of the most influential applications of systems thinking to the study of politics. For Easton, the concept of political system is merely an analytical convenience, which may or may not be useful; it does not correspond to empirical reality:[11]

2

any aggregate of interactions that we choose to identify may be said to form a system. It is solely a matter of conceptual or theoretical convenience . . . this is the only position that will enable us to avoid more problems than the concept would otherwise create.

The political system is defined as the mechanism for providing for 'the authoritative allocation of values as it is influenced by the distribution and use of power'.[12] 'Authoritative' means 'generally accepted as legitimate'; 'values' are 'scarce goods and resources'; the term power is subsequently dropped from the definition, and is nowhere defined. The political system operates by processing inputs received from the environment, and exporting them as outputs. The inputs are classified as demands (for the allocation of goods and services, for the regulation of behaviour, for participation in the system) and supports (taxes, votes). An excess of demands, leading to the collapse of the system through demand overload, is prevented by cultural proscriptions and the watchfulness of system 'gate-keepers'. Supports are focused upon three aspects of the system: the community as a whole, the regime and specific political authorities. These demands and supports are processed by the system, and emerge as outputs – extractions, rules, allocation of values and symbolic affirmations of collective values.[13]

It is obviously impossible to summarize the sociological theory of Talcott Parsons in a brief paragraph, for his theory is highly elaborate, has been evolving and growing more complex over three decades, and there are marked differences in emphasis between the early and the later writings.[14] However, although his general systems theory is obviously relevant to the study of political institutions, less effort has been made by Parsons himself to apply his theory to politics than to economics.[15] Parsons may be regarded as a 'structural functional' systems theorist (although this characterization, despite being widely used, is only partially accurate). According to structural functional theory a number of 'needs' – or 'requisites' (Levy), or 'prerequisites' (Sutton, Aberle et al.) – must be met if society is to survive.[16] In Parsons's terms, these functional needs are for adaptation, goal attainment, integration and pattern maintenance. Four major sub-systems have developed to satisfy these needs: the economy to satisfy the need for adaptation, i.e. the acquisition of necessary resources from the system's environment, the political system to satisfy the goal attainment need, socialization (through the family and through the education system) to satisfy the need for pattern maintenance, and culture, including religion, to satisfy the need for integration – although each system helps to satisfy all four needs.[17] Each sub-system is further divided into four

3

sub-sub-systems, replicating the G A I L schema at a lower level of generalization. More specifically, the political system provides for the authoritative specification of system goals and, to a lesser extent, facilitates the integration of the system through political socialization and the adaptation of the system through the allocation of values and costs.

Society develops through a complex set of exchanges between each sub-system. Hence, the political system produces a resource, power/authority, which it exchanges for the resource created by the economic system, money: the economic system uses the authorization received from the polity to raise capital – capital is in this sense a political resource – and the political system uses the money to purchase material goods. 'The flow from the polity into the economy is the creation of capital funds through credit; the reverse flow is the control of the *productivity* of the economy.'[18] Figure 1 illustrates in simplified form the major processes of societal exchange.[19]

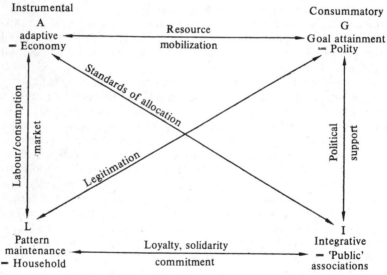

Figure 1 Parsonian Paradigm of Societal Interchanges

The Parsonian framework has been explicitly applied to politics by W. C. Mitchell and, less directly, by G. A. Almond. Almond's work is the more important because he has done more than mechanically apply Parsons's terminology and his writings have been more widely circulated. For Almond the 'systemic' nature of politics is an empirical reality. He defines the political system as:[20]

that system of interactions to be found in all independent societies which performs the functions of integration and adaptation (both internally and *vis-à-vis* other societies) by means of the employment, or threat of employment, of more or less legitimate physical compulsion. The political system is the legitimate, order-maintaining or transforming system in the society.

The parts of the system are interdependent, and possess a definable boundary *vis-à-vis* the rest of the social system. Like Easton, Almond analyses this system as a mechanism receiving inputs, processing them, and exporting them; however, the details are different, and he pays more attention to the internal processes and the outputs of the system than Easton. The functioning of the system can be analysed on three levels: capabilities, conversion processes and system-maintenance and adaptation functions. By capabilities he means the contribution made to the functioning of the larger whole by the political system; its ability to respond to the demands of the citizenry, its ability to extract material and to redistribute resources, and to regulate behaviour. The major conversion processes are the formulation of demands (interest articulation), the combination of demands into strategies for action (interest aggregation), the formulation of authoritative rules (rule-making), the application and enforcement of rules (rule-application), the adjudication of rules in individual cases (rule-adjudication) and the communication of these various activities to the population at large. Finally, the ancillary functions required of any social system, those of adaptation, maintenance and integration, have to be performed; resources have to be obtained from the environment, including personnel, personnel have to be socialized into their roles in the system, and internal disagreements have to be reconciled or moderated.

These are the processes and techniques used by the political system to solve the problems passed to it by the larger social system. The major problems posed for the political system by the social system are, successively, those of state-building, nation-building, participation and distribution. By state-building Almond simply means the drawing of a delimited boundary to the system; by nation-building the development of commitment to that territory; and by distribution the manipulation of pressure from the domestic society for the use of state power to 'redistribute income, wealth, opportunity, and honour'.[21]

The fourth systems theorist considered here, Karl Deutsch, has adopted a cybernetic model, with terminology based explicitly upon Norbert Wiener's[22] classic exposition *Cybernetics*:[23]

5

the viewpoint of cybernetics suggests that all organizations are alike in certain fundamental characteristics and that every organization is held together by communication. Communication is a process different from transportation on the one hand and from power engineering on the other. Transportation transmits physical objects. . . . Power engineering transmits quantities of electric energy. Communication engineering . . . transmits messages that contain quantities of information.

'[*The Nerves of Government*] suggests that it might be possible to look upon Government somewhat less as a problem of power and somewhat more as a problem of communication.'[24] Society comprises a network of channels, along which information, defined as 'patterned relationship between events', flows. Society is 'self-steering', but reacts to the feedback of information from the internal and external environment by providing new resources, or by adapting goals. 'Feedback' is the cybernetic definition of consciousness, according to Deutsch, performing the same function for cybernetic systems theory as equilibrium for functional systems theory – it is the process whereby change occurs. But Deutsch sees four major advantages in using 'feedback' rather than 'equilibrium':[25]

First . . . in feedback processes the goal situation sought is outside, not inside, the goal seeking system. Second, the system itself is not isolated from its environment. . . . Third, the goal may be a changing goal. . . . In the fourth place, a goal may be approached indirectly by a course, or a number of possible courses, around a set of obstacles.

In short, *The Nerves of Government* may be viewed as an extended analogy between advanced forms of engineering, the human nervous system, and society.[26]

One reaction to systems theory is to dismiss it as, at best vacuous and banal, at worst malicious. Max Black in his essay on Parsons reached the former conclusion – that Parsons has simply translated the assumptions of the common man into the jargon of social science: 'I am forced to conclude that [Parsons] . . . has provided us with a web of concepts, whose correspondence with the concepts laymen use for thinking about social relations is barely disguised by a new terminology.'[27] Hugh Stretton reached a more violent conclusion after a detailed examination of the works of Parsons, Dahrendorf and Easton:[28]

[Such theory] neither builds, tests, [n]or applies law. Nor does it serve any useful educational or engineering purpose. Instead, *theory building and eclectic explanation have simply been brought into a relation of mutual service*: they assist each other, and suffice for each other, without serving any reputable purpose whatever. There are not even likely to be the valuable educational effects which arise from, for example, the self-perpetuation of classical studies. Those studies may cultivate accurate, imaginative scholarship, the criticism and appreciation of great works of art, and debate about important moral and social issues. By contrast, the uses of sterile theory prohibit moral or political debate, spurn art and curdle communication, and teach deceptive misapplications of scientific method. Most of the values they insinuate are nasty, some of the facts they allege are untrue. In so far as they claim to be uninterfering general theories of social behaviour, the appropriate tests for them are political criticism of their selections, and systematic searches for detailed historical cases to limit or refute them – but how often are these 'ideological', 'idiographic', and 'pre-scientific' exercises the tests which instructors in sociology encourage? . . . These exercises [in examining general theory] are not unlike the educational uses of Marx's general theory in Communist countries.

Although the prose of systems theorists is tortuous, the style pretentious, the ambitions grandiose, and the normative agnosticism deceptive, such a choleric overall assessment is unjustified. Criticism of systems theories for excessive generality is misplaced, for systems theories are 'pro-theories' rather than theories. 'Much of what is described in text-books as sociological theory consists of general orientations toward substantive materials. . . . The chief function of these orientations is to provide a general context for inquiry; they facilitate the process of arriving at determinate hypotheses.'[29] Pro-theory thus consists of vague general orientations rather than specific hypotheses; it is necessarily abstract and imprecise. However, the concepts used to formulate testable hypotheses can only be interpreted within a general theoretical framework; denial of the need for such a framework involves a conception of theory just as much as the use of systems theory. As Parsons pointed out long ago, 'the element of abstraction is involved in the concept of fact itself. A fact is a theoretically observed aspect, element, or property of a concrete phenomenon.'[30] Failure to adopt an explicit 'pro-theory' results in the unconscious adoption of an inadequate one, or more likely a heterogeneous mixture of pro-theories, resulting in confusion. 'Pro-theory' is thus a necessary

7

preliminary to constructing sociological hypotheses. Evaluating pro-theories involves examining the precision of the terminology to draw out the assumptions involved and to indicate the problems illuminated, or neglected – not denying the value of pro-theories altogether. Pro-theories illuminate, and therefore also cast into shadow, some aspects of political behaviour. Only after this examination is it possible to judge the merits and limitations of systems theory and to assess the need for an alternative 'pro-theory'. In the remainder of this chapter I will attempt a brief and neces- sarily simplified examination of systems theory, focusing upon four major problems: definition; explanatory status; usefulness in explaining social change; and conceptualization of power.[31]

Definitions

Concern with precise definition is not simply pedantry, a debased derivative of linguistic philosophy, but a requirement for the construction of usable sociological theory. Unfortunately, the terminology used by systems theorists is neither clear nor un- ambiguous. This confusion is especially evident in the definitions of the basic concepts of systems theory, system and politics.

The concept of system, in its most general sense, involves simply the view that all the elements in a given area are linked to each other, however indirectly – the 'seamless web' of everyday speech. Hence, Rapoport's definition: 'a system [is] (1) something consisting of a set (finite or infinite) of entities (2) among which a set of relations is specified, so that (3) deductions are possible from some relations to others.' System in this sense is basically a term of convenience, involving no assumptions about *interdependence* (the parts of the system may be connected by mutual antagonism), no assumptions about consensus upon norms and values, and no assumptions about the functions of specific sub-systems for the system as a whole. It is in this sense that both Marx and Parsons may be bracketed together as systems theorists: both view society as a whole.[32] But this weak use of the term is accurate rather than helpful – the differences between Marx and Parsons are far more significant than the similarities, and statements based upon this very extended definition of system are so general as to be trivial.[33]

The systems theorists considered here use the concept of system in a stronger sense, involving, at the minimum, a distinction between system and environment, with specifiable transactions across systems boundaries. This represents the lowest common denominator between the definitions of Easton, Parsons, Almond and Deutsch. Almond and Powell provide a characteristic and succinct statement: 'what do we mean by system? A system implies the interdependence of parts and a boundary between it and its environment.'[34] Parsons has been rather reticent about defining the concept of system, as Gouldner has pointed out,[35] but he does provide a rare definition in the collective volume *Towards a General Theory of Action*: 'The word *system* is used in the sense that determinate relations of interdependence exist within the complex of empirical phenomena. The antithesis of the concept of system is random variability. However, no implication of rigidity is intended.'[36] Although the term 'boundary' is not used, the definition does not make sense without regarding the term as implicit; and W. C. Mitchell has stated categorically: '"System" is therefore definable in terms of certain boundaries that distinguish it from other systems or from its environment.'[37]

Even this parsimonious statement of basic assumptions is problematic, for both the related terms of 'boundary' and 'interdependence' are elusive. The obvious way to specify system boundaries is by measuring the relative frequency of interaction between units: at a specified point the frequency of interaction reaches the level at which system–environment interactions become qualitatively transformed into intrasystem interactions. But the frequency of interaction between units of the 'political system' and their non-political environment may be greater than interaction between intrasystem units. For example, British trade union sponsored MPs may interact more frequently with their fellow union members than with Conservative Ministers, but it would not be sensible to include trade unions within the political system and exclude the executive. More sophisticated measures of interaction, in terms of the significance of interaction for the actor, may be equally misleading, for political actors may be more dependent upon economic actors than upon other politicians. (Or, to adopt Finer's analogy, the human organism is more dependent upon oxygen than upon the pineal gland.)[38] In short, the ability to delineate system 'boundaries' is a prerequisite for any form of systems analysis: without clearly defined boundaries fundamental concepts like boundary-exchanges are meaningless. But systems theorists have not been able to do this.[39]

Definition of the term 'politics' and related concepts has been a concern of writers on political life at least since Plato, and probably earlier: this 'classical' literature is beyond the scope of this study.[40] It is thus not surprising that systems theorists should have failed to provide a definition of politics congruent with their approach yet encompassing the traditional interests of students of politics. Easton, as we have seen, initially defined the political system as the mechanism for 'the authoritative allocation of values as it is influenced by the distribution and use of power', but subsequently deleted the reference to power. The amended definition reads: 'a *political* system can be designated as those interactions through which values are authoritatively allocated for a society.'[41] This corresponds closely with the definition used by Almond (see above, p. 5) and in substance, although not in terminology, with those of Deutsch and (usually) Parsons. According to Deutsch, 'from [my] perspective ... the essence of politics [is] the dependable coordination of human efforts and expectations for the attainment of the goals of the society'.[42] Parsons's conception of politics appears to have shifted, from seeing politics as a specific type of social process, not confined to a specific set of institutions, to seeing politics as tied to a specific set of roles, namely those required for attempts to satisfy society's need for 'goal-attainment', the specification of collective goals.[43]

Although the terms used by different theorists differ, there is a common theme running through these definitions: authority and legitimacy. Resources are allocated 'authoritatively', force is used 'legitimately'. But these terms are both too exclusive, and too inclusive. Too exclusive, in that the allocation of values is not necessarily 'authoritative'; large sections of the population may question repeatedly the distribution of values in society. The military regime which came to power following the overthrow of President Allende in Chile in 1973 was political, in that it allocated values, but hardly authoritative, in that it overthrew by force a popularly elected government. Yet it would be foolish to describe the Chilean military junta as 'non-political'. Political regimes are not authoritative or legitimate by definition. The definition is too inclusive, in that institutions which allocate values authoritatively among specific sections of the population, for example religious organizations with regard to the priesthood, should not be regarded primarily as part of the political system (and are not so regarded by systems theorists in practice).

In short, the terminology developed by systems theorists is confusing and inadequate. An initial source of difficulty is the frequent use of different but overlapping concepts and terminology, as the brief summary of major theorists indicated. More importantly, the basic definitions are inadequate, and do not provide criteria for distinguishing between systems and non-systems, or between politics and non-politics. However, linguistic confusion would not, in itself, be a decisive reason for rejecting systems theory: as Alice knew, words may mean what one wishes them to mean, and even if terms vary systematically with the context the dangers of confusion can be avoided. Before dismissing systems theory as an 'otiose and confusing' piece of obscurantist academic jargon it is necessary to look more closely at the explanatory status of the theory, and its usefulness in examining relevant substantive problems.

Explanatory status

In its most general form systems theory is a form of explanation in terms of consequences, actions being explained by their results for the larger system. This characteristic is common to all varieties of systems theories, but is especially evident in functionalist theories. As Stinchcombe has commented:[44]

> Functional theories explain phenomena by their consequences. They are very generally useful because there are many chains of reverse causation which select patterns of behaviour by their consequences . . . it is always a good bet, in trying to explain a social phenomenon, to look at its consequences.

The input-conversion-output model of Easton can be interpreted in the same way. Explanation consists in showing the role played by the part in the functioning of the whole, not in showing the antecedent conditions for the development of the part. For example, Parliamentary procedure is explained by showing how it regulates discussion, facilitates legislative scheduling, reduces emotional tension by imposing a surface patina of formality, and fits into the whole array of representative institutions, not by tracing its evolution from medieval precedent. A similar explanatory strategy is followed by cybernetic theorists when explaining social change through reaction to the feedback of information.

This explanatory strategy is unacceptable to conventional philosophers of social science, for it denies a basic principle of causal explanation, that causes must precede effects. The first tenet of causal explanation, according to this view, is that A must precede B if A is to be regarded as causing B. Hence there are two assumptions involved in Popper's classic discussion of causal explanation – universalizability, and anteriority:[45]

> [there are] two different kinds of statement which together yield a complete explanation: (1) universal statements with the character of universal laws; and (2) specific statements pertaining to the special case in question, called the 'initial conditions'.

Systems theory attempts to fulfil the first condition, but rejects the second. However, this rejection of the necessity of anteriority does not involve a complete repudiation of causal explanation, for there are several types of 'reverse causation': 'biological evolution; social evolution; individual and collective planning to achieve

11

consequences; satisfaction to the actor from the consequences, with consequent operative conditioning; satisfaction to other, who rewards the actor; and satisfaction to others combined with social selection in a market system.'[46] Each of these processes involves selecting one kind of behaviour rather than another according to its consequences, consciously or unconsciously. Hence it is possible to reconcile systems-type explanations with the requirement that the explanans should precede the explanandum in causal explanations.

Functional systems theories are unsatisfactory for a different reason: the impossibility of linking specific functions to specific institutions. It is impossible to specify precisely the link between (alleged) universal functions and specific social structures. Hence, Parsons sees all the four major institutional areas (polity, economy, latency, integration) helping to fulfil all four major functions, although of course each is concerned primarily with one.[47] Whatever causal value the theory may ever have possessed is undermined by the explicit, yet unavoidable, recognition of 'functional alternatives' and 'dysfunctions'.[48] There are a number of alternative ways in which a given need may be satisfied. For example, the need for goal-attainment mechanisms may lead to the development of a specific set of political institutions, as in modern industrial societies, or such needs may be met more diffusely by institutions whose primary functions are quite different, as among the Bantu Kikuyu of the Kenya Highlands or the Nilo-Hamitic Masai.[49] Functionalist theory does not provide any means for specifying which form of structure is likely to develop, much less which specific institution will develop.

The concept of 'dysfunctions' also raises as many problems as it solves: 'Dysfunctions [are] those observed consequences which lessen the adaptation or adjustment of the system.' 'The concept of dysfunction . . . implies the concept of strain, stress, and tension on the structural level.'[50] However, if institutions persist because of their contribution to the functioning of the system it is difficult to see why systems continue to 'tolerate' institutions which provide strains. It is assumed that such dysfunctions are temporary and that the system will produce adaptive mechanisms to reduce the strain, the grit will be removed from the engine. But this assumption is less plausible than the alternative assumption, that dysfunctions at one level are functions at another – in other words that there is no system, only a number of imperfectly integrated 'sub-systems' in tension with each other.

Despite the difficulties involved in linking specific institutions with specific functions, and the consequent impossibility of explaining the development of specific institutions by the need for the performance of specific functions, functionalism is not totally useless as an explanatory theory. For it is illuminating to examine specific institutions in terms of their manifest and latent functions for the operation of the larger system of which they form a part. Merton's classic discussion of the political machine, where its manifest function is the provision of rewards in exchange for votes and its latent function the absorption of immigrant groups into the American political system, illuminates the political process in the United States in the early twentieth century (although it does not explain why the political machine rather than some other institution emerged to facilitate the process of absorption).[51] But the role of functionalism, and systems theory in general, is more limited than its more enthusiastic proponents suggested: it cannot explain the persistence – much less the origin – of social institutions (or indeed any specific social institution). For explanations must involve adequate causal propositions.

Social change

One aspect of the treatment of social change by systems theorists is non-controversial: the treatment of change originating in the system's environment. The system adapts to meet external challenges, as in Arnold Toynbee's theory of challenge and response in history. Geographical, military and technological changes thus produce accommodating adjustments in the social system. Hence the invention of the stirrup in the early Middle Ages transformed the technology of war, established a new balance of power within society, and the system of land-tenure adjusted to meet the new situation.[52] In functionalist terms, society moved from one state of homeostatic equilibrium to another. Expressed more formally, the principle of homeostasis indicates that, where a given equilibrium is disturbed, countervailing forces will be set up seeking to re-establish that equilibrium. This mechanism operates whether one is talking of social systems, or merely small groups, whether one regards the links between different elements in the situation as communications networks or whatever.[53] This homeostatic model of society can also provide a suitable framework for the explanation of other types of change: purposive and evolutionary (or 'unconsciously purposive'). However, the starting-point for all such explanations is external to the system: the system is responding to external stimuli.

Systems theorists have been less successful in explaining social changes originating *within* social systems. W. J. Buckley commented in his critique of Parsonian functionalism:[54]

The Parsonian model has difficulty in dealing with social

13

change, since the latter tends to be seen . . . as residual – something that happens to the system when the relationships and mechanisms dealt with by the model break down. This often seems to imply that the sources of change are always external to the system, though the model is explicitly declared to allow endogenous change.

How far is this assessment valid?

The starting-point for the Parsonian analysis of social change is the state of equilibrium normally obtaining between social structures, their functions and the environment:[55]

> The concept of equilibrium is a fundamental reference point for analysing the processes by which a system either comes to terms with the exigencies imposed by a *changing* environment, without essential change in its own structure, or fails to come to terms and undergoes other processes, such as structural change, dissolution as a boundary maintaining system (analogous to biological death for the organism), or the consolidation of some impairment leading to the establishment of secondary structures of a pathological character.

Pressure for social-system change may originate within the environment, the organic, psychological or cultural systems, or within the social system itself, in the disturbance of the balance of exchanges between the economic, political, pattern-maintenance and integration sub-systems. Examples of the former, i.e. changes originating outside the social structure, include genetic changes, charismatic personalities, changes in population density, and changes in value patterns; examples of the latter include maternal overprotectiveness and religious fundamentalism. Such external changes or internal strains are contained by 'lower order mechanisms of control' – deviants are destroyed, isolated or accommodated by minor changes in the sub-system. However, pressures are occasionally strong enough to produce changes *of* the system, not merely *in* the system: such changes depend upon the size and incidence of the disturbance, the proportion of systemic units at the relevant levels effected, and the effectiveness of the mechanisms of control. If the change is to be permanent, during the transition period a repertoire of relevant, constructive role models must be in existence, together with mechanisms for the selective rewarding of 'required' role performances. The major processes of change analysed in terms of this scheme are cultural diffusion, for example the transmission of Puritan ideals from England to America during the seventeenth century, structural differentiation, for example the separation of kinship from occupational roles during the process of industrialization, and charismatic

14

invention, as in the influence of St Paul upon the development of Christianity.[56]

The Parsonian approach to the analysis of social change has been expanded by Chalmers Johnson, in his book *Revolutionary Change*.[57] According to Johnson, 'the key to both the study and the conceptualization of revolutionary violence lies in social systems analysis.'[58] There are four functions which must be performed if a society is to survive – socialization, adaptation, integration and goal-attainment – and the division of labour evolves to satisfy them. The precise form taken by the division of labour depends upon the internal and external environments of the system. An integrated value system emerges in response to the need for predictability in role-performance. The relation between the value system and the environment is normally one of homeostatic equilibrium, but disturbances can occur to create disequilibrium. Disequilibrium occurs when exogenous changes (e.g. wars, 'external reference groups'), or endogenous changes (e.g. new technologies), are not synchronized with changes in the value system. For example, the American value system did not change to accommodate the new position of the Southern Negro, whose position had been radically altered by the Second World War, the transformation of the Southern economy by industrialization and the rise of the Afro-Asian states. Disequilibrium leads to the need to use increased force to maintain stability. Extended use of force leads to 'power deflation' – the direct analogue of monetary deflation – and a revolutionary situation. Whether the revolutionary situation leads to revolution or not depends upon the initiative of the oppressed and the reactions of the élite – the 'accidents' of history.

The mechanistic limitations of functionalist attempts to explain social change are clear in Johnson's work. Attempts to restore the *status quo ante* by the use of force are seen to be the automatic response of 'the system' to disruptive environmental changes. But, equally, some 'sub-systems' of the 'system' may attempt to take advantage of external changes, and attempt to extend the disequilibrium (regardless of the attempt to apply force to maintain it): the system contains centrifugal, as well as centripetal, 'components' (e.g. disadvantaged groups). Moreover, it is difficult to explain in functionalist terms why a given value system should ever move out of phase with the environment if the adjustment process is automatic, unless additional assumptions about differential investments in the system are introduced into the model. How does the grit get into the fly-wheel in the first place? In brief, the concept of the disequilibriated social system is not an explanation for revolutionary situations – merely a new terminology for them.

Buckley's criticism of Parsons for failing to provide an adequate account of endogenous change is justified. Although Parsons includes a category of endogenous change, it is largely empty. The paradigm source of such change seems to be imperfect socialization, the failure to internalize appropriate role models – as in the inadequate formation of the super-ego due to maternal overindulgence. The concepts are those of psychology, of deviance and social pathology, not of sociology. (Indeed, in a rare statement of intellectual indebtedness, Parsons explicitly acknowledges his debt to Freud, especially in his discussion of social change.)[59] Moreover, the basic type of *social* change discussed, structural differentiation, is a form of evolutionary change: the social system is selecting the most appropriate means for solving problems posed by the environment. Increased population density, changes in cultural values, improvements in technology, lead to increases in productivity, which ultimately lead to structural differentiation. This form of evolutionary theory contains a number of difficulties in its own terms. How does the process of natural selection operate? How can the point of equilibrium be identified? What constitutes a healthy system? What are the limits of distortion, based upon individual and group interests, possible before the system collapses? But more important is the wide range of social behaviour which it is impossible to explain in terms of such system concepts: the dialectical process of change resulting from conflict between the forces of production and the relations of production; the conflict over the distribution of scarce resources, legitimated in terms of discrepant value systems. The whole process of dialectical social change discussed by Marx is ignored.

Non-functionalist systems theories have provided more satisfactory explanations for social change. Hence Karl Deutsch has replaced the concept of equilibrium by that of feedback: 'by feedback . . . is meant a communications network that produces action in response to an input of information, and includes the results of its own action in the new information by which it modifies its subsequent behaviour.'[60] There are three different kinds of feedback mechanisms: '"goal seeking", the feed-back of new external data into a net whose operating channels remain unchanged'; '"learning", the feed-back of external data for the changing of these operating channels themselves'; and '"consciousness", the feed-back and simultaneous scanning of highly selected internal data.'[61] Easton has adopted a similar strategy, replacing the concept of equilibrium with that of feedback, the political system's means for coping with the stresses created by its attempts to deal with the demands of its supporters:[62]

It is the fact that there can be such a continuous flow of effects and information between system and environment . . .

16

that ultimately accounts for the capacity of a political system to persist in a world even of violently fluctuating changes. Without feed-back and the capacity to respond to it, no system could survive for long, except by accident.

In short, political systems change, not because of an automatic process of homeostatic equilibrium, but because the feedback flow has provided information about the counterproductive effects of outputs on the system's environment. Unfortunately, the theory presents a new terminology for describing what happens, rather than an explanation: the cybernetic model remains a highly elaborate analogy rather than an explanation for what happens in the social world. Moreover, although the mechanistic assumptions of functionalist theory have been modified, the model remains basically one of system responding to environment: modifications occur because of information about the impact of outputs upon the environment. Easton himself is conscious of the dangers involved in assuming an automatic process of adjustment to environmental pressures:[63]

> For any social system, including the political, adaptation represents more than simple adjustments to the events in its life. It is made up of efforts, limited only by the variety of human skills, resources, and ingenuity, to control, modify, or fundamentally change either the environment or the system itself, or both together.

Innovation involves a continuous process of trial and error: 'Channelling mechanisms such as parliaments, interest groups, parties, or responsive administrative organizations did not just emerge as ways of absorbing, communicating and processing demands. They were social mechanisms, gradually worried through, to deal with specific sources of tension.'[64] Nevertheless, despite this relative caution, the assumption is that, in the end, the system will reach some *modus vivendi* with its environment, either by changing the environment or by changing itself. The source of change remains the environment, and the organism's attempt to cope with the environment: there is no recognition of the possibility of the system being at odds with itself and thus changing according to its own internal dynamic. Nor is there any suggestion that different groups within the system might have different views on the appropriate mode of response to environmental change, including the possibility that the system itself might be dispensable.

Conceptualization of power

Systems theorists have either minimized the significance of the

17

concept of power for the sociology of politics, or have redefined it to make it more compatible with their overall theory, or both. Deutsch has adopted a (more or less) conventional definition of power – 'by power we mean the ability of an individual or an organization to impose extrapolations or projections of their inner structure upon their environment'[65] – but denied that power relationships are central to politics. 'Power is thus neither the centre nor the essence of politics. It is one of the currencies of politics, one of the important mechanisms of acceleration or of damage control where influence, habit, or voluntary coordination may have failed, or where these may have failed to serve adequately the function of goal attainment.'[66] Politics is about steering, not about power. Easton has similarly demoted consideration of power relationships, concentrating instead upon authority. The initial inclusion of power in the original definition of politics in *The Political System* has been dropped, and he has subsequently implied that power is an inadequate basis for the analysis of politics by citing, with apparent approval, March's pessimistic essay 'The Power of Power'.[67] The overall theoretical aim of Easton's systems theory is to shift attention away from the allocation questions which have been asked, and answered, in power terms, and towards systemic questions at the most general level.[68]

Functional systems theorists, especially Parsons, have redefined power to accord closer with their overall theoretical schema:[69]

> Power then is generalized capacity to secure the performance of
> binding obligations by units in a system of collective
> organization when the obligations are legitimized with
> reference to their bearing on collective goals and where in
> case of recalcitrance there is a presumption of enforcement by
> negative situational sanctions whatever the actual agency of
> enforcement.

The key phrase (resonant of Almond and Powell's definition of politics as 'the legitimate order maintaining or transforming system in the society') is 'legitimized with reference to their bearing on collective goals': it is collective and not individual goals which are important. This definition is unsatisfactory even when considered in its own unconventional terms, for it rests upon an unsatisfactory analogy between power and money.[70] But power, unlike money, is not a circulating medium: it has only limited liquidity.[71] The power of A over B rarely gives A control over C, although money may be used to obtain resources from B, C, D and E. Similarly, the ability of A to secure compliance from B in one respect may not be equalled by his power to obtain compliance in another. Power depends upon specific relationships, and specific actions. The problem of limited liquidity remains whether power is defined in legitimated terms or not. If power is defined in terms of legitimacy, as by Parsons, its liquidity is limited by the norms and values of society; if power is defined simply in exchange terms, the liquidity of power will be limited by the balance of dependences between ego and alter. In short, power is a specific and not a generalized capacity. Power relations are more comparable to barter than to open-market relations.

But the deficiencies of the Parsonian definition in its own terms are less important than its very limited scope and exclusion of important problems. 'Classical' definitions of power, for example by Weber, have defined power in terms of the ability of A to force B to perform actions which B would not otherwise do.[72] The subject-matter of politics is the use of individual and collective resources to achieve individual and collective ends, if necessary in conflict with other individuals and groups. This range of problems is not encompassed within the Parsonian conception of politics: politics, and power, are seen in unitary, systemic terms, not in terms of conflict and cooperation. As Anthony Giddens has pointed out:[73]

> what slips away out of sight almost completely in the Parsonian analysis is the very fact that power . . . is always exercised *over* someone! By treating power as necessarily (by definition) legitimate, and thus *starting* from the assumption of consensus of some kind between power holders and those subordinate to them, Parsons virtually ignores, quite consciously and deliberately, the necessarily hierarchical character of power, and the divisions of interest which are frequently consequent upon it.

Systems theorists, whether functionalist or not, have thus failed to provide a theoretically satisfactory framework for the analysis of power relations.

Conclusion

Systems theorists have performed an important role in the development of the study of politics since 1950. They have focused attention upon social processes instead of formally defined institutions – upon inputs, conversion processes and outputs, or interest articulation, interest aggregation, rule-making, rule-application, and rule-adjudication – and in doing so have provided a framework for analysing the relation between political and other institutions. This has involved analysing the latent as well as the manifest functions of political processes. By focusing upon functions and processes, rather than institutions, systems theories promise to provide an intellectually defensible basis for comparative politics, revealing the similarities in processes to be discerned beneath differences in structure. At best, systems theory could provide a set of general propositions about political behaviour and ultimately a means of integrating the social and natural sciences: 'the perspectives of a systems analysis serve to link all of the sciences, natural and social.'[74] At worst, systems theories provide a checklist of things to be looked for in examining the politics of different countries.

But there are a number of unresolved problems with systems theories. Least significant, except symbolically, is the apparently non-cumulative character of work in the systems tradition. Easton, Parsons, Almond and Deutsch have each constructed alternative theoretical frameworks, borrowing only from each other when the borrowings could be incorporated within their own existing framework. Systems theorists seem more like a fragmented extended family, sharing common ancestors, belonging to the same blood-brotherhood, but with unequal contact between members and only rare family gatherings, than the conventional picture of the scientific community, where the free flow of ideas makes for cumulative scientific progress. More important are the problems upon which I have focused in this chapter: the unsatisfactory definitions of basic terms, like 'system', the limited explanatory value of teleological theories, the limited range of types of social change explicable within systems terms, and the eccentric conceptualization of power. Such deficiencies reflect, and compound, the fundamentally misleading assumptions made by systems theorists about the character of social life.

Use of terms like 'system' and 'organism' raises the question of the relation between society and the individual. One danger is that of reifying society – attributing to the social system an external, quasi-objective reality which the social system does not possess. Terminology like 'systems responding to environmental pressure', 'organisms developing', 'systemic adaptation', can easily be interpreted in real rather than metaphorical terms. Social systems, and societies, do not react: individuals do. The term 'system' in social science is an abstract collective noun, referring to a number of related processes, not a term for an organism; the term 'society' refers to a specific category of processes. As Marx pointed out long ago, 'It is above all necessary to avoid postulating "society" once again as an abstraction confronting the individual. The individual *is* the *social being*.'[75]

In its crudest form this criticism of systems theory is misleading: systems theorists do not contrast society and the individual in a simple way. According to functionalist theory 'system needs' lead to the development of social institutions, i.e. connected structures of

20

roles, and influence individual behaviour through the pattern of expectations associated with specific roles: roles are of course occupied by individuals, socialized into fulfilling the pattern of rights and obligations associated with a specific role. Individual behaviour is thus interpreted through the perspective of role theory.[76] Role theory is used, with varying degrees of explicitness, by other forms of systems theory. However, this more sophisticated view of the relation between society and the individual is still misleading, for it involves, to use Dennis Wrong's term, 'an over-socialized' concept of man,[77] and ignores four basic features of social life: the conflict of expectations of a given role held by different significant others, the conflicts between the expectations associated with different roles in the individual's role set, and the unpredictability of modes of resolving them, 'deficiencies' in socialization which may result in incomplete internalization of expectations, and the more or less idiosyncratic interpretations individuals bring to role-playing.[78] In short, role theory does not provide a satisfactory approach to the analysis of the relationship between the individual and society.

Systems theories have thus proved a misleading approach to the study of politics. They have stimulated interest in theoretically relevant, rather than simply historical questions, and helped to broaden the concerns of political science by focusing upon the connection between political institutions and their social environment, and by looking at the social system as a whole. But they have not achieved the ends of their authors, the formulation of an empirical explanatory theory of politics, and can never do so. For systems theories say little about human social attitudes and behaviour – and politics without either is a very peculiar subject. An occasionally illuminating metaphor has been transformed into an elaborate theoretical model, without success. A quite different – in some ways more traditional, in other ways more radical – approach is required to the investigation of power relations.

2 Social action theory

The social action approach differs radically from the systems approach in origin, assumptions and tenets. Whereas systems theories have developed from physics, biology and cybernetics, social action theory has developed from history and psychology. Whereas systems theories begin with the assumption that society comprises a more or less interdependent whole, social institutions developing to fulfil the functions necessary to ensure the survival of society, social action theorists see social institutions as the sometimes intended and sometimes unintended result of attempts by individuals to achieve individual and group goals. Whereas systems theorists analyse society in terms of structures, functions, roles and processes, social action theorists analyse society in terms of actors, goals, situations, norms and meanings. Whereas systems theories are concerned with the function of institutions for the persistence of systems, social action theories are concerned with the meanings of action for actors – one with the consequences of behaviour, the other with the reasons for behaviour.

In this chapter I want to examine the basic assumptions and tenets of social action theory, and some of the major problems involved, as an indication of the general orientation towards the sociology of power adopted in the remaining chapters. This examination of social action theory will be highly selective, dealing only with 'mainstream' theorists, especially Weber, Parsons and, to a lesser extent, John Rex, and excluding a number of distinctive 'subgroups' within the tradition, especially symbolic interactionism and ethnomethodology.[1] This exclusion is necessary partly because of the lack of space, and partly because these more 'radical' forms of social action theory have shown relatively little theoretical interest in macro-socio-political questions,[2] concentrating instead upon increasingly detailed analyses of the meanings and mechanisms of everyday interaction.[3]

Systems theorists hope, ultimately, to integrate the natural and social sciences into a single intellectual unity, systems theory. Writers within the social action tradition deny that this is possible, or desirable: human behaviour is not comparable with the behaviour of physical objects, or even non-human primates. 'In the social sciences we are concerned with mental phenomena, the empathic "understanding" of which is naturally a task of a specifically different type from those which the schemes of the exact natural sciences in general can or seek to solve.'[4] Human behaviour requires understanding as well as explanation, appreciation of the actor's point of view, not simply observation of his activity. Sociology is thus the 'science concerning itself with the interpretative understanding of social action and thereby with a causal explanation of its course and consequences'.[5] Sociology thus has a dualistic nature: 'it is both an interpretative and empirical discipline.'[6]

Stated crudely and abstractly, social action theorists assume that actors, with specific needs and goals, will attempt to use available resources to satisfy them, within 'constraints' set by the environment, widely defined to include cultural norms and values and the activities of other goal-seeking actors. These needs and goals are themselves derived from the cultural, social, psychological and biological systems. Norms and values are the expression of often tacit conventions regarding appropriate attitudes and behaviour. If sociology is conceived in these terms, a number of important issues relevant to the sociology of power emerge: what determines the needs and goals of different actors? What determines the distribution of resources? What determines the content of the norms and values regarding appropriate behaviour? However, before investigating some of these issues in the context of different systems of labour exploitation it is necessary to examine briefly a limited number of difficult general theoretical problems: the definition of social action; the appropriate concepts for analysis; the postulate of 'rationality'; and the conceptualization of constraints.

Definition of social action

'We shall speak of "action" insofar as the acting individual attaches a subjective meaning to his behaviour – be it overt or covert, omission or acquiescence. Action is "social" insofar as its subjective meaning takes account of the behaviour of others and is thereby oriented in its course.'[7] Weber's definition of social action in these terms, at the beginning of his monumental *Economy and Society*, is central to the social action approach. There are three different elements involved. First, action is clearly distinguished from behaviour, which may or may not be 'subjectively meaningful': tripping over a paving-stone when walking home alone on a dark night is behaviour, but not action. Second, the meaningful action must be social, i.e. involve others (or symbols representing others), not solipsistic. Gathering blackberries to eat by oneself is action, but not social action. Finally, the phrase 'thereby oriented in its course' is significant, for it introduces the essential elements of intention and purpose. Action may involve others without being purposive, as in random encounters on the street-corner.[8]

Both Parsons and Rex accept this definition of social action. The passage quoted here was endorsed by Parsons in his first major work, *The Structure of Social Action*: 'the concept of action [as defined here by Weber] is substantially the concept dealt with all through this study.'[9] Later in the same work Parsons elaborates his own view of the 'action frame of reference' in the following terms:[10]

First, there is the minimum differentiation of structural elements, end, means, conditions and norms. It is impossible to have a meaningful description of an act without specifying all four. . . . Second, there is implied in the relations of these elements a normative orientation of action, a teleological character. . . . As process, action is, in fact, the process of alteration of the conditional elements in the direction of conformity with norms. Elimination of the normative aspect altogether eliminates the concept of action itself and leads to the radical positivistic position. Elimination of conditions . . . equally eliminates action and results in idealistic emanationism. Thus conditions may be conceived at one pole, ends and normative rules at the other, means and effort as the connecting links between them.

Third, there is inherently a temporal reference. . . . The concept end always implies a future reference, to an anticipated state of affairs, but which will not necessarily exist without intervention by the actor. The end must in the mind of the actor be contemporaneous with the situation and precede 'the employment of means'. . . . Finally, the scheme is inherently subjective. . . . This is most clearly indicated by the fact that the normative elements can be conceived of as 'existing' only in the mind of the actor. They can become accessible to an observer in any other form only through realization, which precludes any analysis of their causal relation to action.

Explanation of social action thus involves examining the actor's goals, the resources available to achieve them, the situation within which the actor is acting, and the means chosen to achieve the desired end-state. Understanding both subjective 'feeling-states' and objective situations is thus required. John Rex also quotes Weber's definition of social action with approval, but does not elaborate upon it.[11]

Such definitions of social action explicitly assume that goals can be separated from means; goals precede the application of means, logically and temporally. Goals are, as it were, in the head, whilst means are resources available in the external world for use in achieving the desired 'end-state'. This use of the concept of 'goal-seeking' (or 'motivation' in the later work of Parsons and in John Rex's *Key Problems*) is justifiable as a more or less arbitrary break in the chain of causation, but questionable as a 'final category'.[12] Goals are conditioned by the means available, past, present and likely future. At the most general level, knowledge of the external world and of the cause–effect chains which operate within it is a necessary condition for the formulation of any goals; goals are not, in this sense, a final category. More specifically, knowledge of the means available, and assessment of the likely chances of success in achieving specific goals, feeds back upon the formulation of goals: they may be redefined in the light of the means available to achieve them.[13] For example, where the economic structure of a specific community provides only limited job opportunities, occupational aspirations are likely to be limited to the kind of jobs likely to be available.[14] Such defeatism or realistic accommodation (depending upon one's point of view) helps to maintain personal stability in an often hostile environment. Moreover, the radical distinction made between 'subjective' goals and 'objective' means ignores the contingent character of means: resources are themselves partially dependent upon the actor's definition of the situation.

The distinction between goals and means also involves more or less arbitrary assumptions about the relevant time-span. Actions may be regarded as means according to one timetable and goals according to another. Distributing leaflets is a means towards the end of increasing electoral support, which is a means towards the end of winning an election, which is a means towards the end of implementing specific policies, which is a means towards achieving the goal of social justice. There is thus the possibility of infinite regress: in the last analysis there is only one goal – salvation, or survival.

Finally, there is a tendency for means to become goals in themselves, through the process of the 'displacement of goals'. This tendency may, in a weak form, be a universal trait of human nature, an attempt to 'hang on' to the certainties of the easily comprehended present instead of attempting to anticipate the needs of an uncertain

25

and sometimes distant future, or may be the product of specific social situations.[15] Merton viewed the process as specifically characteristic of bureaucratic life:[16]

> Adherence to the rules, originally conceived as a means, becomes transformed into an end-in-itself; there occurs the familiar process of *displacement of goals* whereby 'an instrumental value becomes a terminal value'. Discipline, readily interpreted as conformance with regulations, whatever the situation, is seen not as a measure designed for specifiç purposes but becomes an immediate value in the life-organization of the bureaucrat. . . . This may be exaggerated to the point where primary concern with conformity to the rules interferes with the achievement of the purposes of the organization.

Displacement of goals, whether the result of psychological traits or social constraints, makes the application of an ends/means dichotomy dubious.

The distinction between goals and means is thus difficult to draw. Goals are a problematic 'final category', for they are themselves influenced by the means available; goals at one level are means at another; and the performance of actions as means to an end can, through habituation, become an end in itself. Nevertheless, discussion of goals or motivation is necessary for social action theory, for the alternative, viewing action as a more or less automatic response to external stimuli (or what Parsons termed 'biologism'), involves a repudiation of the basic aim of social action theory – the construction of a social theory which recognizes the distinctively human character of social action. For social action theorists the actor's relationship to the environment is active, not passive; and the direction of the activity varies according to the diverse goals of social actors. Passivity is rejected on historical and social as well as on moral grounds.

Ideal-types

Weber's first academic interest was history, rather than sociology, with understanding specific social situations, not with formulating general laws: '[for Weber] the formulation of general explanatory principles is not so much an end in itself as a means which may be used to facilitate the analysis of the particular phenomena to be explained.'[17] However, although Weber never repudiated this pre-occupation with understanding specific events, his attention shifted away from detailed historical studies towards general comparative questions, especially the reasons for the distinctive character of

Western capitalism.[18] But there was no sharp theoretical break between his early historical work and his later sociological work, the latter grew out of the former. The concept which made this difficult accommodation between the historical and the sociological approaches possible was that of ideal-type; for Weber ideal-types provided the necessary basis for comparative sociology. Ideal-types have proved indispensable in the development of social action theory.[19]

An ideal type is constructed by the abstraction and combination of an indefinite number of elements which, although found in reality, are rarely or never discovered in this specific form. . . . Such an ideal type is neither a 'description' of any definite aspect of reality, nor . . . is it a hypothesis; but it can aid in both description and explanation. . . . In formulating an ideal type of a phenomenon such as of rational capitalism, then, the social scientist attempts to delineate, through the empirical examination of specific forms of capitalism, the most important respects (in relation to the concerns which he has set himself) in which rational capitalism is distinctive. The ideal type is not formed out of a nexus of purely conceptual thought, but is created, modified, and sharpened through the empirical analysis of concrete problems.'[20]

The construction of ideal-types is thus a method focusing clearly and precisely upon theoretically relevant aspects of empirical reality. At best, this procedure can provide a basis for comparison, generalization and explanation; at worst, it specifies clearly what historians actually do.[21] However, there has been considerable confusion amongst sociologists about the status of ideal-types, the procedure to be followed in constructing them, and the criteria to be used in assessing their value. Weber, and his commentators, have been more explicit about what ideal-types are not than about what they are. They are not descriptions of reality; they are not hypotheses about reality; they are not averages; nor are they traits common to a given class of objects.[22] This confusion, especially about the relationship between ideal-types and the observed attributes of the social world, has led to the exasperated dismissal of ideal-types as 'ultra-rational intuitions', 'neither derived by a process of deductive rationalization from higher concepts, nor built up from empirical data by relevant inference, nor demonstrably developed as working hypotheses from such data'.[23] This 'profound methodological confusion' led Friedrich to reject Weber's ideal-type concept of bureaucracy.

Despite this iconoclasm, the status, rationale and role of ideal-types are clear in general terms:[24]

The ideal types of social action which for instance are used in economic theory are thus unrealistic or abstract in that they always ask what course of action would take place if it were purely rational and oriented to economic ends alone. This construction can be used to aid in the understanding of action not purely economically determined but which involves deviations arising from traditional restraints, effects, errors and the intrusion of other than economic purposes or considerations. This can take place in two ways. First, in analysing the extent to which, in the concrete case, or on the average for a class of cases, the action was in part economically determined along with other factors. Secondly, by throwing the discrepancy between the actual course of events and the ideal type into relief, the analysis of the non-economic motives actually involved is facilitated. . . . The more sharply and precisely the ideal type has been constructed, thus the more abstract and unrealistic in this sense it is, the better it is able to perform its functions in formulating terminology, classifications, and hypotheses.

Such procedures are followed by conventional historians, with varying degrees of self-consciousness: any assessment of causal relations in history is posited upon an unspoken 'if x had not happened, y would not have happened.' They are also followed by economic theorists, for example in their use of the concept of 'market'. Much of the confusion amongst sociological commentators upon Weber stems from Weber's attempt to provide a basis for generalization without doing violence to the complexity of history; economic theorists have been more successful in preventing their models from being contaminated by the vagaries of human behaviour.

By abstracting logically coherent ideal-types from the morass of historical evidence, and by examining the relationship between specific ideal-types and other aspects of society, it is possible to develop the comparative analysis of social behaviour, as John Rex has emphasized.[25] But the major problem remains: what ideal-types are to be used? For both Weber and Parsons the paradigm example of ideal-type analysis is provided by classical economic theory, with its assumption of economically rational behaviour in a free market economy. A similar model would provide a firm basis for comparative sociology, facilitating the clear formulation of testable hypotheses. Assessing the possibility of constructing sociological models analogous to economic models involves examination of the problem of rationality.

Rationality

According to Weber there are two major types of rationality, formal and substantive, the latter comprising two sub-types, 'wert-rational' and 'zweck-rational'. The concept of formal rationality is relatively clear, referring to 'the extent of quantitative calculation which is technically possible and which is actually applied' (although there is obviously scope for divergence between the 'technically possible' and the 'actually applied').[26] Formal rationality provides an obvious basis for comparative analysis, making possible the construction of detailed models and the formulation of relatively precise predictions. For this reason it has provided the fundamental rationale for 'economic' theories of political behaviour, especially voting behaviour.[27] Political action is viewed as a type of economic action, capable of analysis in terms of a rational choice model borrowed from economic theory: political exchange is a form of market behaviour, with voting as the analogue of consumer choice. For example, according to Downs, voters attempt to maximize the returns to be obtained from voting for alternative parties in terms of the rewards to be derived from the implementation of specific policies, discounted by the costs in effort involved in voting, whilst political parties formulate policies designed to maximize the number of votes. Even in its own terms the model is unsatisfactory: all voting is 'irrational' in terms of the individual's effort–reward bargain, for the individual's vote is unlikely to make any difference to the eventual outcome of the election, whether favourable or unfavourable.[28] Moreover, the model assumes transitivity, the ability to compare the rewards to be derived from alternative courses of action with each other, or with a common denominator – in economic theory this role is performed by money. But there is no *generalized* medium of exchange in politics, no way of satisfactorily comparing the rewards to be derived from more social justice with the rewards to be derived from faster economic growth. If there is no currency there can be no market, and the analogy between politics and economics breaks down at the beginning. However, the specific deficiencies of the economic model are less relevant here than the general limitations inherent in any model based upon formal rationality. The concept of formal rationality refers only to 'technical' considerations, to the criteria for evaluating the effectiveness of alternative means of achieving a given end, not for assessing the value of different ends. But in political life, however defined, this former comparison is secondary to the comparison between different ends, and the resolution of conflicts arising from disagreement over ends. A comparative analysis of power relations could be constructed on the basis of a model of formal rationality; but the precision would be gained at the price of sociological relevance. The model would explain too little.

The concept of formal rationality is clear and precise, but of limited value; the concept of substantive rationality is ambiguous, but more fruitful. 'Substantive rationality' involves the application of 'certain criteria of ultimate ends, whether they be ethical, political, utilitarian, hedonistic, feudal, egalitarian, or whatever, and measure[s] the results of the economic action, however "formally" rational in the sense of correct calculation they may be, against these scales of "value rationality" or "substantive goal rationality"'.[29] An extensive and fluctuating range of criteria may be relevant for evaluating the relative success of alternative courses of action in terms of 'substantively rational' values, not simply those capable of comparison in 'technical' terms. It is therefore necessary to recognize the plurality of relevant values and criteria of assessment, despite the resulting impression of uncertainty and difficulties in generalization.

One reaction to the limitations of formal rationality and the imprecision of substantive rationality is to deny the value of the concept of rationality altogether. For example, according to Pareto logical explanations are merely rationalizations of emotional responses to situations – to use Pareto's idiosyncratic terminology, the 'deviations' which are used to disguise the 'residues' or 'instincts' which motivate political action.[30] Logical explanations are merely a surface dressing, designed to hide irrationality:[31]

> in concrete theories . . . there are, besides factual data, two principle elements. . . . The [first] element directly corresponds to non-logical conduct; it is the expression of certain sentiments. The [second] element is the manifestation of the need of logic that the human being feels. It also partially corresponds to sentiments, to non-logical conduct, but it clothes them with logical, or pseudo-logical reasonings. The [first] element is the principle existing in the mind of the human being; the [second] element is the explanation (or explanations) of that principle, the inference (or inferences) that he draws from it.

Despite the length of *Mind and Society* Pareto presents little evidence or logical argument to support his point of view – only lengthy anecdotes drawn mainly from Greek and Roman history and polemics against Marx.[32] Lasswell, in his study *Psychopathology and Politics*, reformulated the irrationalist thesis in more psychoanalytic terms, arguing that political activity was often the product of 'private motives displaced upon public activities and rationalized in terms of the common good'.[33] Lasswell's evidence was derived from psychoanalytic case studies, and may provide a basis for the explanation of the involvement of some leaders in political life, especially in extremist movements, but hardly of political action in general.[34] Of more general relevance is the evidence presented by Robert Lane, in his detailed study of the political beliefs of the American common man. Following Lasswell, Lane attempted to distinguish between democratic and anti-democratic personalities. He argued that authoritarian and restrictive attitudes were derived from the inability of individuals to control their own impulses, especially sexual: 'Our theory [for the minority of three with relatively extreme views], familiar to psychoanalysis and to commonsense alike, is that men who have trouble in controlling their own impulses will be likely to fear freedom in the personal sense.'[35] The three non-democrats amongst the group interviewed by Lane revealed a lack of self-identity, resulting in an unusual emphasis on stability, and a lack of realism, hence disappointment of excessive hopes, and experienced social isolation due to their low IQ and their second-generation immigrant status.

Political beliefs undoubtedly do perform a number of functions for individuals: evaluating external objects, maintaining or breaking relations with others (social adjustment), and 'externalization', the projection of hated aspects of the self on to others, and resulting hostility to others.[36] Externalization is an important element in explanations of racial prejudice, and other forms of belief not subject to disconfirmation by investigation of the external world.[37] But the emphasis upon irrationality characteristic of Pareto, Lasswell and Lane represents a profoundly unsympathetic form of psychological reductionism: personally unsympathetic because of the arrogant assumption that it is possible to explain what 'really' makes human beings behave the way that they do by stripping away their rationalizations and unmasking their unconscious, intellectually unsatisfactory because it neglects completely the way in which the social structure moulds political attitudes and behaviour.[38] The major issue in the sociology of power is the way in which personal problems are translated into political ones, instead of remaining private. For example, the personality-type frequently referred to as 'authoritarian' is probably distributed randomly throughout different societies, and different groups within society: in some circumstances this type of personality is politically significant, and in others not – depending upon the problems faced by that society and group. Moreover, the beliefs whose measurement provides the basis for constructing psychological indices may be learned through interaction, rather than derived from individual maladjustments.

This denial of rationality is as unsatisfactory as insistence upon formal rational choice models. Social action is variably rational, both as to ends and as to means. In some situations the model of economic man is relevant, either where there is only one goal, or goals are clear and the costs and benefits of alternative courses of action can be calculated in terms of a common currency. But in most situations such clarity does not exist: there are multiple goals, the significance of alternative goals fluctuates over time, and there is only very limited transitivity between alternative goals. It is therefore necessary to substitute the ambiguity of substantive rationality for the clarity of formal rationality, to introduce political, ethical and other criteria into the discussion. Moreover, even in the limited number of situations where goals are clear and the costs and benefits of alternative courses of action calculable, the concept of formal rationality may be of only limited value. Knowledge of the situation, and of the consequences of action, is likely to be limited in practice, because of distorted perspectives and the costs of acquiring information from multiple perspectives, and by the psychological tendency to 'satisfice', to be willing to accept the first solution which satisfies minimum criteria, rather than to maximize.[39] Formal rationality can provide a basis for predicting behaviour in the limited number of situations where knowledge is complete, in practice not simply in theory, and where actors are also willing to spend the time and energy required to achieve optimal results. For the rest, sociologists must rely upon the more ambiguous concept of 'substantive rationality'.

Conceptualization of constraints

Social action theorists have been concerned to stress the creativity of human behaviour, the ability of individuals to make their own history. 'Man participates in *meaningful* activity. He creates his reality, and that of the world around him, actively and strenuously. Man *naturally* – not supernaturally, transcends the existential realms to which the conceptions of cause, force, and reactivity are easily applicable.'[40] But this ability to create reality, to transcend nature, is only limited: as Marx said, 'Life is not determined by consciousness, but consciousness by life.'[41] Actors are subject to constraints, factors external to the actor which enjoin certain courses of action which the actor would otherwise avoid taking, and which prevent other forms of action which he might wish to take.[42] These constraints may be biological, psychological, social or cultural. Social constraints include the scarcity of desired resources, the prevalence of competition between actors for desired resources, and lack of knowledge of the means required to obtain resources. Especially important is the distribution of power in society, rendering some forms of action necessary for some groups, but dispensable for others: constraints for some are facilities for others.

This emphasis upon constraints is not intended to imply a mechanical determinism; the environment is negotiable, and constraints do not automatically determine action. Responses to constraints are essentially active, and may involve the expenditure of additional resources in attempting to minimize or to avoid the constraint, or in constructing explanations for changes in goals following adaptive readjustment, as well as simple acceptance. For example, cooperation between actors facing similar or complementary problems is an obvious way to increase strength and thus to increase power over the environment; the familiar process of adjustment of expectations is an example of the second reaction to constraints. But the concept of constraints, or some equivalent, is necessary as a means of relating the actor to the environment within which he is acting, and to avoid the idealist excesses of some forms of 'naturalism'. The actor's meanings cannot be understood apart from the context within which the actor is acting. Marx and Engels' discussion of Feuerbach remains the classic expression of this perspective:[43]

> In direct contrast to German philosophy, which descends from heaven to earth, here we ascend from earth to heaven. That is to say, we do not set out from what men say, imagine, conceive, nor from men as narrated, thought of, imagined, conceived, in order to arrive at men in the flesh. We set out from real, active men, and on the basis of their real life-process we demonstrate the development of the ideological reflexes and echoes of this life process . . . men, developing their material production and their material intercourse, alter, along with this, their real existence, their thinking and the products of their thinking. . . . [The] premises [of this approach] are men, not in any fantastic isolation and rigidity, but in their actual, empirically perceptible process of development under definite conditions.

Conclusion

In this chapter I have attempted to outline the social action approach, as developed by Weber, Parsons, and to a lesser extent Rex, and to examine some of the problems involved. The discussion is not exhaustive, and I have not examined the relationship between the 'classical' social action approach and phenomenology, as developed by Husserl and Schutz, and ethnomethodology. Following Weber, social action has been defined as subjectively meaningful behaviour which takes into account the behaviour of others, and is thereby oriented in its course. Social action can be analysed through the construction of 'ideal-types', logically coherent models, based explicitly upon the premise of 'substantive rationality'. Explanations for social action are grounded in the actor's perception of his social situation, and the subjectively rational behaviour necessary to achieve desired goals. The social action approach is not a theory – in itself it explains very little. Rather, 'it is a set of near tautological assumptions which structure the mode of cognition of social inquiry, which is, on the whole, concerned with the conditions and the products of social interaction.'[44] These propositions direct attention towards the goals of actors, the meanings of situations for them, and the purposive character of social behaviour. It avoids the misleading assumptions involved in systems theory, the elaborate analogies between the social system and machines, organisms and species, and provides a framework within which historically variable goals and methods of achieving them can be viewed. Society is seen as a congeries of individual human actors, with human goals, bound together by a complex pattern of interdependence, not an elaborate machine. By focusing attention upon this conception of society the social action approach provides a useful orientation towards the sociological analysis of power relations, as I hope the following chapters will show.

3 The sociology of power: problems of definition and measurement

'Power', like 'love', is a word used continually in everyday speech, understood intuitively, and defined rarely; we all know what 'the power game' is. In many instances sociologists have been no more precise than this. Yet it is possible to define power precisely without losing touch with the commonsense meaning of the term. In the first section of this chapter I want to review some of the ways in which the concept of power has been defined, before presenting my own definition, and then to discuss more briefly some of the other major terms used in the study – compliance, coercion, authority and influence. The second section deals with measurement problems.

In the most general sense power may refer to any kind of influence exercised by objects, individuals or groups upon each other. As Dahl puts it in his *International Encyclopaedia of the Social Sciences* survey article, 'power terms in modern social science refer to subsets of relations among social units such that the behaviours of one or more units depend in some circumstances on the behaviour of other units.'[1] Or, more succinctly, 'for the assertion "A has power over B" we can substitute the assertion "A's behaviour causes B's behaviour".'[2] However, these broad and deceptively simple definitions represent a grave dilution of the concept; collapsing power into cause robs the term of precision, and consequently of utility. Moreover, the concepts of power and cause are not interchangeable. For example, A may 'cause' B to jump out of the way of an approaching car by shouting a warning, but this has little in common with the situation in which A 'causes' B to patrol the South Vietnamese forest. And if the terms are not interchangeable additional terms are required. These additional terms are not provided, and the definition is therefore incomplete. Precision,

35

y and traditional sociological usage (as well as the desire to
immediate submergence in the epistemological quagmires
surrounding the concept of cause), all militate against such an
inclusive definition of power.

Most sociological theorists have defined power in more restricted
terms, as a specific type of relation between objects, persons and
groups. The most influential definition remains that of Max Weber:
'power is the probability that one actor within a social relationship
will be in a position to carry out his own will despite resistance,
regardless of the basis on which this probability rests.'[3] This provides the starting-point for most modern discussions of the concept,
whether referred to explicitly or not. Dahl, for example, states in his
influential paper 'On the Concept of Power': 'My intuitive idea of
power, then, is something like this: A has power over B to the extent
that he can get B to do something that B would not otherwise do.'[4]
The Michigan social psychologists French and Raven use a similar
definition in their Lewinian field-theory of power: power is the
potential ability of one group or person to influence another within a
given system.[5] But perhaps the most influential recent refinements of
the Weberian concept are those of Ralf Dahrendorf and P. M. Blau.
Both suffer from specific defects, as well as from the common defects
of developments of the Weberian approach.

After explicitly endorsing the Weberian definition, Dahrendorf
goes on to argue that power is a contingent property, a property of
individuals, rather than a property of social structures:[6]

> The important difference between power and authority consists
> in the fact that whereas power is essentially tied to the
> personality of individuals, authority is always associated with
> social positions or roles . . . power is merely a factual relation,
> authority is a legitimate relation . . . we are concerned
> exclusively with relations of authority, for these alone are part
> of social structure and therefore permit the systematic
> derivation of group conflicts from the organization of total
> societies and associations within them . . . [such group conflicts]
> are not the product of *structurally fortuitous* relations of power.
> (My italics.)

This formulation defines out of existence non-legitimate structural
or recurrent power relationships, an important source of social
conflict. Moreover, the distinction between power and authority
in these terms is a false one, for definitions of legitimacy are themselves contingent upon power relations, as the author subsequently
recognized.[7] The introduction of the derivative concept of authority
in this way confuses rather than clarifies the problem of definition.

Blau defines power as 'the ability of persons or groups to impose their will on others despite resistance through deterrence either in the form of withholding regularly supplied rewards or in the form of punishment, inasmuch as the former, as well as the latter, constitute, in effect, a negative sanction'.[8] The capacity to produce intended effects despite resistance has given way to the capacity to produce intended effects despite resistance through the use of negative sanctions. However, despite the expansive caution of this definition, it fails to solve major difficulties. Specifically, how regular does a reward have to be before its loss becomes a negative sanction? More generally, what distinguishes a negative from a positive sanction? It is not the content of the sanction *per se*, for the ultimate negative sanction of physical force has been distinguished from power and defined as coercion. Instead, Blau adds in a footnote, 'it is necessary to decide, depending on the purpose at hand, whether the defining criterion is the subordinate's expectation or the superior's intent.'[9] However, this relativism appears to be at odds with the formulation of the definition, for the cessation of the regular provision of rewards must constitute a benefit for the superior in a relationship. The definition, I think rightly, views the sanction from the perspective of the subordinate; the explanation suggests something different. Precision is difficult with such definitional uncertainty.

Despite widespread use the Weberian definition and its derivatives suffer from a number of weaknesses. There are two major problems. As Parsons has argued, the assumption of conflict and antagonism is built into the definition: A overcomes the resistance of B, implying that the interests of B are being sacrificed to the interests of A.[10] But this ignores the possibility that power relations may be relations of mutual convenience: power may be a resource facilitating the achievement of the goals of both A and B – in the same way as money may facilitate the achievement of the goals of both borrower and lender in a credit relation. Transposed on to a societal level, power may be seen as a generalized means for the achievement of collective goals, instead of a specific means for the satisfaction of limited, sectional interests. Weber defines this possibility out of existence.

The second major difficulty with the Weberian definition of power is that it transposes a property of interactions, of interrelations, into a property of actors. In part this may be merely a matter of terminology and grammatical construction: Weber is explaining the meaning of an adjective instead of defining an abstract noun. (Although this in itself is curious: it is as if mass were defined in terms of the probability of people of a given size being a given weight, instead of as weight over volume.) But the sleight of hand is more significant than that. Instead of defining the term 'power',

Weber is providing the basis for a comparison between the attributes of actors: actors become more or less powerful to the extent that the probability of obtaining compliance with their wishes increases or decreases. It is an easy step from this definition to the view that power is a generalized capacity rather than an attribute of a specific relationship. But although power may be possessed as a capacity and is only revealed in action, it is the property of a relation. To revert to the metaphorical language which has perhaps plagued analysis of the concept of power, it is the electric current rather than the electric generator.

In an attempt to avoid defining power in terms of conflict Parsons has suggested a completely different conceptualization, viewing power as a system resource. 'Power then is generalized capacity to secure the performance of binding obligations by units in a system of collective organization when the obligations are legitimized with reference to their bearing on collective goals, and where in case of recalcitrance there is a presumption of enforcement by negative situational sanctions – whatever the actual agency of that enforcement.'[11] The key terms in this definition are generalization, legitimation, and 'negative situational sanctions'. 'Generalization' means simply the ability to transfer power from one relation to another, the political equivalent of the economic distinction between bartering and market relations; 'legitimation with reference to their bearing on collective goals' means the acceptance of the relation by both sides because of its function in achieving social system goals; and 'negative situational sanctions' means the use of material deprivations as distinct from moral blackmail. Unfortunately, as I have argued earlier (p. 19), the new Parsonian definition creates more difficulties than it resolves, for Parsons places consensus where Weber placed conflict. Parsons defines out of existence the problems which have usually preoccupied sociologists of power.

Thus the two major strands in contemporary discussions of power, the Weberian and the Parsonian, both suffer from major problems of definition. By building the element of conflict into his definition, by seeing power solely in zero-sum terms, Weber disregarded the possibility of mutually convenient power relations. Moreover, by seeing power as a capacity, he transformed an attribute of a specific relation into a generalized facility, confusing form with substance. On the other hand, the Parsonian conceptualization suffers from the opposite difficulty. By defining power in terms of consensus and legitimacy Parsons defines out of existence the problems students of power have been attempting to resolve. Moreover, the reliance upon the monetary analogy ignores the limited liquidity of power, its inseparable links with specific patterns of dependence. Does this mean that the only solution is a formalization of Dahl's 'intuitive conception'?[12]

I think not. W. J. Buckley, in his book *Sociology and Modern Systems Theory*, suggests a way in which power may be reconceived, namely as a specific form of communication flow. According to Buckley society comprises a system of interrelated mechanisms, organisms and socio-cultural sub-systems, linked together by physical, energy and information flows. At the level of the social and cultural systems the physical and energy components of the flow are of only marginal importance, the system being linked 'almost entirely by conventionalized information exchange'.[13] Such information flows can 'trigger' action at any level, organic, social or cultural. In these modified cybernetic terms, therefore, power may be defined strictly, at the most general level, as *that type of information flow which symbolizes non-self-regarding action for the recipient*. The purport of the first clause is obvious: it is to emphasize that power is a specific type of information flow, whose meaning depends upon the 'coding' practices of the recipient. But the summary and anachronistically moral sounding term 'non-self-regarding action' requires amplification. It is intended to exclude purposive action showing a surplus of benefits over costs. The reason for excluding such action is that groups and individuals will seek to achieve at least a balance of costs and benefits in their relations with others, and that action which succeeds in doing so in terms of the actor's frame of reference will not be the result of a power relationship. The relation of domination and subordination is reversed when subordinates gain more from the relation than superordinates. Action outside this category constitutes *prima facie* evidence of a power relation: the signals must then be examined.

This convoluted but recognizable definition has three advantages over the standard definitions. First, it makes clear that power is the property of a relationship, not of the individuals in that relationship: power *is* a specific mode of communication, a signal. But, second, signals have meaning only in terms of the frame of reference of the actors in a situation – the senders and, especially, receivers of the signal or information flow. Third, the relevant frame of reference, as Blau's emphasis upon negative sanctions rather left-handedly suggests, is that of the subordinate, for it is the limitation upon his self-regarding activity which indicates the existence of a power relation.

Despite these advantages, this definition of power can still be criticized for failing to permit the recognition of situations in which subordinates fail to realize that their actions are non-self-regarding, although they are judged to be so by external observers. According to this view subordinates may be socialized into accepting a false conception of their own interests, and may therefore misinterpret their own activity. Superordinates may use their influence over the formulation of social values, and over the processes of communication, to persuade subordinates that their actions are in their own best interests, strictly defined, and therefore not the result of power relations. Such persuasion is likely to be especially successful in societies which derogate compliance as 'unmanly'. 'Those who obey because they are afraid do not like to think themselves unmanly or cowardly; in an effort to maintain a decent regard for themselves, the fearful frequently find ingenious ways in which they can define almost any demand made upon them as legitimate'.[14] This view has been elaborated most recently, although in slightly different ways, by Steven Lukes, John Westergaard and, in more specific detail, by Ruth Elliott.[15] Steven Lukes, for example, proposes a 'radical', 'three dimensional', definition of power, focusing upon interests: 'I have defined the concept of power by saying that A exercises power over B when A affects B in a manner contrary to B's interests, interests being defined as what men would want (between alternatives) if they were given the choice, not what they actually do want.'[16] Westergaard similarly sees power being wielded most effectively when subordinates fail to understand their own interests correctly, interests being 'inherent in structural positions irrespective of whether and how the incumbents happen to see them at any given time'.[17]

I will consider the implications of this *genre* of definitions more fully in the final chapter, as one aspect of current Marxist approaches to the analysis of power. However, in brief, this criticism and the theoretical superstructure which accompanies it, is unacceptable, for it runs counter to the basic assumption of the social action approach outlined earlier; the actor's own interpretation of his situation, and the *grounded* explanations for that interpretation, should be the primary focus of attention. Put briefly and crudely, there are at least four major reasons for rejecting such criticisms. First, the reasons for the actor's action lie in his own consciousness, not in that of the observer; any causal explanation must therefore be in terms of the actor's goals, and perceptions of the situation in which he attempts to achieve them. This inevitably involves examining the external situation within which the actor operates, including the agencies of socialization: investigation, not presumption. Second, there is no criterion for deciding between alternative definitions of interest provided by different observers; it is only rarely that the actors' 'real' interests will be so obvious to observers that they all agree, except where such interests are also obvious to the actors themselves. Third, there is no adequate theory specifying the processes whereby the actor acquires false consciousness. Finally, the intellectual confidence – or arrogance – implied by the assertion that my view of your interests is true but your view of your interests is false, is more apposite to political propaganda t academic analysis.

Power is the central concept in this study, and has therefore received most attention. But there are four other related terms which will be used frequently below, and which require definition: compliance; coercion; authority; and influence.

Compliance refers to the attitudes and behaviour caused by power, or, more formally, to the 'non-self-regarding actions performed at the behest (direct or indirect) of others'. This definition is significantly more restricted than the standard definition of compliance formulated by Etzioni: 'compliance refers both to a relation in which an actor behaves in accordance with a directive supported by another actor's power, and to the orientation of the subordinated actor to the power applied'.[18] This composite definition is difficult to use, for it includes two different perspectives – of the observer (in the first clause), and of the subordinate participant (in the second clause). These perspectives may, or may not, be the same. Where the observer sees behaviour 'in accordance with a directive supported by another actor's power', and therefore presumptively causally related to the superordinate's power, the participant may see intelligent calculation of the prospective benefits to be gained by a given course of action, regardless of the superordinate's power. It is therefore necessary to disentangle the two perspectives, and in the present work compliance refers simply to action interpreted as non-self-regarding by the subordinate.

Coercion is relatively easy to define, although difficult to measure. It comprises 'the application, or the threat of application, of physical sanctions such as infliction of pain, deformity, or death; generation of frustration through restriction of movement; or controlling through force the satisfaction of needs such as those for food, sex, comfort, and the like'.[19] There are two major problems involved in this definition, as in the later definition of authority. First, it is difficult to distinguish between behaviour in response to implicit threats, and behaviour regarded as appropriate to a given status: fear of the consequences of non-compliance and belief in the rectitude of compliance are often difficult to distinguish (as in the Indian peasant's acceptance of Spanish domination in Guatemala in Tumin's study).[20] Similarly, behaviour may be conditioned not by violence, or threat of violence, but by *anticipation* of unfavourable reactions from powerful others. Second, the use of an 'etc.' clause inevitably produces difficulties: is deprivation of happiness (a frequent result of fulfilling moral obligations) a form of coercion? Despite these difficulties, which indicate that Etzioni's definition

41

is far from watertight, it remains a valuable initial classification. The essential element in the concept of authority is 'legitimacy'.[21] 'However authority is defined, few writers fail to see it as being bound up in some way with legitimacy. Authority is said to lie in the *right* to expect and command obedience.'[22] Hence Parsons defines authority as that type of superiority 'which involves the legitimized right (and/or obligation) to control the actions of others in a social relationship system'.[23] It is important to remember that this legitimation does not necessarily extend to the whole relationship, but only to certain aspects of it, whether specified precisely or not. Hence, under later feudalism, the vassal's legitimation of the lord's superior status did not involve acceptance of the lord's right to exact more than customary labour dues. Legitimized domination, in contrast with coercive domination, is norm-governed. The superordinate's right to exact compliance is based upon the consent of the subordinate. This consent may be founded upon a number of different bases – tradition, charisma or legal-rationality, to use Weber's terms – as the more detailed discussion of authority in chapter 6 indicates (below, pp. 75–83). In short, in general terms, authority relationships exist where subordinates consent to their own non-self-regarding actions, regardless of the basis for that consent.

The concepts of coercion and authority do not provide an exhaustive typology of the bases of compliance. For compliance may result from a fear of the consequences of non-compliance, even where the deprivations likely to follow are not physical, or where the relationship is not legitimized. For example, industrial managers may comply with the wishes of their superiors and act in a non-self-regarding manner where the legitimacy of the wish is denied, out of a fear of the loss of future promotion opportunities. It would be misleading to call such behaviour the result of coercive power, for there is no physical deprivation involved; it would be equally misleading to attribute legitimacy to the compliance. The term 'influence' is used to refer to such relationships.

Coercion, authority and influence are all derived from imbalances in dependence relations, and it is with these concepts that this study is primarily concerned. But non-self-regarding action can occur even where dependences are balanced, or where the balance is in favour of the compliant actor. Where dependences are balanced compliance is the result of exchange, in the narrow sense of the term: equals are exchanging one good for another. When the payoff from the compliance is direct, specific and short-term, the behaviour can be regarded as 'economic'; when the payoff is indirect, long-term or unspecific, the exchange can be regarded as 'social'. Moreover, superordinates can perform non-self-regarding actions at the behest of their subordinates, perhaps out of a normative commitment to humility or some other supernaturally sanctified value. In one sense such relationships are power relationships – there is a signal involved, non-self-regarding actions *do* occur. But, as there is no imbalanced dependence, it is very different from the power relationships based upon coercion, authority and influence. As such relationships are not part of a system of domination they are not examined in this study.

Measurement

The definition of power adopted in this study focuses upon compliance, and therefore upon the action of subordinates. Attempts to measure the distribution of power therefore involve measuring the attitudes and behaviour of the recipients of power signals; in the most general terms, the amount of power involved in a given relation may be measured by the difference the receipt of a power signal makes to the attitudes and behaviour of the recipient. This difference, in turn, comprises three elements: scope, frequency and probability.

The measurement of 'scope' poses difficult problems. In general terms 'scope' refers to the extent (breadth and depth) of the attitudinal and behavioural changes caused by the receipt of the power signal. Unfortunately there is no standard of measurement to use in comparing the extent of different forms of non-self-regarding behaviour: to use a trivial example, what measure can be used to compare the non-self-regarding action involved in repairing the boss's motorcar free of charge with that involved in reading *The Structure of Social Action* instead of playing football? Such measurement must be in terms of the subordinate's opportunity costs, i.e. the value to the subordinate of the activities forgone by carrying out the superordinate's wishes. (This may result in different conclusions from those based upon measures which focus upon the benefits accruing to the superordinate: the 'amount' of power involved will depend upon the perspective adopted. The cost to the subordinate may exceed the benefit to the superordinate.) Opportunity costs can only be calculated in terms of the subordinate's scale of values, his own experienced deprivation. What value does he place upon the activities he would have done had he not mended the motorcar? Once scope has been measured it is relatively easy to measure frequency, in terms of a standard unit of time. The measurement of probability involves comparing the actions of the subordinate following the receipt of power signals with the actions he would have taken anyway, without the signals. This involves obtaining information both about the attitudes the subordinate would possess or the way he would act in terms of his own independent need satisfaction and opportunity cost calculations if he had not received the power signals, as well as his actual attitudes and behaviour. Dahl has expressed this in a convenient formalization. We define A's power over a, with respect to the response x, by means of w, as M, or more fully:

$$M(A/a:w,x) = P(a,x/A,w) - P(a,x/A,\bar{w}) = P_1 - P_2.$$

If there is no difference in the probabilities of action with or without the intervention of alter, i.e. if $P_1 = P_2$, then there is no power relation. Power is at its maximum when $P_1 = 1$ and $P_2 = 0$, at its minimum when the reverse is the case.[24]

Unfortunately, there have been no successful attempts to measure power precisely in these terms because of the difficulty of establishing the hypothesized probability. The most precise measures of power have been developed by social psychologists in their studies of inter-personal and small-group relations. Power is measured by the changes in B's attitudes following interaction with A in an experimentally controlled situation. For example, Lippitt *et al.*, in their famous summer-camp experiments, measured manifest power by the proportion of successful influence attempts, and attributed power by responses to questions regarding ability to secure compliance.[25] More complex experimental techniques and measures have been developed subsequently, for example by Bandura, Ross and Ross in their test of the status envy, secondary reinforcement, and social power theories of learning.[26] However, although the experimental approach to the study of social power yields relatively precise measures of the distribution of power in small groups, the attribute measured is a rather peculiar one. The artificial and often arbitrary nature of the experimental interpersonal or small-group situation undermines the sociological relevance of the findings. If power is a property of a specific relation between specific individuals or groups in a specific situation, the frequency of the occurrence of that situation is of crucial importance. If it happens rarely or not at all outside the experimental situation, the results are of limited interest. The non-social experimental situation does not distil the essence of a social relation, it destroys it.

The experience of students of community power indicates more directly the problems of measuring power encountered in socio-logical research. Although none of the contributors to the community power debate have approached a fully satisfactory level of rigour, none having compared actual with predicted behaviour, the debate reveals clearly the difficulties involved in moving from conceptual exegesis to the construction of empirical tests for theoretically relevant hypotheses. Neither of the two major approaches adopted by community power analysts, the 'reputational' or the 'event analysis', is fully satisfactory.

The essence of the reputational approach, although not its more subtle refinements, is presented in Hunter's now classic study, *Community Power Structure*.[27] The managers of civic organizations in Regional City were asked to provide four lists of community power holders; the community council provided a list of leaders in community affairs; the chamber of commerce provided a list of business and financial leaders; the League of Women voters provided a list of political and governmental leaders; and the editors of the local newspapers provided a list of social leaders. This list of 175 was then whittled down to 40 by asking a panel of 14 knowledgeable judges to name the 10 most important members of each list. Twenty-eight of this group of 40 were then interviewed.

This method of measuring the distribution of power in a community possesses numerous methodological advantages, in addition to relative cheapness. There is evidence, from studies of hospitals and elsewhere, that there is a substantial congruence between attributed power and actual power over a number of different issue areas, and *prima facie* it is likely that the systematic collection of informed opinions would give a reliable guide to the distribution of power in a community. Moreover, the reputation for power is one source of power, just as the reputation for wealth may be a help in obtaining a favourable credit rating – if only in default of more precise information. However, there are both conceptual and methodological weaknesses. Conceptually, the reputational approach does not distinguish between the ability to exercise power (power potential) and the actual exercise of power; abilities may or may not be used, depending upon predispositions and opportunities. Moreover, it assumes that power is an object much like money, which is possessed and recognized by all. But it may be recognized only by the actual performers of non-self-regarding actions. Methodologically, the approach suffers from a number of inadequacies, carrying approximation to unacceptable extremes. No attempt is made to define power for the interview respondents. Respondents may interpret in a number of randomly varying ways, which may or may not correspond to their own interests, the question which was asked – 'If a project were before the community that required *decision* by a group of leaders – leaders that nearly everyone would accept – which ten on this list of forty would you choose?' – nor was any attempt made to specify the scope of the behaviour in question. Moreover, the form of the question presupposes its answer: by asking for a specific, in practice small, number of community leaders, the question assumes that there is such a group, even where there may not be. Few respondents have the temerity to say that the interviewer has asked the wrong question.[28] Finally, the intercorrelation between attributions is not always high, and there is rarely any external validation of the responses given – for example, by comparing the reputation for the possession of power with actual influence on a specific decision-making process.

The opponents of the reputationalists have adopted a more historical approach in their attempt to counter the conceptual confusion between potentiality and actuality and the methodological problems of ambiguity and arbitrariness. Questions about the distribution of power can only be answered by looking at what actually happens in respect of specific issues. Interviews with opinion leaders are irrelevant except as a first step towards discovering what issue areas are worth investigating. In *Who Governs?*, still one of the most sophisticated studies, Dahl employed six methods in assessing the relative power of different statuses; changes in the socio-economic background of incumbents of community political positions; measures of the nature and extent of the participation of particular socio-economic groups; determination of the influence of particular individuals in a specific set of issue areas; a random sampling of community political activists and voters; and an analysis of changing voting behaviour.[29] The most important method of measurement for the present discussion is the assessment of the influence of different individuals and groups in key issue areas, and as the most precise attempt to measure power within a large institutional setting is worth examining in detail.

The detailed reconstruction of the events in four issue areas was intended to 'penetrate the veil of official position and overt participation in order to determine, as far as possible, who *really* influences decisions'.[30] Attention was focused on comparable respondents who 'directly' participated in a single issue area and decisions were examined where the number of participants was more or less the same over the period of the investigation. It was assumed that: 'the following collective actions are responses of roughly the same strength or extent; when a proposal initiated by one or more of the participants is adopted despite the opposition of other participants; when a proposal initiated by one or more of the participants is rejected; when a proposal initiated by one or more of the participants is adopted without opposition.' The number of successful initiatives or vetoes and the number of failures was assessed for each participant. Participants were ranked in terms of the relative frequencies of their successes out of all successes, or the ratio of a given participant's successes to total attempts. The issue areas chosen were political nominations, public schools and urban redevelopment.

Like Hunter's *Community Power Structure, Who Governs?* suffers from a number of methodological weaknesses. In particular, the choice of three issue areas 'because they promised to cut across a wide variety of interests and participants', has been criticized for its inadequate theoretical basis, and for leading to biased findings. Issues which arouse controversy are by definition issues which have aroused concern and conflict, in which the interests of one group are challenged by another. More important may be the ability to secure acceptance of particular proposals as non-controversial, and therefore acceptable. without the actual exercise of power. Moreover, power does not have to be seen to be active in order for it to operate; the receivers of power signals may anticipate the exercise of power, and act accordingly. Groups may effectively exercise a veto power without being called upon to act, or may forestall action which might otherwise have taken place: the failure of given individuals or groups to act may be due to their expectations of the exercise of power, the success of the power wielders being indicated by non-behaviour. The exclusion of certain political solutions as illegitimate (even if they are not illegal), and the restriction of the range of search for viable solutions (especially likely if individuals have a tendency to 'satisfice' rather than maximize), may be the result of unexercised power.[31] Finally, there is no definition of scope, no means of deciding who are comparable respondents, and no way of weighting the significance of particular decisions for initiators or vetoers.

Many of these criticisms, although important, are open to the charge of infinite regress, and raise insoluble problems of verifiability. How can the hidden manipulators of the scope of legitimacy be discovered? And who manipulated the manipulators? The manipulators of the manipulators of the manipulators? Other criticisms are more directly relevant to measurement problems: the historical approach adopted in the New Haven study fails to reach the level of rigour demanded of the reputationalists, and lacks the methodological rigour of Dahl's own conceptualization. There is no attempt to compare what happened with what, but for the intervention of x, might have happened. Specifically, there is no discussion of what the Mayor of New Haven might have done had his proposals not had to be approved by the lay Citizens' Action Committee; the Mayor had to tailor his proposals to their known views, and mayoral caution may have been responsible for the fact that the Committee never challenged his proposals. Power is measured by the difference between predicted and actual behaviour: there is no way of avoiding this comparison.

The significance of the community power debate for sociologists interested in formulating a theory of power relations is twofold.[32]

First, and most obviously, it illustrates the complexity of the measures needed: it is possible to pick substantial methodological holes in research as well designed and carried out as the New Haven study More interestingly, it illustrates the central importance of definitional precision. The methodological polarization which occurred in the community power debate was based upon conflicting definitions and only intensified by disciplinary affiliation and ideological commitment. For the reputationalists power is a capacity, an ability to obtain compliance based upon the possession of desired facilities, especially income and prestige. For the event analysts power does not exist independently of its use: if businessmen do not actively intervene in the political life of New Haven, they are not politically powerful. Different research procedures and measures derive directly from different definitions.

For our purposes, the amount of power involved in a relation may be measured by the difference in probabilities of action of a given scope with or without the receipt of a given signal. This involves comparison between a hypothesized sequence of events and the actual sequence of events, and constitutes a more elaborate form of event analysis. However, the explanation for the difference made by the signal is likely to be found in the sanctions available to the sender to punish non-compliance, the resources he can withdraw from the subordinate. These resources, whatever their form, may be regarded as capacities, and may be measured reputationally.

Constructing a sociology of power relations involves serious difficulties of definition and measurement; but they are not insuperable. In this study power refers to symbols denoting non-self-regarding behaviour, compliance to the non-self-regarding behaviour itself. There are three different bases of power: coercion, authority and influence. In addition, non-self-regarding action may be the result of non-power relations. Coercion exists when compliance is based upon physical deprivation, or the threat of physical deprivation; authority refers to legitimated compliance; influence is a residual term, referring to non-legitimate non-coercive compliance. It follows from these basic terms that attention should focus upon the subordinate in power relations, upon the opportunity costs of his compliance. The amount of power involved in a relation is measured in terms of the compliant actions of the subordinate, their scope, frequency and differential probability.

The definitions and measurements proposed in this chapter require elaborate and precise data about communications, attitudes and behaviour, and evaluations of likely attitudes and behaviour in hypothetical situations. Such data is, in principle, obtainable, and the models of action with which action is to be compared can be constructed. But, at the present time, the data is rarely available: research into power relations is a particularly contentious activity, for obvious moral reasons. It is therefore impossible to expect to construct a theory of power relations possessing the precision and rigour allegedly characteristic of economic theory, or to amass comprehensive statistical or documentary data. The following chapters leave a great deal to be desired in the precision of the evidence presented. But this does not undermine the value of an attempt to discuss the sociology of power relations, for sociology should, of course, be concerned with what is important and interesting, not with what can be measured or documented. The result lacks the precision and rigour of economic theory; but so does social action.

4 Power relations and dependence

In the broadest sense power relations arise out of interdependence, alter possessing resources which ego requires in order to achieve his own goals, and which ego can obtain only by performing non-self-regarding actions. The major elements in any explanation of power relations are actors' goals and the distribution of resources required to achieve them. Although the range of possible goals is almost infinite, certain general goals have remained important, especially in the conditions of scarcity which have characterized most of human history: acquisition of the basic necessities of life and competent performance of basic social roles – although of course more complex sets of goals exist in all historical situations, especially in the relative material abundance of contemporary industrial society. Asymmetric patterns of dependence, and thus the need for compliance, results from differential control over access to the resources required to achieve these goals. This differential control is based partly upon the degree of 'criticalness' of specific attributes or resources at specific times, and partly upon ancestral inheritance – the local chief typically evolved into the feudal lord, the feudal lord into the capitalist entrepreneur, the capitalist entrepreneur into the industrial manager. Criticalness is a function of centrality and scarcity, and differs according to the prevailing forces of production and availability of natural resources. In summary terms: technology and natural resources determine criticalness; criticalness and inheritance lead to differential control over resources; differential control over resources leads to dependence where resources are desired; imbalanced dependence and limited possibilities for escape lead to compliance.

The interrelationship between the factors involved in determining the amount of power in a given relationship can be briefly summarized in Figure 2.

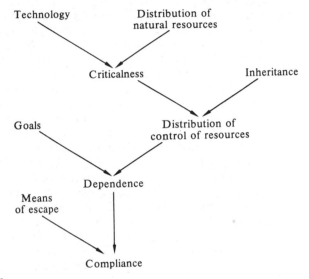

Figure 2

Power relations are thus the result of a long causal chain (although the metaphor of a chain is misleading, for each process is linked with more than two others). A comprehensive theory of power relations would specify the variables relevant to understanding each stage of the process, the reasons for their variation, and the ultimate consequences of such variations for power relations. It is impossible to present such a comprehensive theory here, for the value of *a priori* theorizing is limited and the relevant sociological evidence is lacking. Nevertheless, before examining power relations in specific systems of labour exploitation, I would like to comment briefly in general terms upon the variables in the model.

The term 'technology' refers to the physical actions involved in treating and manipulating raw materials, the organization of the labour force thus employed, and the knowledge used in combining the two: it does not refer simply to a set of physical objects.[1] According to the school of thought caricatured in the unhappy Marxist slogan 'the hand-mill gives you society with the feudal lord; the steam-mill society with the industrial capitalist' technology is the basic determinant of inequalities, including inequalities of power. For example, Lenski has argued that different types of technology create different patterns of social stratification, the degree

51

of inequality increasing with technological development, until the trend is partially reversed in industrial society.[2] Such technological determinism is misleading (as well as being alien to Marx's own sociological work). For it ignores the extent to which technology itself incorporates particular intellectual assumptions about the character of the causal processes operating in the physical world, and the 'feedback' effects of the distribution of power upon the development of technology.[3] Groups benefiting from the distribution of resources produced by a given system of technology will attempt to 'hold' technology at its current level in order to avert threats to their own positions and perquisites; at the very least, their struggles will have a delaying effect upon technological innovation, and by causing delays influence outcomes. Technology should thus not be seen as a final cause, but as a particularly important variable in a more complex multi-directional system. It develops out of attempts to satisfy perceived needs, or to achieve perceived goals, and is constructed according to specifiable intellectual principles. Human desires, ingenuity and willingness to cooperate produced the hand-mill and the labour organization accompanying it. Once established the most profitable operation of the hand-mill 'required' a specific arrangement of work relations and, around that, a particular pattern of social relations, including power relations.

Technology can be classified more or less precisely according to the purpose for which the classification is required. At the most general level technology may be classified into 'pre-industrial' and 'industrial', as in conventional sociological theory textbooks, or into 'pre-neolithic' and 'post-neolithic', as in Gouldner and Peterson's *Notes on Technology and the Moral Order*.[4] More elaborately, technology may be divided into an almost infinite number of types based upon refinements in the application of physical and human engineering principles, as in Meissner's comprehensive work *Technology and the Worker*.[5] The classification of Gouldner and Peterson is too crude, that of Meissner too complex, for the level of analysis involved in this study. For present purposes technologies can be most conveniently classified into five types, based upon the predominant instrument of production: hunting and gathering, simple horticultural (based upon the digging stick), advanced horticultural (based upon the metal hoe), agrarian (based upon the plough, harness and more advanced metallurgy), and industrial.[6] These five technologies will produce different characteristic distributions of control over desired resources, and thus different typical patterns of asymmetric dependence relations. The connections between advanced horticultural societies and slavery, between agrarian society and feudalism, and between industrial society and capitalism are discussed below, p. 63, p. 92, p. 101 respectively.

The extent and distribution of natural resources affects both the general pattern of power relations, and the place of particular individuals and groups within that pattern. Where resources are relatively scarce interdependence, and therefore the possibility of imbalanced dependence is greater than where they are abundant; there is an evident contrast between societies characterized by abundance, like late eighteenth-century America, and those characterized by scarcity, like late twentieth-century Bangladesh. Precisely which natural resources are fateful for power relations will depend, of course, upon non-social factors like geology and climate, and upon quasi-social factors like technology and the residential distribution of the population.

'Criticalness' comprises two elements, centrality and scarcity. Some resources are vital, but not scarce, like land in nineteenth-century Canada; other resources are scarce but not central, like diamonds in seventeenth-century England; neither are nearly as important for power relations as resources which are both vital and scarce. The scarcity of resources depends upon the distribution of natural resources and the technology available to exploit them. Hence well-watered land is a critical resource when irrigation is primitive, but ceases to be so critical with the development of irrigation systems: such technological changes either produce a more balanced set of dependence relations, and thus less power, or change the distribution of power by changing the critical factor from well-watered land to irrigation technology.

The amount of asymmetric dependence in society is mainly influenced by 'criticalness' and inheritance. Inheritance affects dependence in two ways. First, the intergenerational transmission of control over resources affects the degree of concentration of control; there is an obvious difference in the concentration of control over resources between societies which permit intergenerational transmission of control, those which partially permit it, and those which prohibit it. The degree of concentration of control was greater in late nineteenth-century Britain, when maintenance of the family estate was the first obligation upon a gentleman, than in the late twentieth century, where the intergenerational transmission of control is regarded by some as an infringement upon the principles of equality of opportunity (although of course other factors have helped to counter this trend). The fragmentation of control over resources is obviously greater where intergenerational transmission of control is proscribed, as in the Soviet Union.

Second, control over resources is affected by the partibility of inheritance. There is an important difference between societies following principles of partible inheritance and those following principles of primogeniture or ultimogeniture: the dispersal of control is greater in the former than in the latter. This is most apparent in comparisons between societies in which the degree of 'criticalness' of a given resource is similar. The importance of different inheritance principles is evident from a comparison between the pattern of development of control over land in Kent and other parts of England in the late Middle Ages.[7] Adherence to the principles of partible inheritance in Kent resulted in a fragmentation in control over land, the persistence of the yeoman farmer after he had largely disappeared elsewhere, and consequent delay in the development of capitalist agriculture. In this way different inheritance principles affected not simply the distribution of control over resources, but also, through their influence upon the rate of capital investment, the development of agricultural technology.

Neither inheritance customs, technology, nor even the distribution of natural resources, should be regarded as 'final' causes of the distribution of power. Attitudes towards familial responsibilities and towards equality, especially equality of opportunity, influence inheritance practices. Technology is dependent upon the state of knowledge of the material world, knowledge which is partly dependent upon the resources men are willing to spend in acquiring it; and the distribution of relevant natural resources is partly dependent upon technology and the time and effort men are willing to devote to developing new technologies. All three categories of factors are thus influenced by the beliefs and values of members of society. Nevertheless, for analytical purposes, it is most helpful to see members' attitudes as primarily effecting the connection between the distribution of control over resources and dependence. For control over resources is not important in itself: it is control over *desired* resources – and desires obviously vary within and between societies. The range of desires is obviously very extensive – for material goods, prestige, 'ego expansion', love, affection, and so on. Any single desire may be obscured by other desires, an obscurity often impenetrable even by the actor himself; the reasoning behind Shelburne's request for a political job in 1761 must have been opaque even to himself: 'The only pleasure I propose by the employment is not the profit, but to act a part suitable to my rank and capacity, such as it is.' Goals may be common, or highly idiosyncratic. Where common they may be complementary with the goals of others, and thus provide a basis for collective action, or conflicting, thus leading to antagonism. All these, and other factors, will influence the distribution of power. However, it is impossible to consider all possible goals, and simplifying assumptions are necessary. Although the whole range of human goals and aspirations is relevant, I have assumed that the most important goals, especially under slavery and feudalism, are the acquisition of material goods, prestige and power. This extended utilitarian assumption obviously grossly oversimplifies human motivation, ignoring the extent to which the pursuit of material goods, prestige and power may be inhibited by other values, including religious beliefs and group loyalties. Nevertheless, such goals do have importance for dependence and therefore for power relations, especially in conditions of scarcity. This utilitarian emphasis is especially justifiable since I am concerned only with goals which lead to interdependence; purely personal goals, like the pursuit of salvation through self-denial, have relatively little importance for power relations.

The distribution of control over desired resources leads directly to dependence; but dependence does not automatically lead to compliance. For compliance only occurs when escape routes are not available. There are four major strategies of escape available to subordinates. First, they can provide resources to the superordinate which are costless to themselves, or persuade the superordinate to modify his own goals so that he is willing to accept costless goods in exchange. Hence subordinates have a direct interest in persuading superordinates that their prestige would be increased by generous and considerate treatment; for the subordinate deference can be a relatively cheap exchange for more material favours. Alternatively, the subordinate may attempt to find elsewhere the resources which create his dependence: the availability of such alternative sources of supply will obviously affect his willingness to comply. Or the subordinate may attempt to combine with others with similar or complementary dependences and attempt to modify the relevant exchange rate between dependence and compliance. Or, finally, he may decide that his non-self-regarding actions are more costly to himself than forgoing the resources which create the dependence, and thus modify his own goals in order to limit his dependence. In short, asymmetric dependence only leads to compliance when escape routes are unavailable, or when their pursuit would lead to imbalances even greater than those involved in the initial exchange.

The amount of power in any relationship is directly determined by the relevant distribution of dependence and the availability of escape routes: *ceteris paribus*, the greater the imbalance and the more difficult the escape, the greater the amount of non-self-regarding action required in order to obtain the resources, and therefore the greater the amount of power involved.

The amount of power influences, but does not directly determine, the basis of power: the relation between the two is more complex. In general, the greater the amount of power, the greater the probability that compliance will be based upon coercion, the lower the probability that the subordinate will willingly consent to the relationship. Conversely, the smaller the amount of power involved, the lower the probability that power will be coercive, the greater the probability that it will be based upon authority, especially legal rational authority. The validity of these generalizations is, however, influenced by the constitution of the power relation, the basis of dependence, and the type of compliant action superordinates require of subordinates.

Power relations are based directly upon two elements, asymmetric dependence and the difficulties of escape. Even where the amount of power, measured by the scope, frequency and differential probability of action is the same, there is a difference between situations in which compliance results from a high degree of dependence and relatively easy escape and situations in which compliance results from relatively low dependence but little chance of escape. This difference has important implications for analysis of the bases of power. Where the degree of imbalance in dependence is great, but escape easy, compliance is likely to be based upon coercion: the subordinate has few ties to the specific relation, whilst the superordinate must use coercion to protect himself and to maintain the relationship with the specific subordinate. Where the imbalance in dependence is great, and there is little possibility of escape, the relation is likely to be based upon authority: the subordinate must resign himself to necessity and maintain his self-respect by consenting to his subordination, whilst the superordinate finds authority a cheaper and more effective means of obtaining compliance than coercion. In this situation coercive force is only a form of insurance against the breakdown of authority. Where dependences are balanced, and it is relatively easy for subordinates to escape, power is likely to be based upon authority: the relationship can only be preserved with the consent of the subordinate. Finally, in the relatively unusual situations in which dependence is balanced, but escape difficult, compliance is likely to be based upon influence. For subordinates will have little incentive to perform non-self-regarding actions and no need to preserve self-respect by granting consent; superordinates will find it difficult to use coercion to enforce compliance, whilst any claims for authority are likely to be questioned. In the absence of coercion or authority, a highly unstable relation based upon influence is likely to develop.

These general propositions are likely to hold when the source of dependence is differential control over desired material resources. However, they are less likely to hold when the dependence results from the desire for prestige or recognition: where such goals are involved, relations are more likely to be based upon authority than upon coercion or influence. For prestige or recognition is not so much a goal in itself, but rather a means of increasing self-esteem; it is the self-image constructed from the reflection in the mirror, and not the reflection itself, that matters. But the performance of non-self-regarding actions is itself a source of personal disesteem, involving external restrictions upon the individual's autonomy and signifying relative weakness. Subordinates are likely to minimize this by granting consent to subordination wherever possible, whilst superordinates are likely to collude with this definition of the situation because authority is a cheaper and more effective basis for compliance than coercion or influence. Where material resources are concerned subordinates must balance damage to self-esteem against more tangible material gains; this balancing is less likely to occur when the initial dependence is based upon status or prestige goals. Prestige or status considerations therefore rarely lead to non-authoritarian power relationships.

A final factor complicating the relation between the amount of power and the basis of compliance is the content of the non-self-regarding action to be performed, especially the amount of discretion involved. Superordinates require subordinates to perform tasks of varying complexity; some tasks can be programmed for supervision or correction by machines or other people, some cannot be programmed. Most human action is too complex to programme easily, and necessarily involves subordinates using their own judgment and discretion: even the most routine work in industrial society involves some degree of personal judgment. The greater the discretion required in the performance of the subordinate's task, the greater the need to base power upon authority, for subordinates will seek to minimize their effectiveness where compliance results from coercion, as studies of slavery and of prison labour spectacularly demonstrate.[8] The greater the amount of discretion involved, the more difficult the supervision and the easier the non-performance of required tasks.

In this chapter I have briefly discussed the relationship between dependence and power in general terms, and outlined the interrelated factors which determine that relationship. The amount of power is determined by the degree of imbalance in dependence and the relative ease of escape for subordinates. This imbalance results from differential control over desired resources; control over desired resources is determined by the distribution of natural resources, the technology available to exploit them, and inheritance practices. The basis of compliance is determined by the amount of power, the way power is built up, the character of the dependence, and the degree of discretion involved in the performance of the task required of the subordinate.

Such general propositions have only limited value in themselves. It is necessary to show how general processes relate to specific structures and events, and in doing so to provide empirical evidence for the propositions outlined. This task can obviously be approached by either or both of two strategies: by examining variations in goals and resources within one system, or by examining a more limited range of goals in different systems. I have attempted to follow the second strategy, tracing the significance for power relations of attempts to pursue a limited range of goals in a number of different social systems. This strategy seemed appropriate for a sociological study more concerned with social processes and structures at the macro-level than with the dynamics of interpersonal relations. This emphasis upon macro-level analysis is particularly necessary in the study of power relations, for previous work has paid a disproportionate attention to interpersonal relations and failed to relate dyadic interaction in the laboratory to processes observed in the external social world. To focus upon a limited range of goals and to emphasize the need for macro-level analysis does not necessarily involve a repudiation of the social action approach outlined earlier, for I recognize that different patterns of power relations would have emerged if I had concentrated upon different sets of goals; but such power relations would have been of much less sociological interest.

The following chapters examine power relations under different systems of labour exploitation, slavery, feudalism and capitalism. The choice of such units for comparative analysis is not accidental, for such systems of labour exploitation, or efforts to 'produce materially', comprise more or less integrated structures of technology, labour organization, and norms and values, with characteristic patterns of power relations. This classification is not without problems. The three systems are not mutually exclusive; slavery has existed within feudal and capitalist societies, just as feudal elements have survived in capitalism. Moreover, some systems of labour exploitation are excluded – not all primitive societies were based upon slavery, even after the invention of private property. Slavery was comparatively insignificant in hunting and gathering societies. Nevertheless, the related concepts of slavery, feudalism and capitalism provide a relevant set of 'ideal-types' for comparative analysis. As I hope the following chapters will show, different systems of labour exploitation do produce different characteristic patterns of power relations.

5 Total power: the sociology of slavery

The greatest power differential between roles in any system of labour exploitation is that between master and slave: the slave performs continuously extensive services which he would never have performed but for the existence of his master. The slave is literally his master's creature, from whom he derives his very identity, whilst the master is only minimally dependent upon the slave. In Aristotle's words, 'The master is only the master of the slave; he does not belong to him, whereas the slave is not only the slave of his master, but wholly belongs to him.'[1] This asymmetric dependence is based upon the slave's lack of any access to the resources required to achieve his own goals, and subordination to his master's monopoly over the means of violence. The master invests capital in his slaves, and relies upon them for the fulfilment of labour services: but this reliance is comparatively small for the individual slave is substitutable.

Slavery originates in the forced depersonalization of the slave as a result of capture during war, enslavement for debt or the gradual erosion of customary rights. It persists to the extent that superordinates continue to profit from it, and subordinates are unable to escape from it. This profitability depends upon the relative efficiency of alternative methods of labour exploitation at a specific stage in the development of the forces of production, the plantation economy of advanced horticultural societies, and the availability of new slaves to replace worked out 'capital'. The ability of the slave to modify the dependence is conditioned by the possibilities of combination and rebellion, or escape: it is by definition impossible to find alternative sources of supply, and difficult to deny the value of the resources controlled by the master. Rebellion or escape is obviously determined by the effectiveness of repression, itself influenced by the locale and the way in which slave labour is utilized.

Despite its attractions for superordinates, and their control over the means of violence, slavery has proved to be only a temporary phase in the development of systems of labour exploitation: in both the Ancient and the Modern world slavery failed to adapt to competition from less rigid systems, was eroded by ideological changes, or decayed as a result of its own internal tensions. This transience was due partly to 'external' changes – in the Roman Empire to the spread of Christian ideals, the drying up of the most convenient sources of supply of captives, the economic decline of free farmers and their gradual merging into a semi-servile mixed population (*coloni adscripti*), in Latin America to the national independence movements, in the West Indies to the hostility towards the slave trade felt by influential sections of opinion in the metropolitan countries, and in the United States to the hostility of the abolitionists and the Civil War. But, even without external pressure, slave societies would probably have proved transient, for total power did not always lead to the maximization of rewards for superordinates: it involved expensive overheads in the form of elaborate and often ineffective institutions of repression, and proved inflexible in the face of market and technological changes. Moreover, although rebellion and escape were often difficult, passive resistance through limited cooperation was common. The effectiveness of slavery as a system of labour exploitation, if not as a system of political repression, proved limited.

In the remainder of this chapter I want to examine power relations under slavery using the general approach sketched in chapter 4. This involves outlining the basic elements of slavery and slave societies, the physical and technological situations in which they operated most successfully, the dynamics of dependence relations within slavery, and the tensions which limited its effectiveness. Finally, since our concern is with power relations in general, not simply with slavery in particular, I want to discuss the relevance of total power and powerlessness for a general theory of power.

Slavery constituted 'a kind of ultimate limit in dependence and loss of natural freedom ... that condition in which man most closely approximates the status of a thing'.[2] The slave had no social existence apart from his master, he was an item of property, devoid of legal personality: 'of property, the first and most necessary kind, the best and most manageable, is man.'[3] The slave's legal non-existence apart from his master had four major direct consequences for the slave: he could not establish a family, nor own property, nor move, and he was totally subordinated to the discipline of his master.[4] The impact of these legal prohibitions varied, and could be blunted by custom or, occasionally, religious pressures; but neither custom nor countervailing institutional pressures could change the total dependence of the slave upon the master, and the enshrining of that dependence in the legal concept of a chattel. In the words of a Jamaican Act of 1674: 'All Negroes lawfully bought as bond-slaves shall here continue to be so and further be held and judged and taken to be goods and chattels and ought to come to the hands of Executors . . . as other assetts do, their Christianity or any Law, Custom, or Usage in England or elsewhere to the contrary notwithstanding.'[5] This lack of legal personality was shown in the clearest possible way: masters could kill their slaves without being charged with murder in Homeric Greece, Ancient India, the Roman Republic, Saxon England, Kievan Russia, the British West Indies, as well as in some of the Southern States of the United States.[6] As the Virginia slave code of 1669 stated, 'it cannot be presumed that prepensed malice (which alone makes murder felony) should induce any man to destroy his own estate.'[7]

The essence of slavery was the non-human status of the slave, his transformation into an *object*. But there were significant differences in the legal status of slaves in different slave systems, as well as in the social conditions which permitted and fostered slavery. Indeed, the major authority on slavery in the Ancient world, W. L. Westermann, concluded that slavery was a multiple, not a single, social institution: 'The term "morphology" and "pattern" of slavery are here consciously avoided as misleading . . . the institution has no single pattern and no single *morphe*. It takes many forms which are determined by the social ideas and external circumstances under which the specific system has developed.'[8] Hence, in the Ancient world, there were significant differences between the legal status of slaves in Greece and in the Roman Republic, as well as differences between the Roman Republic and the Roman Empire. In Ancient Greece slaves were permitted to marry, to own property, and to buy their freedom (even, in some circumstances, to join loan associations to raise money to purchase their freedom); Roman slaves were not permitted to marry, and their property rights were limited. There were also important differences between slaves in different parts of the Modern world. In Latin America slaves were encouraged to marry by the church, and owners were unable to resist, and manumissions were permitted, although property ownership was rare. In Anglo-Saxon North America the logic of the slave's lack of personality was carried further than elsewhere: marriage could only be recognized by custom, not by law, property ownership was illegal (although slaves were often granted small plots of 'provision-land' to cultivate in their spare time), and manumission was only permitted in limited circumstances. Nevertheless, despite important differences between systems of slavery in the extent to which the humanity of the slave was recognized, there were common features in the social institutions of slavery which make it possible to talk of a sociology of slavery, of total dependence and thus total power.

Slavery was, by definition, a legal status, the absence of specific rights. But this legal status was the formal recognition of the complete *de facto* dependence of the slave upon his master. This dependence derived from a complex of social relations whose core was a specific form of labour exploitation. Slavery was essentially a *labour* system, as Stampp has emphasized in his analysis of American Negro slavery.[9] Slavery survived only where it was an effective way of expropriating surplus labour: its core was the total expropriation of the product of the labour power of one man by another. This core relation affected the whole society: slave societies comprised an interlocking set of relations to ensure the subordination and dependence of the slave. Ideology, as well as legal and political institutions, sustained the master's domination. Social philosophy and social science, as well as theology, legitimated the subordination of slaves to their master. Aristotle's arguments, if not his precise terminology, have been echoed in the Modern world:[10]

> is there any one thus intended by nature to be a slave ... ?
> There is no difficulty in answering this question, on grounds
> born of reason and of fact. For that some should rule and
> others be ruled is a thing, not only necessary, but expedient;
> from the hour of their birth, some are marked out for
> subjection, others for rule. ... For he who can be, and therefore
> is another's, and he who participates in reason enough to
> apprehend, but not to have, reason, is a slave by nature.
> Whereas the lower animals cannot even apprehend reason;
> they obey their instincts. And indeed the use made of slaves
> and of tame animals is not very different; for both with their
> bodies minister to the needs of life.

The innate inferiority of the slave, and therefore the legitimacy of the denial of his humanity, was a recurrent theme in theological, philosophical and social discussion in the American South, as in George Fitzhugh's *Sociology for the South: or the Failure of Free Society*, published in 1854, one of the first works in American social science.[11] The need to maintain the subordination of the slave was a constant preoccupation of politicians and the judiciary. Under the influence of small-scale uprisings, and the increasing number of runaways succoured by Northern sympathizers, Southern legislatures passed a number of extensive slave codes in the 1830s, far more severe than the codes current in Greece and Rome. Even U. B. Phillips, a generally sympathetic historian of American slavery, admitted that the State and local laws regulating slavery were stringent, although he went on to argue that they were 'rarely enforced in the spirit'.[12] The judiciary endorsed the master's view that 'without discipline there cannot be profit to the master or comfort to the slave', and that 'insolence' was a recurrent threat to the social order.[13] As one judge Catterall commented, 'insolence [may] be a look, the pointing of a finger, a refusal or neglect to step out of the way when a white person is seen to approach. But each of such acts violates the rules of propriety, and if tolerated would destroy that subordination upon which our social system rests.'[14] 'That subordination' was maintained by summary punishment on the plantations – 'on our estates we dispense with the whole machinery of public police and public courts of justice. Thus we try, decide, and execute the sentences in thousands of cases, which in other countries would go into the courts – by the granting of power of arrest to all white persons, by an extensive police force, and by the gallows and the lash.'[15] The major symbol of slavery throughout the American South was not the grinning household servant but the lash, what the *Richmond Engineer* described in 1859 as a 'great institution for stretching negroes' skins and making them grow good'.[16]

Slavery flourished as a system of labour exploitation under specific ecological and technological conditions. It did not flourish in hunting and gathering societies, or in agrarian societies in infertile areas. This was for both political and economic reasons. The political problem of security was acute in societies obliged to move from place to place, either in pursuit of game or because of low fertility. Hence slavery did not flourish in Northern Europe in antiquity, except where slaves could be used as trading objects with the Romans: elsewhere it proved too difficult to prevent escapes. Even where permanent cultivation was possible slavery flourished only in relatively fertile areas, because of its low productivity.[17] In less fertile areas slavery existed either as a form of security, or as a means of performing household services, but not as a major system of labour exploitation.

Even in relatively advanced horticultural and agrarian societies slavery was of only limited effectiveness. For slavery was an efficient form of labour exploitation only when an uncommitted labour force could be coerced into action. Slaves could not be trusted to operate complex or expensive machinery without very close supervision. Strabo lamented upon the unprofitability of slaves because of their 'apathy and insensibility', whilst Phillips commented: 'in the work of a plantation squad no delicate implements could be employed, for they would be broken; and no discriminating care in the handling of crops could be had except at a cost of supervision which was generally prohibitive. The whole establishment would work with success only when the management fully recognized and allowed for the crudity of the labour.'[18] Slaves could perform hard, repetitive, unskilled, but not dangerous, tasks in the field, like picking grapes or cotton, or cutting sugar cane, or even the routine operation of the cotton gins; but they were too valuable to perform dangerous tasks, and too apathetic to perform responsible ones. One Southern planter summed up the feelings of many when he advised his son to change from sugar to cotton production: 'it was trouble enough to have to manage negroes in the simplest way, without having to over-look them in the manufacture of sugar and the management of Machinery.'[19]

These reservations about the usefulness of slaves were even more common amongst industrial managers. In the United States in the nineteenth century boosters for the Southern way of life proclaimed the virtues of industrial slavery:[20]

> When the demand for agricultural labour shall be fully supplied then of course the labour of slaves will be directed to other employment and enterprises. . . . It may be commanded and combined with more facility than any other sort of labour; and the labourer, kept in stricter subordination, will be less dangerous to the security of society than in any other country, which is crowded and over-stocked with a class of what are called free labourers (*De Bow's Review*, 1851).

Slaves *have* been used in manufacturing industry: in the Roman Empire the famous pottery works at Aretium were manned by slaves, and in the United States the Tredegar Iron Works, in Georgia, were a regular tourist attraction for visitors to the South. But the supposed advantages of slave over free labour were not recognized by the men who mattered, prospective industrialists. The workshops in the Ancient world were mainly small craft enterprises, whilst manufacturers in the American South preferred free to slave labour, even in the ante-bellum period. Freemen could be trained to perform more complex operations, required less supervision, could be used for dangerous work for which slaves were too valuable, and they could be sacked when not required. Hence, there were only 198 cotton mills in the South in 1860 employing slave labour, and they were relatively small, with an average labour force of only 71 workers, slave and free. Industrial slavery represented only a small proportion of total slavery in the American South.[21]

The fear of damage to valuable machinery, the costs of supervision, the rigidity in manpower planning, and the large sums needed as working capital, largely explain the limited use of slaves in

American manufacturing industry. Similar difficulties, on a smaller scale, had influenced the use of slaves in industry in the Ancient world. But there was a wider, related problem: industry was concentrated in urban areas, and the retention of control over slaves was considerably more difficult in urban than in rural areas. Total control over slaves was possible in rural areas – even if difficult – through the creation of segregated compounds and rigid restrictions upon movement. Such control was much more difficult in urban areas: 'Slavery is from its very nature eminently patriarchal and altogether agricultural. It does not thrive with master or slave when transplanted to cities.'[22] It was possible to maintain patriarchal domination in the city if slaves were employed only as domestics and kept within the confines of the household, as many were: the bijou town houses in the narrow streets of Charleston, with their main doors facing inwards, were once the outhouses inhabited by slaves (though later occupiers have added windows on to the streets). This inclusive domination became difficult when slaves were allowed out of the house on their master's business, and impossible once the practice of 'hiring out', and later even 'living out' had developed. As the *Savannah Republican* commented on living out in 1845: 'It is the beginning of the end and unless broken up in time will result in the total prostration of existing relations.'[23] It is not surprising that the number of runaways was far higher in urban than rural areas, although there are no reliable figures. Attempts to control the situation by segregating slaves, residentially and occupationally, by tightening manumission laws, and by selling young male slaves 'up country' were palliatives rather than solutions; segregation increased contact between slaves, thus facilitating the organization of rebellion, manumission laws could not effectively prevent masters from freeing slaves when they wished to do so, especially in areas where 'free Negroes' existed, and selling young males up country obviously lessened the contribution slaves could make to the urban economy. It is thus not surprising that, despite the continued demand for slaves in the cities, especially as domestics but also as handicraft workers, the number of slaves in Southern cities declined sharply between 1820 and 1860, and:[24]

by 1860 the institution of slavery was in great disarray in every Southern city. The number of negroes had declined precipitously. Discipline over those remaining proved difficult to sustain. The network of restraint so essential to bondage no longer seemed to control the blacks nor wholly govern the whites. The distance between the races as well as the separation of the free coloured from slave could not be maintained in the kinetic world of the city.

Ecological and technical conditions thus limited the extent of slavery in both the Ancient and the Modern world. Slaves were mainly used for domestic service, in mining and, especially, in plantation agriculture. The greatest concentrations of slaves in the Ancient world were in the Greek silver mines, and in the extensive plantations of Southern Italy and Sicily, although slaves were also used in the Near East. In the modern world, in Latin America, the West Indies, and the United States, slaves were used mainly in plantation agriculture: sugar cane and coffee in Brazil, sugar cane in the West Indies, sugar cane, tobacco and, especially, cotton in the United States. Slavery was not confined to these sectors – in Greece slaves were used in nearly all occupations except the 'liberal' professions (like law) and the armed forces, in Rome slaves were often important officials, for they were regarded as more trustworthy than freemen, in the Southern States they were often skilled craftsmen like silversmiths – but it was most extensive in them. For 'servile labour must be unskilled labour and unskilled labour must be dispersed over land.'[25]

The development of slavery was fostered by the practice of primogeniture, allowing the accumulation of capital and the preservation of 'the estate' over several generations. For slavery required a larger amount of working capital than feudalism or capitalism, and involved a higher ratio of fixed to variable costs. This need for a high level of capitalization was increased by dependence upon international markets, and the consequent need to cushion against the effects of changes in the pattern of demand or against the discovery of new sources of raw materials. The intergenerational transmission of undivided capital resources, and reverence for 'the estate', were essential for the survival of slavery, for without them the accumulation of capital and the creation of economically viable plantations would have been difficult. In the United States partible inheritance would probably have led to the development of a free peasantry on mid-Western lines in the South.

Slavery flourished in specific ecological and technological conditions, and its survival was assisted by a specific inheritance custom. But it was not a direct product of those conditions: it depended upon the extent to which the goals of relevant social actors led to imbalanced dependence within the framework of those conditions. For the slave the distinction is academic; his participation in the relationship was the result of coercion, usually capture during war, and he could only obtain the means of physical survival from his master. For the master the question turns upon the profitability of slavery and the personal satisfaction and social status derived from upholding traditional patterns of life. Unfortunately it is difficult to calculate the profitability of slavery, for any useful calculation involves comparison between slavery and alternative systems of labour exploitation, distinguishing between the economics of slavery and the economics of plantation agriculture, and making allowance for increased profitability due to changing levels of demand rather than improved productivity: these requirements have not been met by even the most sophisticated econometric work on the economics of slavery, that of Fogel and Engerman on the economics of slavery in the ante-bellum South.[26] Unsatisfactory evidence, and logic, suggest that slavery was not a very profitable form of labour exploitation, especially in the long run: inefficiency and the high cost of supervision in the short run, and barriers against innovation in the long run, more than made up for direct savings in wage costs. However, slave-owners had neither the wish, nor the knowledge, to make calculations about the absolute profitability of slavery, for their satisfactions derived from maintaining patriarchal domination rather than from maximizing economic returns. For masters, slavery constituted at worst a satisfying form of labour exploitation, especially if allowance is made for the physical comfort and personal status provided by domestic slaves. As Stampp concluded in his analysis of American slavery:[27]

> For a small proportion of Southern whites the pattern provided the economic rewards and social prestige of the plantation. For the great majority of slave-holders it provided the more modest advantages of moderate sized agricultural units. For the nearly three quarters of the Southern whites who owned no slaves it provided less tangible things: a means of controlling the economic and social competition of Negroes, concrete evidence of membership in a superior caste, a chance perhaps to rise into the planter class.

The most common form of escape from the constraints caused by complete dependence was 'internal withdrawal', the development of a destructive form of infantilism caricatured by the Quashee figure of Jamaican folklore and the Sambo figure in the United States.[28] The Sambo figure was a recurrent image in slave societies – 'the Sambo personality [is] neither more nor less than the slavish personality; wherever slavery has existed, Sambo has also.'[29] Slaves were regarded as childlike by nature, and the master's role that of the responsible patriarch with wilful children. Hence Calógeras in his standard *History of Brazil*: 'the Negro element in general revealed a perpetual good humour, a childish and expansive joy, a delight in the slightest incidentals of life. . . . Filled with the joy of youth, a ray of sunshine illumined his child-like soul.'[30] Southern slave-owners were agreed that slaves were by nature loyal, cheerful, submissive and deferential, if also evasive and lazy. In

67

Phillips's words: '[slaves] possessed a courteous acceptance of subordination, an avidity for praise, a readiness for loyalty of a feudal sort, and . . . a healthy human repugnance toward overwork.'[31] This slave personality can be interpreted in psychoanalytic terms (as Elkins does), as the natural result of the destruction of the slave's original personality and the substitution of one all-powerful other, the master, for all previous significant others. But it can be represented more plausibly as a form of passive resistance; infantilism minimized responsibility and legitimated often destructive stupidity. By appearing to be 'stupid, bungling, exasperating, and completely inefficient' the slave protected himself, confirmed his master's stereotype of the cheerful, childlike fool, and reduced his economic value.[32] Slave-owners were aware of this subterfuge – one Virginia planter commented that slaves made 'dupes' of their masters 'under the cloak of great stupidity': 'The most general defect in the character of the negro is hypocrisy; and this hypocrisy frequently makes him pretend to more ignorance than he possesses; and if his master treats him as a fool, he will be sure to act the fool's part. This is a very convenient trait, as it frequently serves as an apology for awkwardness and neglect of duty' – but were incapable of circumventing it.[33] Infantilism and internal withdrawal were the easiest ways to escape from the burdens of continuous non-self-regarding action.

Individual withdrawal also took other forms – malingering, illness and even suicide. The proverbial laziness of the slave, captured in the widespread Southern aphorism 'it takes two slaves to watch one slave do nothing', was the most common means of non-cooperation. But illness, physical and psychological, was also frequent, especially amongst women of child-bearing age. One Virginian claimed that female slaves lost much of their value when they reached 'breeding age' because of the frequency of 'female complaints' and the impossibility of disregarding them for fear of permanent damage. Masters were fearful of injuring their own property – more so than they were of injuring other freemen. (As one river-boat captain explained, 'the niggers are worth too much to be risked here; if the Paddies are knocked over-board, or get their backs broke, nobody loses anything.')[34] It is impossible to guess at the number of slaves who took their own lives to escape their bondage, but suicides did occur, especially among slaves newly arrived from Africa (the most common method in the West Indies was simply by eating dirt).[35]

Active attempts were made to escape from dependence, either by running away or by rebellion. It is impossible to estimate the proportion of slaves who escaped from bondage in any society, but it has been suggested that over 60,000 escaped from the South to the North in the period before the American Civil War. The possibility of escape obviously depended upon the ease with which it was possible to merge into the local population (hence the disadvantages of buying slaves from local populations and of permitting manumission) or to escape to a safe destination. Both means depended heavily upon the sympathy of local populations, willing to forgo the rewards offered for the return of runaways and to disregard the legal penalties incurred for harbouring escapees; as the repetitive complaints of slave-owners in both the Ancient and the Modern world indicated this sympathy was often forthcoming. Escape was easier in urban areas than in rural areas, especially where members of the same race were already legitimately at liberty.

The combination of slaves to exert pressure upon their masters, either as a small group or in a full-scale rebellion, did not prove very successful. There were no major slave risings in Ancient Greece, or in Israel; the major Roman revolts were successfully contained; there were no successful risings in Latin America; and the revolts by American slaves led to repression and reaction rather than to liberty. (The successful revolt in Haiti remained exceptional.) The reasons for this lack of collective rebellion did not lie in the basic personality of the slave, his 'nature', but in the conditions of his social existence: the lack of weapons, the difficulty of communications, the lack of leadership skills, and the sensitiveness of slaveowners to any development likely to weaken their dominance. Total domination usually succeeded in preventing collective rebellion; where it failed owners could retain control by sacrificing part of their capital to retain the rest. The severity of the repression which followed the small-scale Vesey's revolt in South Carolina in the 1820s showed the extent to which owners were prepared to destroy their own property to retain their control: terror worked.

Despite the profitability of slavery for masters, and the difficulties for slaves of escape, slavery was an unstable system of labour exploitation. This instability stemmed partly from the economics of the plantation system, and partly from the sociology of slavery itself. Plantation agriculture was a form of productive system developed in response to national and international demand for primary products – sugar, tobacco, coffee, cotton – which required highly intensive cultivation. It was not a form of subsistence agriculture. Dependence upon markets, especially dependence upon international markets, rendered the plantation system highly vulnerable to the disruptive effects of the trade cycle, as well as to long-term changes in the patterns of supply brought about by the discovery of new sources of primary products. This vulnerability was most obvious in the cotton plantations but it was also evident in the pattern of development of the coffee plantations in Brazil and the sugar plantations in the West Indies. The slump of 1837 caused large numbers of bankruptcies amongst slave-owners in the American South, whilst numerous bankruptcies followed the collapse of world demand for Brazilian coffee and West Indian sugar. Such disruption has been a characteristic of plantation economies throughout the world, whether based upon slave or free labour, and is not in itself a direct result of slavery. But the effect upon slave-owners was more serious than upon employers of free labour owing to the inelasticity in the supply of labour in slave systems.

Employers of free labour can obviously adjust to changes in patterns of demand by dismissing unwanted labour (even if political and trade union opposition to unemployment is increasing the difficulty of this solution in the developed world). At the very least land can be allocated to free labourers for use in subsistence farming without losing control of the situation. Neither solution was possible for slave-owners. The slave constituted a form of fixed capital which the owner could not temporarily alienate from himself (and hiring out had considerable difficulties, including the danger of excessive 'wear and tear' and thus rapid capital depreciation); and the allocation of provision-land increased the difficulties of maintaining control. The ratio of fixed to variable costs was thus higher in slave plantation agriculture than in free plantation agriculture. The significance of this factor obviously depended upon the relative cost of slaves compared with alternative forms of labour, in turn a function of demand and supply. In both the Ancient and the Modern world the price of slaves tended to increase over time, partly because political stability reduced the supply of captives, and partly because the actual demand did not seem to vary directly with the economic demand for slaves – they were too important an indicator of social prestige. Roman writers commented on the inflation of slave prices and their lack of relation to the economic worth of slaves. Similarly, despite fluctuations in the demand for cotton the price of slaves continued to increase in the ante-bellum South from 1820–60, the price reaching its peak immediately before the Civil War, when it had already become evident that slavery would have difficulty in expanding.

The first source of instability in slave plantation agriculture was thus narrowly economic, the unpredictability of market forces. But even where market forces were favourable – or manipulable – total power proved to be an unsatisfactory basis for labour exploitation. Since the slave could only be cajoled or coerced into working, constant supervision was necessary. As Adam Smith commented, 'the experience of all ages and nations ... demonstrates that the work done by slaves, though it appears to cost only their maintenance, is in the end the dearest of any. A person who can acquire no property, can have no other interest but to eat as much and to labour as little as possible'.[36] This was certainly the experience in the American South. 'My negroes have the reputation of being orderly and well-disposed; but like all negroes they are up to anything if not watched and attended to.'[37] 'Hands won't work unless I am in sight. . . . I left the field at 12.00 [with] all going well, but very little done after that.'[38] The need for very close supervision was doubly inefficient, involving the employment of special overseers or the removal of the most trusted field-hands from directly productive work, and limiting the use of slaves to tasks in which close supervision was possible. Slaves could be used most conveniently where the 'gang' system of labour organization was possible – attempts to individualize tasks and to force slaves to work to individual quotas generally proved unsuccessful. There was thus a tendency to use the gang system whenever possible, including situations in which it was wasteful, or to fail to do, or hire others to do, tasks which required more individual action. Where free labour had to be hired, relations between slaves and freemen were a constant source of friction.

The conflict between the need for strict supervision and the desire to use slaves profitably, or at least conveniently, was most evident in the city. At the least slaves had to be allowed to leave the master's house to run errands; at the most they were permitted to live and work out of the house, earning their own wages and paying only a levy to their owners. This dilemma is well-illustrated by the conflicts among Southern slave-owners over the issue of educating slaves. Educating slaves, or at least teaching them the rudiments of reading, writing and arithmetic increased the efficiency and value of the slave; it also increased the danger of combination and rebellion. To deal with the problem many local authorities, like the Charleston City Council, made it illegal to teach slaves to read and write: 'To be able to read and write is certainly not necessary to the performance of those duties which are required of our slaves and on the contrary is incompatible with the public safety . . . this knowledge [will permit them] to carry on illicit traffic, to communicate privately among themselves, and to evade those regulations that are intended to prevent confederation among them'. The ordinances were largely ignored.[39]

Even during periods of relatively slow change in the methods of production slavery was a very inefficient system of labour exploitation – the Romans, as well as the Americans, agreed with Adam Smith's verdict. During periods of change in the methods of production this inefficiency increased: slaves were very resistant to doing anything new, and could effectively sabotage innovations. In the American South attempts to make marginal adjustments to the gang system proved ineffective. Moreover, innovation usually involved either the use of machinery, or increased reliance upon the judgment of the slave: both increased the vulnerability of the master to the slave's aggressive apathy. Nevertheless, tied to external markets, slave-owners were obliged to attempt to improve productivity to keep up with competition from other systems, including free labour. Hence the increased sophistication of the basically simple technology of the cotton gin. Such technological changes further heightened the tension between the need to increase productivity and the need to maintain control.

This tension stemmed from the basic character of the slave relationship and the slave's lack of 'interest' in its maintenance. As Adam Smith commented, the slave had 'no other interest but to eat as much and to work as little as possible'; the master had the opposite interest. For the slave-owners the problem had two alternative solutions: denial of the existence of any 'interest' for the slave, and persuading the slave that his interests were identical with those of his master. If slaves were capital, then the possibility of a conflict of interests between slaves and their masters could not arise: 'by making the labour itself into capital, the conflict of interests, so evident in other labour systems, lost its foundation. This unity was effected because slave labour was the property of slave capital.'[40] As one pro-slavery writer, John Fletcher, put it in his *Studies on Slavery, in Easy Lessons* (1852): 'Capital and labour can exist in but two relations: congenerous or antagonistic. They are never congenerous only when it is true that labour constitutes capital, which can only happen through slavery.'[41] Other owners recognized that this assimilation of labour to capital was little more than an intellectual conjuring trick, not a solution, and that the only way to resolve the tension was by persuading the slave that his interests were the same as his master's, and were not served by doing as little work as possible. As one Southern journalist commented: 'to moralize and induce the slave to assimilate with the master and his interest, has been and is the great desideration aimed at.'[42] It is hardly surprising that he went on, 'but I am sorry to say I have long since desponded in the completion of this task.' The paternalism of the Southern gentleman was an elaborate strategy for achieving this identity of interest.

Thus, despite the extent to which slavery satisfied the goals of the master, and the master's monopoly over the means of violence, slavery proved only a transient system of labour exploitation. This transience was due partly to external factors – to the economic difficulties deriving from reliance upon a limited range of primary products, to the economic and military problems posed by rival nations and economic systems, to the ideological problems posed by the evident contrast between a religion stressing God's relation to all men through Christ and the denial of the slave's humanity – and partly to internal tensions. External factors affected the chronology of the decline of slavery, but did not determine its outcome. The most important tension was between the desire to increase productivity and the desire to maintain control. For slavery constituted a rigid and inelastic method of labour exploitation, resistant alike to increased efficiency in the use of customary methods of production and to experimentation with new methods. Any change in the methods of production involved increasing the resources under the control of subordinates, and thus a change in the balance of power. In view of slaves' lack of 'interest' in the relationship any such change could only corrode the whole structure of domination.

The development of slavery illustrates clearly the complex interaction between the forces of production and the relations of production, to use the basic Marxist terms. The ecological and technological characteristics of advanced horticultural societies favoured the development of slavery, which the availability of prisoners of war made possible. Once established the system of labour exploitation developed a dynamic of its own, an increasing elaboration of the means of violence to maintain the basic structure of total domination. Increased resources were required to maintain the domination, without which the flow of resources would have ceased. Slavery, from being a means of developing the forces of production, became a 'fetter'. Yet it would be a mistake to see this as an inevitable evolutionary process, the result of social systems adapting inexorably to changing ecological and technological conditions, for it merely represented attempts by specific dominant groups to maintain their position by preserving a given method of distributing rewards. This attempt involved dominant groups in assessing the importance they attached to domination rather than productivity: the latter could often only be gained at the expense of the former.

The major significance of the analysis of slavery for the study of power relationships is the limited effectiveness of total power. Total power provided a very unsatisfactory basis for labour exploitation, as large-scale comparative research, as well as detailed studies of prison workshops, has confirmed.[43] On the surface coercion appears to provide the cheapest way for superordinates to achieve their goals, for they are not called upon to provide resources in exchange. However, coercion proved a costly form of labour exploitation for superordinates. The costs involved in ensuring compliance with the terms of the 'unilateral exchange' (to use a common if contradictory term) proved to be high, for subordinates had no 'interest' in maintaining the relationship and therefore no interest in acting according to the terms of the exchange. Recognizing this, dominant groups

73

have attempted to provide subordinates with an interest, to persuade them that their own interests are best served by compliance. By this means relations of coercion are translated into relations of authority. Authority constitutes a cheaper basis of compliance for superordinates, and a more self-respecting basis for subordinates, than coercion.

6 Authority

In slave societies the compliance of subordinates was based solely upon coercion, the slave's fear arising from his master's monopoly of the means of violence. In feudal and, even more, capitalist societies coercion is complemented by authority. A relationship of authority exists when 'the subordinate extends "consent" to the order giving role of the superior, i.e. legitimizes the norms governing this relationship'.[1] To the extent that subordinates consent to their inferior hierarchical position and thereby grant it legitimacy, coercion is supplemented by authority. Hierarchical relations thus have a mixed character in both feudalism and capitalism. In feudal societies the lord's domination was based largely upon the serf's fear, ignorance and bondage to the soil; but the serf's subordination was limited – the lord as well as the serf incurred obligations. Although the lord did not seek his serf's consent, serfs retained their humanity, their right to oppose unilateral changes in custom was generally recognized, and they could appeal outside their lord's jurisdiction in limited circumstances. With the breakdown of the inclusive domination of the lord over the serf, and the evolution of the money-based market economy of capitalism, a less predictable situation developed, with fewer fixed hierarchies. New patterns of dependence and therefore new power relations developed. Winning – or creating – consent assumed new significance, for coercion could not guarantee effective compliance when the pattern of dependences was constantly shifting and the tasks required of subordinates involved a high degree of discretion.[2] Under capitalism compliance does not result simply from a fatalistic acceptance of overwhelming domination but, at least in part, from consent. The need to win consent, and to completely transform coercion into authority, has emerged as a fundamental problem for dominant groups under capitalism only slowly, and still incompletely: but in contemporary

75

society hierarchical relations not based upon authority will always remain unstable.

The starting-point for any examination of authority must be Weber's typology of the three sources of legitimacy: tradition, charisma and legal rationality. Weber defined the three bases for claims to legitimacy in the following terms:[3]

1. Rational grounds – resting on a belief in the legality of enacted rules and the right of those elevated to authority under such rules to issue such commands (legal authority).
2. Traditional grounds – resting on an established belief in the sanctity of immemorial traditions and the legitimacy of those exercising authority under them (traditional authority); or finally,
3. Charismatic grounds – resting on devotion to the exceptional sanctity, heroism, or exemplary character of an individual person, and of the normative patterns revealed or ordained by him (charismatic authority).

I will not be concerned with traditional authority in this study, for the concept is of only limited value. One aspect of traditional authority can be subsumed under charismatic authority, 'sanctity': tradition is one basis for sanctification, and only precedents which have been sanctified are incorporated into tradition.[4] A second aspect of traditional authority is inseparable from legal rational authority, the legitimation of established precedent: tradition constitutes a repository of relevant rules, whose binding power is ultimately derived from legality and is only increased by repetition. There is some 'traditionalism' in many relationships, a variable acceptance of precedent: 'the regular recurrence of certain events somehow confers on them the dignity of oughtness.'[5] But tradition is not in itself an explanation, for not all precedents provide legitimacy: the sociologist's task is to break down the inclusive concept of tradition into its constituent parts, and to explain why some precedents rather than others are endowed with 'oughtness'. This explanation is to be found in the related concepts of charismatic and legal rational authority, the 'non-rational' and the rational.

'The term "charisma" will be applied to a certain quality of an individual personality by virtue of which he is considered extraordinary and treated as endowed with super-natural, superhuman, or at least specifically exceptional powers or qualities. These as such are not accessible to the ordinary person, but are regarded as of divine origin or as exemplary, and on the basis of them the individual concerned is treated as a "leader".'[6] For Weber charisma is not simply an attribute of the leader's personality; it is a social relationship: the leader is termed 'charismatic' because he is *seen* as possessing 'the gift of grace'. Extraordinary actions, like the performance of a miracle, validate this perception. Acceptance of charismatic authority is, according to Weber, irrational (although a more accurate term would be non-rational): 'charismatic authority is specifically irrational in the sense of being foreign to all rules . . . in the pure type charismatic authority disdains and repudiates economic exploitation of the gift of grace.'[7] But this authority will eventually collapse if the charismatic leader fails to provide at least minimal satisfaction for his followers: 'if proof and success elude the leader for long, if he appears deserted by his God or his magic or heroic powers, above all, if his leadership fails to benefit his followers, it is likely that his charismatic authority will disappear'.[8] Charismatic authority is essentially revolutionary, repudiating all claims to authority based upon established conventions, or upon standard conceptions of value:[9]

> Charismatic belief revolutionizes men 'from within' and shapes material and social conditions according to its revolutionary will . . . charisma, in its most potent forms, disrupts rational rule and tradition altogether. . . . Instead of reverence for customs that are ancient and hence sacred, it enforces the inner subjection to the unprecedented and absolutely unique and therefore Divine. In this purely empirical and value-free sense charisma is indeed the specifically creative, revolutionary force in history.

Weber's use of the concept of charisma was often confusing, and he did not present a fully developed theory of charismatic authority. One writer has concluded: 'Weber's . . . treatment of charismatic authority is the weakest link in his typology [of authority]. It is quite apparent that his analysis of charisma lacks the depth and systematic exploration that he gave to both the traditional and rational-legal types of authority . . . [Weber] had no theory of charisma.'[10] These confusions have been reflected in the writings of later commentators, both those attempting a textual exegesis of Weber and those attempting to use the concept in empirical research. It is thus not surprising that the concept has been severely criticized, and even ridiculed.[11] There are indeed serious weaknesses in the original presentation. The 'gift of grace' is not defined precisely; the reasons for followers accepting leadership claims to extraordinary powers are not fully examined. Is it possible to distinguish between truly charismatic leaders and false pretenders? The focus upon the character of the leader can lead to an exaggeration of the significance of the claimed extraordinariness of the leader at the expense of detailed investigation of the needs of subordinates and of the way in which the leader satisfies those needs. It can lead to a crude Carlyle-esque 'great man' theory of history, or to historically naïve psychoanalytic theories of leader–follower relations. But these ambiguities and criticisms do not destroy the value of the concept. It is necessary to examine the meaning of the leader's claimed extraordinariness for his followers and the way in which the followers depend upon their leader, and to attempt to relate personal qualities to social processes.[12] This requires both synchronic and diachronic analyses.

Subordinates legitimate claims for compliance on charismatic grounds when leaders help followers to satisfy their needs or to achieve their goals. Charismatic authority is distinguished from legal rational authority by the character of the needs and the way in which the leader helps to satisfy them: the needs are non-rational and the processes involved are not rule-bound. The paradigm case is that of the leader and the crowd during a mass rally. The needs may be analysed in strictly psychoanalytic terms, as the result of the malfunctioning of the super-ego, or more loosely in terms of extreme anxiety, guilt, insecurity and anxiety (although of course obedience to a charismatic leader is not the only way of resolving such problems). The processes involved are those of projection, identification and transference. In Downton's words:[13]

> seeking some way to either reduce the distance between his ego and his ego-ideal or to find a positive identity, the follower legitimizes the leader's authority by clothing the leader in the sanctifying garments of a transcendental source of power. Seeing the leader as God's spokesman or as chosen by history to work out a plan of destiny gives the follower a strong identification with the leader.

Downton is right to stress the psychological dimension of charismatic authority relations; but his stress is exaggerated, deriving from a restricted definition of charisma, and he misleadingly generalizes from the psychodynamics of crowd behaviour to less direct leader–follower relations. Although the needs satisfied by charismatic leadership ·may be psychological, the origin and distribution of those needs is, at least in part, social. For example, political and social instability during periods of decolonization may produce anxieties classifiable in clinical psychoanalytic terms amongst 'prone' sections of the population, and lead to support for charismatic leaders: but any full explanation would involve analysing the social as well as personal bases of insecurity. Moreover, acceptance of charismatic authority is based upon instrumental as well as therapeutic success: in Friedland's analysis of leadership during the struggle for independence in Tanganyika charisma was attributed to leaders on the basis of their success in the struggle, not simply their personal mystique.[14]

The highly charged charismatic leader–follower relation is only fragile; charisma provides only a temporary source of legitimation, as Weber recognized – the charismatic leader needs to place his authority upon a securer footing than that provided by divine grace. Hence the 'routinization of charisma'. This transformation usually occurs through the evolution of personal charisma into charisma of family or followers, and eventually into charisma of office: the evolution from the sacred birth of the king, to the sacred descent of the royal family, to the sacred status of the monarchy. This process can be seen operating amongst both leaders and followers.

The process of the institutionalization of charisma can be analysed into six stages corresponding to changes in the character of the relations between leader and follower. At leadership level there is an evolution from person to office, at follower level from sentiment, to unpredictable rewards, to predictable rewards. This sequence can be summarized schematically:

1 Hero–audience relation. The sentiment binding followers to leaders is primarily the recognition of the extraordinary character of the leader by subordinates: a process of transference accompanied by only minimal rewards to followers. Such a relation exists between Gairey and his followers in British Grenada.[15]

2 Hero–follower relation. The sentiment binding followers to leaders is still primarily that of transference, but increasingly associated with material rewards in the form of booty. Such a relation existed between Nkrumah and his followers in the early stages of the People's Progressive Party in Nigeria.[16]

3 Chosen group-following relation. The original charisma has been transferred from the single leader to his chosen followers, whilst they have gathered round themselves a further group of followers, bound partly by charisma and, more importantly, by the prospects of booty.

4 Chosen group-movement. The charisma of the leader has been dispersed amongst the group, and the chosen group has gathered about itself not simply a band of followers but a coherently organized movement, bound together in the hope of obtaining reward, if necessary in the distant future. Such ties bound the leadership and the rest of the membership together in the early days of the Russian Bolshevik party.

5 Office-movement. The charisma or sense of 'other-worldliness' has been transferred from the group to the office held by the group, the executive committee. The movement remains, as before,

organized in terms of a common ideology, designed to obtain power. The unifying tie to the leadership remains the desire to achieve a remote goal.

6 Office-organization. Charisma has, by this stage, been transferred completely to the office. The relation corresponds to that referred to by Eisenstadt and Shils as the institutionalization of charisma in the 'order-affecting' roles in society.[17] The subordinate is tied to the superordinate by the expectation of predictable rewards. The organization is based upon principles designed to maximize such rewards.

This tendency to develop from hero–audience to office-organization is not necessarily an evolutionary one: the process can be stopped, or even reversed by the abilities of specific leaders or followers, by fratricidal conflicts amongst the 'chosen', or by the intractability of the environment. But there is a tendency for the relationship between leader and followers to develop in the direction of greater predictability, and in so doing to move from stage 1 to stage 6. In doing so the relevance of charismatic authority diminishes, that of legal rational authority increases.

In relations of legal rational authority subordinates accept the supremacy of superordinates because it is legitimated in terms of mutually accepted rules:[18]

> In this type, an individual who holds authority does so in virtue of impersonal norms which are not the residue of tradition, but which have been consciously established within a context of either purposive or value rationality. Those who are subject to authority obey their super-ordinate, not because of any personal dependence on him, but because of their acceptance of the impersonal norms which define that authority. . . . Those subject to legal authority owe no personal allegiance to a super-ordinate, and follow his commands only within the restricted sphere in which his jurisdiction is clearly specified.

Although authority is accepted because it is grounded in legal norms, Weber did not assume that legal norms were themselves necessarily the product of agreement – 'any given legal norm may be established by agreement or by imposition, on grounds of expediency or value-rationality or both' – although they are normally agreed and accepted by the subordinate as a means of achieving his own ends. The ends which the subordinate wishes to satisfy by compliance are, for Weber, variable – they may be narrowly economic, political, religious or whatever. The characteristic organizational structure created by relations of legal rational authority is bureaucracy, government by experts according to formally rational rules. The function of such rules is to ensure predictability and equity.[19] Bureaucracy was regarded by Weber as the characteristic form of administration in capitalist society, especially in democratic capitalist societies, for it represented the apotheosis of rationalization, suited the market economy, and incorporated the democratic premises of equality before the law.

The essence of legal rational authority, for Weber, was the acceptance of the authority of the superior because it was legitimated by reference to an accepted overall rule. Any edict falling within the scope of the area covered by the relevant impersonal norms was accepted. But, for the subordinate, this was more legal than rational: it was *not* necessary that the edict should be rational from the perspective of the subordinate. Edicts were to be accepted because they were legal and *therefore* rational (a view lying at the centre of the Eichmann defence). This view is, of course, implausible: the relation between legality and the subordinate's substantive rationality is contingent and unpredictable. Weber avoided this confusion by excluding 'expedient' behaviour from his discussion of authority; expedient behaviour was the province of the sociology of economic life, not the sociology of domination.[20] The problem of rationality, rather than legality, thus did not arise for Weber in this context. However, acceptance of the overarching norms upon which legality is based involves consent, and consent cannot be classified into 'expedient' and 'inexpedient', with legal rational authority arising over inexpedient actions. An authority relation exists whenever subordinates grant consent to the superordination of others and the consequent rightfulness of compliance, regardless of the basis of that consent.

There are two types of legal rational authority, corresponding to two types of subordinate interest: of procedure, and of outcome. Compliance may occur because the superordinate fulfils a role whose maintenance the subordinate feels is necessary to ensure the survival of the society or group to which he belongs, not because he consents to the specific decision. Hence supplicants may comply with the unfavourable decisions of the judiciary, even when the decisions are against their direct 'outcome' interests, because they recognize that the role of the judiciary is to uphold the rules of the game, and that the game could not survive without rules. In these circumstances the acceptance of judicial decisions is legal and rational, but not expedient. Similarly, trade union leaders may accept the outcome of a specific sequence of collective bargaining not because they believe that the outcome meets their demands, but because the refusal to accept the outcome might prejudice the survival of the institution of collective bargaining. (This concept of 'procedural legal rationality' is not the same as Parsons's term

81

'legitimated with reference to collective goals', for there may be little collective support for the role.) Alternatively, subordinates may consent to their subordination simply because it is in their direct interests to do so: it may be personally advantageous to accept present subordination in return for present or future reward, as in the conventional capitalist wage-labour contract.

Weber's typology of authority comprised a set of 'ideal-types', each forming a logically coherent 'pure-type' not found empirically. As I have argued earlier, an ideal-type is a theoretical model, a vocabulary from which to construct a coherent account of social dynamics, not a set of empirical generalizations about the real world;[21] 'none of these three ideal types . . . is usually to be found in historical cases in "pure" form.'[22] Authority relations, under all societies, have been based upon a mixture of all these types of legitimation – charismatic, traditional and legal rational – the precise mixture depending upon the character of the social system and of the specific relationship within it. 'Groups approximating to purely traditional types have certainly existed. But they have never been stable indefinitely and, as is also true of bureaucratic authority, have seldom been without a head who had a personally charismatic status by heredity or office.'[23] For Weber the ideal-typical basis of authority in industrial organizations in capitalism was legal rationality: but in practice he expected it to include traditional and charismatic elements. Such expectations were justified, as the discussion below, p. 107, shows.

Despite its limitations Weber's typology remains the best starting-point for investigating the problem of authority. Authority relations exist when subordinates consent to the dominion of others. There are two bases of consent, non-rational and rational, corresponding to two broad classes of subordinate goals. There are two corresponding types of authority, charismatic and legal rational. In turn, there are two types of legal rational authority, procedural and outcome. The distinction between charismatic and legal rational authority is based partly upon differences in subordinate goals and needs, and partly upon parallel differences in the grounds of super-ordination: charismatic rulers obtain compliance through acceptance of their claimed personal extraordinariness, legal rational leaders because compliance is seen as being substantively rational by subordinates. Charismatic authority is likely during periods of rapid social change, when extraordinary qualities are required to deal with unusually disorienting conditions. Legal rational authority is characteristic of more stable or predictably evolving societies, in which subordinates develop exchange relations susceptible to rule.

Hierarchical relations under feudalism and capitalism contain both authoritarian and coercive elements: the existence of authority does not necessarily exclude coercion. Any given hierarchical relation may be based upon authority but, when the compliance is not forthcoming, superordinates may use their greater resources to obtain compliance by coercion. Moreover, consent constitutes a very slippery 'end-term', for consent may be based upon the hopelessness of non-compliance, not the recognition of interest; indeed consent is more likely where the balance of dependence is extreme and the prospects of avoiding compliance limited than where the balance is finer and there are real prospects of avoiding non-self-regarding action. Nor is the amount of power involved in a relationship of authority necessarily less than that involved in coercion: the legitimation of a relation may increase the power of the superordinate by changing the rate of exchange between dependence and compliance. Subordinates may be prepared to perform more non-self-regarding actions when they believe that the superordinate's position is legitimate than when they do not. At the very least the motivation to escape is undermined, and the costs of supervision reduced. The balance between coercion and authority, and its impact upon power relations, is an empirical matter.

7 Power relations under feudalism

Slavery involved an extreme form of asymmetric dependence, in which the slave ceased to exist except as an expression of his master's will; the slave had no alternative but to perform continuously non-self-regarding actions at the behest of his master. The master's domination could only be sustained by coercion, attempts to persuade the slave that it was in his own interest predictably failing. The feudal serf retained his humanity, but was similarly obliged to comply with his lord's demands. The dependence of the serf upon his lord was only slightly less than the dependence of the slave upon his master, for the lord monopolized control over the major means of subsistence, the land; indeed, the distinction between the freeman and the slave was negligible in the early stages of feudalism, especially in Italy. The serf surrendered himself into the hands of his lord, in return for protection and maintenance, and was obliged to carry out his lord's will. Nevertheless, although the amount of power involved in master–slave and lord–serf relations was similar, the bases of power and therefore the character of the relation were different. The serf's compliance stemmed basically from his lack of access to the means of survival; but coercion was supplemented by authority. The serf became the lord's man; but the lord was reciprocally obliged to provide protection and maintenance. The ties between lord and serf were a complex of customary obligations, on both sides. Either party could appeal to the lord's lord, the king, if customary rights and obligations were not fulfilled, unlike slavery, where no slave could appeal against or give evidence against his master. In addition, the immunities of the church provided legitimate sanctuary for wronged serfs. In short, power relations in feudalism were more complex than under slavery.

The term feudalism may be used in either an extended or a restricted sense. For St Simon and, following him, Marx feudalism was used in an extended sense, to refer to any society in which land was the decisive factor of production, and where the major relation of production was that of land-owner and tenant. As such it constituted the intervening stage in the development of society from the slave-society of the Ancients to the capitalist society of the Moderns.[1] This extended usage is, however, too imprecise, disregarding significant variations in degrees of domination deriving from different types of land-lord and tenant relations and from different forms of land-tenure. Instead, I will use the term 'feudalism' in a more restricted sense, to refer to that form of society possessing the following characteristics:[2]

> [the] development pushed to extremes of the element of personal dependence in society, with a specialized military class occupying the higher levels in the social scale; an extreme sub-division of the rights of real property; a graded system of rights over land created by this sub-division and corresponding in broad outline to the grades of personal dependence just referred to; and a dispersal of political authority amongst a hierarchy of persons who exercise in their own interest powers normally attributed to the State.

Feudal society was militaristic, landed and fragmented.

Feudalism was a highly complex social system, whose structure varied considerably throughout Europe: English feudalism was very different from German, and there were several varieties of French feudalism. But the core of the system comprised two personal relationships, that of crown and vassal or lord, and that of vassal and peasant. The essential characteristic of the feudal system was the surrender of one man into the hands of another, in return for which he received protection and maintenance, usually through the grant of a fief over land, in the case of king and vassal, or the direct grant of land, in the case of vassal and peasant. This surrender occurred at two levels of society: the king received the surrender of his vassal, the lord, and the lord received the surrender of his vassal, the peasant.[3] Essentially, 'feudalism may be regarded as a body of institutions creating and regulating the obligations of obedience and service – mainly military service – on the part of a free man (the vassal) towards another free man (the lord), and the obligations of protection and maintenance on the part of the lord with regard to his vassal.'[4] Such ties were personal, particular and diffuse.

This dual submission formed the central relationship in feudal society, endowed with economic, political, religious, and in the widest sense, social significance. As Marc Bloch summarized the relationship between lord and peasant:[5]

> To this lord . . . the cultivators of the soil owed, first, a more or less important part of their time; days of agricultural labour devoted to the cultivation of the fields, meadows, or vineyards of his demesne; carting and carrying services; and sometimes service as builders and craftsmen. Further, they were obliged to divert to his use a considerable part of their own harvests, sometimes in the form of rents in kind and sometimes by means of taxes in money. . . . The very fields that they cultivated were not held to be theirs in full ownership, nor was their community – at least in most cases – the full owner of those lands over which common rights were exercised. Both were said to be 'held' of the lord, which meant that as landowner he had a superior right over them, recognized by dues owed to him, and capable in certain circumstances of overriding the concurrent rights of the individual cultivators and of the community.
>
> Finally, the lord did not merely draw from his peasants valuable revenues and an equally valuable labour force. Not only was he a *rentier* of the soil and a beneficiary of the services; he was also a judge, often – if he did his duty – a protector, and always a chief, whom . . . those who 'held' their land from him or lived on his land were bound, by a very general but very real obligation, to help and to obey. Thus the *seigneurie* was not simply an economic enterprise by which profits accumulated in a strong man's hands. It was also a unit of authority, in the widest sense of the word; for the powers of the chief . . . affected a man's whole life and acted concurrently with, or even in place of, the power of the State and family.

Ties of vassalage were supreme over all other ties. According to the court of the Count of Barcelona: 'In law-suits brought by parents against sons or by sons against parents, the parents shall be treated for purposes of the judgement as if they were the lords and the sons their men, bound to them by the rite of homage.'[6]

Around this central relationship developed congruent political, economic, and religious systems, although none were peculiar to feudalism: a fragmented polity, a manorial economy, and an hierarchical conception of the universe.

Under feudalism rights of sovereignty and political functions did not belong to the prince, the state, or the nation, but to lordships and fiefs – indeed Strayer sees this fragmentation as the distinctive feature of feudalism, in my view mistakenly: 'political power is monopolized by a small group of military leaders, but is rather unevenly distributed among members of the group. As a result no leader rules a very wide territory, nor does he have complete authority even within a limited territory – he must share power with his equals and grant power to his subordinates.'[7] The indivisibility of sovereignty was not a principle recognized by feudalism, as the highly complex jurisdictional disputes, especially between the church and secular authorities, indicate.

The major unit of production in feudal society was the manor, although the manor existed before feudalism and survived long after its disintegration: it cannot be regarded as a defining characteristic of feudalism:[8]

> The manor in itself has no claim to a place among the institutions which we call feudal. It had existed (as it did again later on) with a stronger State, with less numerous and less solid relationships of clientage, and with a much freer circulation of money. Nevertheless, in the new conditions of life which arose from approximately the ninth century onwards, this ancient method of social organization was destined not only to extend its grip over a much larger proportion of the population, but also to consolidate to a remarkable degree its own internal structure.

The manor comprised the lord's 'demesne', worked by serfs as part of their labour service and by a minority of landless labourers, especially in later feudalism, together with the serf's strips of land, held of the lord and worked by the serfs in combination. The emphasis upon hierarchy characteristic of medieval theology and social philosophy was not peculiar to feudalism either; but it reached its apogee in Europe during the feudal period. Social hierarchy reflected moral hierarchy, which reflected Divine hierarchy. The conventional teaching of the Schools of the early twelfth century is well summarized by an anonymous member of the circle of Anselm of Laon:[9]

> Servitude is ordained by God, either because of the sins of those who become serfs, or as a trial, in order that those who are thus humbled may be made better. For servitude is of great help to religion in protecting humility, the guardian of all virtues; and it would seem to be pride for anyone to wish to change that condition which has been given him for good reason by the divine ordinance.

Any assessment of the extent of feudalism obviously depends upon the definition adopted. If feudalism is defined in the extended Marxist sense, it refers to virtually all forms of pre-capitalist society subsequent to the collapse of the Asiatic mode of production, being found in Ancient Egypt, in India, throughout the Turkish empire, Russia, Japan and elsewhere. In this vein *The Great Soviet Encyclopaedia* of 1956 stated that feudalism lasted in Western Europe until the eighteenth century, in Russia until 1861, in Soviet Asia until 1917, and in China until 1949.[10] In similar vein President Nixon referred to the 'feudal princes' of South-East Asia. However, if the term is used in the more restricted sense adopted here, feudalism flourished in France, Germany, the Low Countries, England, and parts of Italy in the eleventh and twelfth centuries, and in Japan during the same period. Elsewhere there developed elements of feudalism, as in Russia, but not feudalism proper. To illustrate the significance of feudalism as a system of power relations I have concentrated upon the classic 'high' feudalism of eleventh- and twelfth-century Europe.

The transition from the slave society of the late Roman Empire to the feudal society of the Carolingian and post-Carolingian period was a confused, chaotic process. Little is known in detail about the history of Europe between the fifth and the ninth centuries. But a profound transformation took place during that period in the basic relations between dominant and subordinate groups. By the ninth century former 'free' peasants and slaves were merging to form free and servile possessors of 'manses', the characteristic tenancy of feudal society; gradually, the economic and social distinction between these two categories diminished in importance, until both became referred to by the same old Justinian name, *coloni adscripti*. Servitude to the soil was substituted for servitude to a master.

There were six major factors responsible for the transformation of both free and slave into this semi-servile status: the disintegration of slavery as a form of labour exploitation, the continued need of the weak for protection against the strong, the inability of either blood kin or central government to provide such protection, the elaboration of the technology of war associated with the spread into Europe of the stirrup, and the continued importance of local chieftains, with power inherited from antiquity. Economic, political and technological changes worked in the same direction.

As I have argued in chapter 6, slavery is of only limited value as a system of labour exploitation, expensive both in its demand for working capital and for effective supervision. These pressures began to undermine European slavery from the beginning of the second century AD. As the supply of slaves dried up their capital cost increased, with increased risks to their masters, whilst the problems of administration worsened with the disintegration of the Roman Empire. Moreover, although the Christian church did not proscribe slavery as such, it did proscribe the enslavement of 'true Christians', i.e. Catholics. By the ninth century the only sources of new slaves were the Far West (Ireland), the North (Finland and the Baltic), North Africa, and the Middle East – sources too distant to sustain an intensive slave system. The high capital cost of slaves, and the risks involved in their administration, led to the development of tenancies as 'the line of least resistance':[11]

> Labour kept itself; the families, each settled on its scrap of land, grew in the natural way. It was merely necessary to take care that the days of work on the demesne were duly given – and that was mostly done for you by custom. As soon as slaves, at the places of sale, were no longer a commodity attractive because abundant, and therefore cheap, the new tone of social life and the new habits of mind were all against any effort to maintain the old, and far too complicated, methods.

Moreover, the grant of tenure of land bound the individual peasant to a specific place far more effectively than direct repression, a central advantage during a period of labour shortage.

The inability to maintain the slave system was not, however, the decisive reason for the development of feudalism: slavery was never the predominant form of labour exploitation in areas where feudalism developed furthest, north of the Alps. More important was the need of the weak for protection, against tax-gatherers or military service, or against foreign marauders. The period between the fourth and ninth centuries saw an elaboration of the system of patronage which had existed throughout Roman history.[12] Hunger, fear of the erratic extortions of representatives of central administration, who were strong enough to levy charges upon the weak but too feeble to protect the weak against the strong, and straightforward coercion were responsible for the peasant placing himself in the hands of his lord, through the contract of commendation. At the same time the strong had obvious incentives to undertake protection of the weak – prestige, power and services.

The peasant was thrown upon his lord for protection because of the inadequacy of the two alternative sources of security – the crown, and the kinship group. By the eleventh century the crown had effectively surrendered the claim to direct political authority over the peasant, and had granted to the lords rights which it recognized it was itself incapable of exercising effectively. This had occurred through the granting of legal 'immunities', rights to jurisdiction over lands and men living on them, even where the residents were nominally free. As the number of immunities increased the central administration grew weaker, and incapable of resisting further pressure for more immunities.[13] The kinship group similarly failed to retain

POWER RELATIONS UNDER FEUDALISM

solidarity, and thereby failed to provide protection. Kinship failed to provide an adequate bond partly because the outlines of the group were vague and variable, partly because of the duality of descent through the male and female lines, fragmenting the potentially cohesive effect of property inheritance, and partly because of changes in the technology of war, which increased the use of war materials, transformed the military position of the peasantry, and thereby undermined the effectiveness of horizontal kinship groupings.[14]

The blood group could, in itself, form a protective community when the possession of arms was widespread, in other words when the technology of war was relatively simple. However, the technology of war was transformed in 733, with Charles Martel's realization of the military potential of the stirrup. The stirrup made the development of a new style of cavalry warfare, the charge with lance at rest.[15] The success of this new style of warfare led inevitably to the diminution of the significance of infantry: military prowess became a monopoly of a single class, the knightly class. Without the necessary technical equipment, the blood group was powerless to provide protection against outsiders; and once the equipment had been obtained, an inevitable process of social differentiation occurred. This inherent tendency was exacerbated by royal policy, especially in France. The new style of warfare was expensive – horses were costly, and armour became heavier: military equipment for one man cost the equivalent of twenty oxen. In an age when money was becoming increasingly scarce, the central taxation authorities were unable to raise money; the only means of paying for the new technology was therefore through the grant of rights over land. At the same time, the military preponderance of the knight made it likely that he would be in a position to maximize the value of his grant, and that the peasantry would be incapable of resisting. In short, 'the requirements of the new mode of warfare which the stirrup made possible found expression in a new form of western European society dominated by an aristocracy of warriors endowed with land so that they might fight in a new and highly specialized way.'[16]

Economic, political and technological developments made it likely that the form of hierarchical differentiation and dependence characteristic of feudalism would develop, but did not determine who would be dominant and who dependent. Here, as elsewhere, the already powerful became more powerful. Village chieftains existed in Gaul before Caesar, in Germany before the invasions, and in Celtic Britain; it was they who became the knights and vassals of the new feudal system: 'in spite of repeated remodellings of social rise and fall and the luck of all sorts of adventurers, the old core of the noble

90

class was formed by the descendants of these rustic chieftains, among whom were recruited – for they had to be recruited somewhere – most of the vassals and most of the knights.'[17] Feudalism represented only a new stage in the evolution of relations between dominant and subordinate.

The pressures which originally led to the development of feudalism naturally continued to sustain it once it had emerged, especially the continued need of the weak for protection. For, despite the attempts of individual vassals to establish islands of order, violence remained an integral part of early medieval society. In part this derived from customary brigandage, which has survived throughout history in rural areas. But the violence was more extensive than that endemic to rural society. For the knights violence was the quickest way of becoming rich, as the knightly troubadour recognized: 'Trumpet, drums, flags, and pennons, standards and horses white and black – that is what we shall shortly see. And it will be a happy day; for we shall seize the usurers' goods, and no more shall beasts of burden pass along the highways by day in complete safety; nor shall the burgess journey without fear, nor the merchant on his way to France; but the man who is full of courage shall be rich.'[18] This natural tendency was exacerbated by the law of 'seisin', by which any usurpation was eventually recognized. But violence was not the prerogative of a single warrior class: respect for the widespread practice of private vengeance, and violent drunkenness, were common throughout the population. As Burchard of Worms commented, violence was part of the contemporary way of life: 'Every day murders in the manner of wild beasts are committed among the dependents of St. Peters. They attack each other through drunkenness, through pride, or for no reason at all. In the course of one year thirty-five serfs of St. Peter's, completely innocent people, have been killed by other serfs of the church.'[19] The knightly class remained the only source of protection for the peasant, with the continued fragility of central administration and the weakness of horizontal bonds of solidarity. The position of the vassals continued to be reinforced from above, by the continued need of the monarchy for military assistance, whether in wars between themselves (as in the continued conflicts between the English crown and the French in France) or in defence of Christendom against the Saracens. The crown was obliged to continue granting fiefs, often burdening the same land, with the same peasantry, with a multitude of cross-cutting feudal obligations (a tendency which was to seriously weaken feudalism later).

But, once established, feudalism drew upon additional sources of strength: custom, primitive communications, religion and the manorial economy. Once established, practices continued unless redefined through the use of superior force. Although the relation between lord and peasant was expressed in contractual terms, the 'contract' made sense only within a system of custom. The texts of agreements which have survived are usually vague, not defining precisely the liabilities of the land, or the length of time the recipient was to hold it. Moreover, customs, once established, became permanent – for example, military service became standardized at forty days per year – and eventually formalized. In the long run such standardization was to facilitate the commutation of services; in the short run it merely reinforced the weakness of the peasantry.

Custom was preserved by the lack of communications characteristic of medieval Europe. The mode of communications did not prevent individuals, especially clergy, from travelling long distances, primarily from monastery to monastery, and thus disseminating very general ideas. However, frequent intercourse between neighbours was impossible, partly because of the danger of violence, and partly for simple technical reasons – the inadequacy of dirt roads, usually passable only in summer. Moreover, the four-wheeled waggon, with pivoted front axle, was not used widely until the end of the thirteenth century, thus restricting the economic viability of commercial transport. Even during the Roman Empire transport costs trebled the price of grain for every hundred miles it was transported: the destruction of this imperial infrastructure meant that by the eleventh century the risk of non-arrival was added to the costs of movement.

Economic developments facilitated the maintenance of feudalism, with the increased agricultural productivity of the eleventh and twelfth centuries making possible the maintenance of an increased population without substantial emigration and labour mobility. Extensive labour mobility would have eroded feudalism rapidly. Feudalism depended, in the first instance, upon fertile soil: where the soil was infertile, for example in Russia, permanent cultivation was impossible and the inevitable labour mobility made the development of the elaborate structure of feudalism impossible. Similarly, feudalism did not develop extensively amongst hunting and gathering societies, or amongst pastoral groups, for similar reasons: the Pyrenees, for example, remained outside feudalism. But fertile soil was a necessary, not a sufficient, condition for agricultural prosperity. Three related technological developments led to an improvement in agricultural productivity in the thirteenth century, which in turn facilitated the maintenance of feudalism: the use of the heavy plough (rather than the scratch plough), the harness (which permitted the ox, and even more the horse, to work more efficiently) and the nailed horseshoe. These three developments were important both generally, because they provided a viable economic infrastructure for the manor, and specifically, because they facilitated the development of the strip system of farming. The heavy plough required eight oxen to be used effectively, no peasant had eight oxen, therefore co-operation was necessary. Moreover, the ancient square field was unsuitable for the heavy plough, because of the turning circle: hence an additional impetus was given to the development of strip farming, with each peasant owning strips dispersed throughout the village. Such improvements in technology and social organization enabled the manorial economy to survive the pressure of increasing population.

Feudalism thus rested securely on the foundation of a specific political, technological and economic basis. But this basis contained within itself the seeds of its own destruction. In periods of disorder the strong inevitably became stronger, the weak weaker – a trend evident amongst the knights as well as in the relations between knights and peasants. The accretion of custom into contract facilitated commutation, and the disintegration of the originally personal character of the bond between lord and vassal, or especially, between vassal and peasant. This disintegration of the personal link was further hastened by the customary recognition of hereditary rights, and by the elaboration of conflicting obligations, which obviously undermined the whole structure. Finally, the technical changes which initially helped to foster manorialism and thus feudalism progressively undermined it; with the increased use of the heavy horse in ploughing in the thirteenth century the radius of cultivation around a settlement increased, leading to an increase in the size of the village, with resultant differentiation of labour, horizontal solidarity and enhanced ability to maintain security without the assistance of the knight. It is necessary now to examine the factors which led to the disintegration of feudalism more fully.

Feudalism centred upon a specific act, the act of homage, an act symbolizing a personal surrender. As feudalism developed the personal character of this relationship changed. Although the 'contract' was renewed at the death of either party and the accession of his heir, it became customary for the oath to be a direct repetition of the previous one. Hence the subordinate developed rights beyond those explicitly granted to him, the right to expect that the oath would be as before, 'customary'. It was only a short step from enshrining obligations in custom to enshrining them in more formal 'contracts', stating clearly the conditions under which the 'contract' was to be binding. This process of formalization occurred throughout the twelfth century: military service was standardized at forty days a year, labour services were standardized at variable amounts. Formalization naturally facilitated commutation: specific rights could be given a price.

Commutation was made possible by the revival of a monetary economy in the twelfth century, primarily in the towns but also, to a lesser degree, in the country. Technical changes, as we have seen, led to increased productivity on the farm, which in turn led to the creation of a surplus, and to the development of trade, even in grain. This was facilitated by simultaneous improvements in land, and especially, water transport. Such increases in productivity also led to an increase in the size of villages, and to the development of a division of labour in the village, for example the emergence of the specific craft of blacksmith. Increased size, and increased division of labour exerted a corrosive effect upon the relationship between lord and peasant, for the specialized worker had to perform services for his peers; he ceased to be economically related solely to his immediate family and his lord. Increased size also led, inevitably, to the development of markets, which further stimulated 'commercial' relations at the expense of the personal relations of lord and peasant.

The redevelopment of a money economy had a further important effect: it enabled the monarchy to obtain services without granting fiefs. Twelfth-century England saw the beginnings of a 'professional civil service', bound to the monarchy by monetary reward rather than by grant of a fief. Money also made possible the raising of a professional army, directly subordinate to the king. Although the lords remained a significant source of military assistance for the crown until the end of the Middle Ages, their role was undermined by the development of a nucleus of 'king's men', a process which went further in some countries (England) than others (Germany). The final blow to the military preponderance of the knight was to be given by the revival of the use of the bow and arrow in the fourteenth century.

The revival of a money economy was accompanied by the revival of city life. Cities had never completely disappeared following the disintegration of the Roman Empire, but they had declined significantly in size. The decline of barbarian conflicts, and the commercial and political revival which this made possible, stimulated economic expansion, which in turn facilitated the revival of urban life. Although there was no city in medieval Europe to equal the size of Ancient Rome, important cities developed, especially in Northern Italy and Flanders: in Flanders, Ghent, Bruges and Ypres all had populations over 20,000 by 1300, in France Paris had a population of 80,000, and even the least developed country,

England, had nine large towns. Urban development eroded feudalism indirectly, by providing an alternative source for royal support, and directly by providing a haven for peasants escaping from their bondage. The revival of cities was in part the result of the slow re-assertion of royal power. In England, for example, the crown never completely surrendered to the holders of fiefs jurisdiction over all crimes, retaining responsibility for felons under the jurisdiction of the assize court. In the twelfth century Henry II was largely responsible for translating this right into a reality; the assize court re-emerged as the focus of justice. At the same time the crown developed a more energetic taxation policy, and in general attempted to curb the position of the feudal aristocracy – a struggle which was to continue at least until the sixteenth century. Even some of the feudal aristocracy were persuaded that justice in the king's court was preferable to the frequently contested justice of the fief-holder.[20] Such a process occurred most clearly in England, but similar tendencies were evident in France (although not in Germany).

The effect of political, economic and technological changes was to replace the vertical ties of feudalism with the horizontal ties, not of class, but of estate. Feudalism had effectively destroyed the ancient distinction between slave and free; it was to give birth to the classic distinction between the three estates, and within the third estate the distinction between landed and landless peasant. By 1300 feudalism had been effectively destroyed, partly by the elaboration of its own logic, up to the point at which it had become internally contradictory, and partly by the changing environment. Disorder was giving way to political order, barter was giving way to the money economy, villages were growing larger, cities were re-emerging. In the new situation the rigidities of feudalism were out of place.

Like slavery, feudalism was the product of a specific stage in the development of the forces and relations of production. It developed fully only in settled agrarian societies, where limited geographical mobility made the development of an elaborate and inflexible system of land-tenures possible. The distribution of control over the critical factor of production, land, was largely determined by military technology, the superiority of the mounted knight over the foot-soldier. The rural society which emerged out of this military situation survived because the productivity of the plough, especially the heavy plough, created an economic surplus sufficient to maintain a military class. Without the heavy plough feudalism could not have sustained the growing population of Europe in the thirteenth century within the restrictions imposed by a 'natural' rather than a market economy, a fragmented system of land-holding, and a large military class.[21] Inheritance played relatively little part in determining the distribution of resources in early feudalism, for the relationship between the lord and his man was a personal one, renewed at the death of either party; however, the principle of the heritability of tenures gained increasing acceptance during the late thirteenth century, signalling the breakdown of personal ties of allegiance.

The ceremony which accompanied the serf's avowal of allegiance to his lord symbolized their mutual dependence. The serf depended upon his lord for protection and for access to the critical factor of production, the land. He ensured his survival by accepting the grant of a fief, comprising small strips of land worked individually and shared rights to use common land. The lord relied upon his men to fulfil his military obligations to the crown, to provide goods and labour services, and in general to enhance the prestige of his name. The lord's own position depended directly upon the military might and economic efficiency of 'his' men.

The serf possessed only limited means of escape from this asymmetric dependence. Collective action, whether violent or non-violent, has always been rare in peasant societies because of the small size of the productive unit, the difficulties of communication in rural areas, and the reluctance of peasants to leave 'their' land:[22]

> The small-holding peasants form a vast mass, the members of which live in similar conditions but without entering into manifold relations with one another. Their mode of production isolates them from one another instead of bringing them into mutual intercourse. The isolation is increased by France's bad means of communication and by the poverty of the peasants. Their field of production, the small-holding, admits of no division of labour in its cultivation, no application of science, and, therefore, no diversity of development, no variety of talent, no wealth of social relationships. Each individual peasant family is almost self-sufficient; it itself directly produces the major part of its consumption, and thus acquires its means of life more through exchange with nature than in intercourse with society. . . . The great mass of the French nation is formed by simple addition of homologous magnitudes, much as potatoes in a sack form a sack of potatoes.

Marx's eloquent account of the nineteenth-century French peasantry is equally apposite to the European peasantry of the early Middle Ages. Collective action was especially difficult under feudalism, especially early feudalism, because of the extreme fragmentation of interests and the personal character of the ties between the serf and his lord. Even where lords failed to fulfil their obligations resistance was usually individual rather than collective; there was little basis in either interests or sentiment for combined group action. The serf found it difficult to escape from his dependence individually, for he derived his social identity from his lord; serfs who reneged upon their oath of allegiance became social isolates (unless they escaped to start a new life in the towns). The search for alternative sources of supply of land was fruitless, for any lord accepting the allegiance of a man already under oath to another lord violated the basic principles of feudalism, and was likely to provoke bloodshed. Finally, it was impossible for the serf to modify his beliefs and minimize the value of the resources controlled by his lord for the land was the fundamental means of subsistence; existence off the land was difficult to conceive.

The lord's power was based upon his control of access to the land, and ultimately upon military force. The serf's subordination to his lord was in some ways comparable to the slave's subordination to his master. The lord could do with his serfs exactly as he pleased, except to maim or murder them; he could sell his serfs and their families. Such ownership rights were symbolized by the right of *merchat*, the right to demand a fine of the serf on the marriage of the serf's daughter (since the lord thereby lost future offspring). But there were important limitations upon the power of the lord, the limitations differing in different parts of Europe. The serf's labour dues were gradually standardized, and by the early thirteenth century serfs in England were protected against arbitrary increases in dues, and against excessive brutality. The dual character of the dependence relation between the serf and his master, and the serf's acceptance of his subordination, was symbolized in the ceremony of the oath of allegiance: the serf surrendered himself and his heirs in perpetuity 'so that they should for ever serve the abbot and monks of this place in a servile condition. And in order that this gift might be made more certain and apparent, he put the bell rope round his neck and placed four pennies from his own head on the altar of St. Martin in recognition of serfdom.'[23] The bell rope and the placing of money on the head were both signs of submission: freemen tendered rent by hand.

Such relationships, based upon increasingly ambiguous custom, were inherently unstable. Any ambiguity in social relations is likely to prove transient, to be replaced by certainty based either upon coercion or upon contract; in this sense Parsons is correct in emphasizing the importance of 'complementarity' of expectations. The erosion of ambiguity in feudalism could have led to the emergence of labour relations based either upon coercion or contract. There were several pressures upon both dominant and subordinate groups which might have been expected to lead to the re-emergence of slavery. Dominant groups might have been expected to maximize their superordination, especially when outside the power of superiors with competing jurisdiction or the influence of peers competing for clients. Subordinates might have been expected to accede to this pressure, either because of inability to resist, or inability to escape, or because it represented the lesser of two evils in a threatening and uncertain environment. But feudal relations developed into wage-labour relations, not into slavery.

The diffuse act of subordination symbolized by the act of homage and the swearing of the oath of fealty gradually developed into the more specific wage-labour contract of employer and employee. In very general terms, a personal and diffuse relation evolved into a personal and specific relation, and eventually into an impersonal and specific relation – although of course even under capitalism this process has not been completed. Feudalism witnessed an increasing specificity of obligations and services on both sides. The lord's obligations to provide protection and maintenance evolved rapidly into the custom of granting rights over land, eventually of a certain size (although there does not appear to have been any very general norm). Similarly, the peasant's labour services became defined more specifically, in terms of work to be done on certain days, or at certain times of year. The dues to be paid on succession also became defined clearly. As the reciprocal obligations became more specific, they became more 'negotiable': labour services could become translated into the obligation to provide goods, and eventually money, equivalent to the goods that would have been produced during the appropriate labour time. The process of commutation was gradual, its speed varying in different parts of feudalism, extending farthest in England, least far in Germany. But by the beginning of the fourteenth century the process of commutation had significantly undermined feudalism in England.

This transformation in the character of relations between lord and peasant was partly the result of the 'logic of the situation', the transformation of the essentially unpredictable into the predictable. Uncertainty evolved into custom. But custom in itself could only provide the basis for social relations during periods of stability, and it is only to the ethnocentric eyes of twentieth-century sociologists that the twelfth century appears static. Social relations were transformed in the twelfth century by the revival of the money economy, the re-emergence of cities, and the consequent possibility of the re-emergence of centralized state power. Both in England and in France the monarchy took advantage of the new conditions, developing a centralized 'civil service', a professional military cadre, and re-asserting its rights of jurisdiction over 'immunities'. The revival of the monetary economy undermined the power of the lord at two levels, at the top, by increasing the power of the crown, and at the bottom, by providing the means for the peasant to dispose of his surplus produce independently of his lord. The revival of a monetary economy made it difficult for the lord to retain his power; it also undermined his desire to maintain custom, for it provided alternative goods to those directly available to him from 'his' men. He was thus willing to accede to pressure for the commutation of dues in kind to monetary tribute, and in doing so to unshackle the peasant. At least in the short term, the lord as well as the peasant gained from the transferability of resources, and increase in choice, which participation in a money economy provided.

Under feudalism a partial solution to the problems which had preoccupied slave-owners was evolved – the reconciliation between unfreedom and personality, and the translation of coercion into interests. In the early period of feudalism the peasant was bound to the soil, and in effect to his lord, without losing his personality and thereby assaulting theology. Moreover, the peasant's link with his land was more effective than any system of repression in preventing the peasant from leaving. At the same time, the peasant had little incentive to deny his lord, for the man without a lord was rootless, both practically and theoretically. In practice he was likely to be oppressed by everyone, in theory he lacked a place in society. It was thus in the peasant's interest to remain his lord's man.

Feudalism had solved some problems inherited from slavery, but at the cost of creating new ones. At a time when labour shortage was a central problem for dominant groups the practice of binding the peasant to the soil was obviously in the interests of the lord. However, by the thirteenth century this had ceased to be a major problem: an increase in population was one of the concomitants of the development of the money economy. In these new circumstances flexibility in the use of resources, especially of labour, was a more salient priority. Feudalism was, of course, based upon principles alien to this. New ways of securing compliance were needed to meet the new situation. In chapter 8 I want to turn directly to such new forms – the character of relations between superior and subordinate characteristic of capitalist industrial society.

8   Power relations under capitalism: industry

The distinguishing feature of capitalism as a system of labour exploitation is not the private ownership of capital, which of course existed in both slavery and feudalism, but the application of the principles of 'market rationality' to the organization of production.[1] In this context 'rationality' means simply the use of the technically most efficient means to achieve given ends, 'market' to the method used to achieve this, individual exchange and competition. The factors of production are allocated according to the principles of profit maximization: capital is invested where it will bring the highest rate of return, labour will seek to find the most profitable employment. Although these free-market principles of classical liberalism are not achieved in practice, and neither capital nor labour markets operate without restriction, interference needs to be justified in terms of vital social interests like the need to maintain social cohesion in national emergencies (as in Britain during the Second World War) or to be defended as the best means of maximizing output in difficult circumstances, as during a recession. The free market of nineteenth-century liberalism is the 'natural' if utopian economy of capitalism.

The overall distribution of power within capitalism is determined by its ecological and technological basis, its inheritance practices, the goals of its members and the distribution of control over desired resources, and by the means available to subordinates to escape from the dependences created by the distribution of this control. Capitalism involves a dense and expanding population, with rising levels of consumption, and a rising demand for raw materials. The pressure of increasing demand upon limited natural resources is relieved by territorial expansion and by technological and social innovation, including increased sophistication in the social organization of labour. The distribution of control over resources is determined by these ecological and technological factors, and by the degree of intergenerational transmission of such control; despite the ideology of the 'open society' and social democratic attacks upon inherited wealth through the imposition of estate and death duties, inheritance remains an important factor in the distribution of control over resources, especially wealth.[2] Such factors lead to a high degree of concentration of control over wealth in modern capitalism: for example, in the United Kingdom in 1971 the richest 5 per cent owned 47 per cent of aggregate personal wealth.[3] The distribution of control over wealth does not lead to an identical distribution of dependence, because.of the large number of goals possessed by both super- and subordinates and the resulting complexity of patterns of dependence. Controllers of wealth require the assistance of the controllers of other resources, including knowledge and votes. Moreover, the rapid rate of innovation, the complexity of the the division of labour, the availability of alternative superordinates, and the relative ease of combination, provide means of escape from dependence, increase the exchange rate between dependence and compliance, and thereby reduce power differentials. The result is a complex, dispersed and unequal distribution of power under capitalism.

Whereas the structure of power relations was essentially unitary under both slavery and feudalism, the domination of master over slave and lord over serf overruling claims to social, political and even legal citizenship rights, the structure of power relations under capitalism is fragmented. Although power in one area of social action is usually associated with power in another, the relation is contingent and not necessary: the organic symmetry of hierarchical relations in slavery and feudalism has been replaced by a more confused situation, in which the distribution of power within industry does not directly determine the distribution of power in political life, although of course the two are influenced by each other. Dahrendorf interprets this development as the 'institutional isolation' of politics from industry, and argues that 'in post-capitalist society industry and society have, by contrast to capitalist society, been dissociated'.[4] But it is more helpful to define capitalism in market terms (as Dahrendorf himself does on occasion) than to introduce the historically dubious concept of the evolution of capitalist into industrial society and to foreclose by definition the discussion of interinstitutional power relations. For analytical purposes industry and politics should be regarded as separate institutional orders and power relations examined separately within each: it is only then possible to discuss power relations within capitalism as a total system of labour exploitation. The discussion of power relations under capitalism is therefore divided into three sections: industry, politics and the links between the two: the remainder of this chapter comprises the first section.[5]

Hierarchical relations within capitalist industry are both simpler and more complex than such relations within feudal agriculture – simpler because less inclusive, more complex because of the increased elaboration of the division of labour. Relations between the incumbents of different roles in capitalist industry are based primarily upon a single strand, the cash nexus. But that single strand weaves a complex pattern – the more elaborate the division of labour, the more complex the relations of dependence and power. Moreover, although capitalist productive relations are based ultimately upon the cash nexus and the need of labour to obtain the material for physical survival, they also provide the means for the achievement of subsidiary goals: the rewards to be derived from work, and therefore the patterns of dependence built up, are more complex than those implied by the crudest forms of Marxist theory.[6] To simplify this complexity I have concentrated upon three sets of power relations, amongst managers, between managers and workers, and between different groups of workers.[7]

Power relations within management

Recent research into power relations between managers has focused upon the patterns of dependence created by the distribution of resources required to achieve organizational goals: in general – almost platitudinous – terms those groups within management who provide the resources most crucial to the success of the organization are the most powerful. More specifically, the power of different groups is seen to depend upon 'contingencies ensuing from varying combinations of coping with uncertainty, substitutability, and centrality'. 'Those sub-units that cope most effectively with the most uncertainty should have most power within the organization, since coping by a sub-unit reduces the impact of uncertainty on other activities in the organization, a shock-absorber function'. Substitutability refers simply to 'the ability of the organization to obtain alternative performance for the activities of a sub-unit'; centrality refers to two separate items, 'the pervasiveness of the work-flow of a sub-unit', and 'the immediacy of the work-flow of a sub-unit'.[8] Since all departments are, to varying degrees, both substitutable and central (or they would not exist), coping with uncertainty is seen as the most important, although there is as yet little reliable evidence to substantiate this suggestion.

The precise group likely to emerge as the most powerful sub-unit depends upon the environment within which the organization is operating, and the dominant coalition's interpretation of the most pressing problems – which may, in turn, be partly based upon the previously mentioned factors and partly upon inherited position. Firms operating in an uncertain market situation, with a slowly developing technology, face different 'strategic contingencies' from firms operating in a seller's market, with a rapidly developing technology. In the first instance it is likely to be sales departments which possess the greatest amount of power, in the second perhaps research and development. The most powerful management group appears, in fact, to be the sales department; in one American investigation sales dominated in eleven out of twelve companies.[9] Sales departments absorbed more uncertainty, in more critical areas, than any other department:[10]

All groups – sales, production, R & D, finance and accounting – contribute to satisfying customer demand, of course, or there would be no need for them to exist. But sales is the main gate between the organization and the customer. As gate-keeper, it determines how important will be prompt delivery, quality, product-improvement, or new products, and the costs at which goods can be sold. Sales determines the relative importance of these variables for the other groups and indicates the values which these variables will take. It has the ability, in addition, of changing the values of these variables, since it sets pricing (and in most firms adjusts it temporarily to meet changes in opportunity and competition), determines which markets will be utilized, the services that will be provided, and the changes in products that must be made.

This 'strategic contingencies' approach to the analysis of power relations provides only a limited, if important, perspective: the problem is defined in organizational and interdepartmental terms, and therefore necessarily solved in those terms. 'The concept of work organizations as *inter-departmental systems* leads to a strategic contingencies theory explaining differential sub-unit power. . . . As the goals, outputs, technologies, and markets of *organizations* change so, for each sub-unit, the values of the independent variables change, and patterns of power change'[11] (my italics). Hence, the definition of substitutability involves the ability of the *organization* to obtain alternative performances, not the ability of different actors within the organization to obtain alternative performances. This represents a misleading translation of individual into collective terms, an overdeterministic view of social action, and a neglect of managerial choice. Organizational problems are solved by human actors, not cybernetic robots, and there is therefore no necessary 'best fit' between the solutions adopted and the posited requirements of the organization as a whole. Organizational goals are only one dimension, alongside other dimensions.

All members of industrial organizations possess individual and group, as well as organizational goals, with varying degrees of importance and salience: one of the major tasks of higher management is to limit the development of individual and sub-unit goals at the expense of organizational ones.[12] For managers the major goals are the personal one of individual career success, the group one of an increased share of collective resources, and the organizational goal of increased total resources. Patterns of dependence develop from the distribution of control over the resources required to achieve each type of goal, leading to power relations. Such power relations may be based upon coercion, authority or influence. All three types are relevant. Coercion exists when subordinates comply out of a fear of losing their livelihoods. Authority exists when compliance is based upon the acceptance of the right of superordinates to issue specific directives necessary to achieve organizational goals. When compliance is based neither upon coercion nor upon authority we can talk of relations of influence.

A more elaborate and comprehensive approach to the analysis of managerial power is thus necessary than that provided by conventional 'strategic contingencies' theory. In general terms the distribution of power is determined by the dependences created by the control over resources necessary to achieve individual, group and organizational goals, and the means available to escape from them. This general issue can be divided into four subsidiary sections: the bases of power; the amount of power; the strategies used to augment or reduce the amount of power; and the relationship between the distribution of power and the environment.

The primary basis of power in relations between managers is authority, managers usually regarding compliance with the wishes of their superiors as legitimate, a necessary condition of maintaining their relationship with the organization: at the very least, questioning their superiors might undermine their own authority over others. However, coercion and influence are also present. Coercion arises when managers unwillingly comply with the wishes of others out of a direct fear of dismissal. Direct coercion in this sense is rarely used because of the need to deal considerately with the difficulties of other members of the in-group, the corrosive effect of coercion upon the trust necessary for effective performance in the often highly discretionary work required of middle and lower managers, and the cost of replacing dismissed personnel. (The degree of consideration shown depends, of course, upon the absolute amount of power possessed by the subordinate: board members require more consideration than departmental supervisors.) More important than the direct use of coercion is the diffuse atmosphere of fear and unease amongst middle managers created by competition and uncertainty:[13]

there is the constant possibility of being planned out of the present job. The management hierarchy is regularly re-organized. A pendulum swings from central control to regional autonomy. New advisers; liaisons with accounts or finance; development teams; executive development programmes are all on the drawing board. Management is always susceptible to rationalization and middle management positions especially. A middle manager is a junior in a big department or the senior of a sprawling department. In either situation rationalization can make him technically redundant. A new norm may be decided 'on consultants' advice' . . . it involves 'a bit of a shake-up', 'a complete face-lift', or 'an organizational set for the seventies'.

But it is easy to misinterpret the effect of such fears upon compliance, for coercion shades imperceptibly into authority as fear of dismissal shades into resigned acceptance of the risks of the game; custom, and self-respect, incline managers to interpret their problems as the latter.

Influence exists when managers do not willingly consent to their subordination, but are not coerced into compliance. Between managers this arises over attempts to achieve personal and group goals, or where the official allocation of resources fails to match that required for the achievement of organizational goals. Managers are dependent upon their direct superiors, and the personnel function, for the fulfilment of their personal goal of career success, whether this involves salary increases, more interesting work assignments, or promotion. Similarly, as members of specific departmental groups, managers are variously dependent upon other groups for a share in collective resources. For example, managers in a specific production department may ask sales managers to ensure that their salesmen push their department's products at the expense of other products produced by the same firm as a means of increasing their share of total output and thus their share of collective resources. Managers may wish to escape from these dependences (and thus an influence relation exists), may grudgingly accept them as an unfortunately necessary part of the 'system' (marginal), or may consent either because they regard the relation itself as right or for instrumental reasons (authority). Influence relations arise from incompleteness when official rules fail to specify priority between two competing but equally legitimate demands upon collective resources at the same time, as when two production departments simultaneously claim the exclusive assistance of a single maintenance group.

Despite the importance of coercion and influence the major basis of power between managers is authority, especially legal rational authority. Where power is based upon legal rational authority subordinates comply because they believe that superordinates are acting according to rule within recognized legally defined spheres of competence. Consent is granted to subordination because it is legal and because it is rational. The essential characteristic in the Weberian analysis of bureaucracy, the institutional exemplification of legal rational authority, is domination through knowledge:[14]

> this is the feature which makes it specifically rational. This consists on the one hand in technical knowledge which, by itself, is sufficient to ensure it a position of extra-ordinary power. But in addition to this, bureaucratic organizations, or the holders of power who make use of them, have the tendency to increase their power still further by the knowledge growing out of experience in the service.

This bureaucratic interpretation of capitalist administration has been extensively criticized on theoretical, empirical and normative grounds. However, my concern here is not with this view of bureaucracy in general, but only in so far as it provides an outline of the distribution of authority within the industrial enterprise. Even here the Weberian model has limitations. The distribution of authority between roles, and between levels, is more flexible than Weber suggested: the degree of hierarchy varies according to the size of the enterprise, its task, and its operating technology.[15] The larger the organization, the greater the degree of bureaucratization, although this may take the form of a high degree of centralization or a high degree of decentralization in accord with fully specified rules.[16] The more uniform the product, and the slower the rate of technological development, the greater the degree of bureaucratization.[17] Moreover, the emphasis upon knowledge as the basic source of legitimation for authority within management is only partially valid, for there are often conflicts within management over the relative value of different kinds of expertise, especially between formal expertise, acquired in educational institutions and validated by degrees and certificates, and practical expertise acquired on the job. As Parsons has argued on theoretical grounds, and as empirical work on managerial behaviour has confirmed, one of the major conflicts within management is between officials with authority acquired on the basis of formal expertise, and those with authority based upon practical experience.[18] This conflict occurs both within general management, and, to an even greater degree, between general management, oriented to the goals of the firm, and scientific personnel, oriented to the goals of the scientific community as a whole.[19]

The actual distribution of legal rational authority is thus less clear-cut than Weber indicated in his ideal-type of bureaucracy. Moreover, legal rational authority is not the only type of authority in industrial organizations; there is often a charismatic element in capitalist administration, especially in relations between the chief executive and his direct subordinates. This charisma was evident in the relations between Henry Ford and his subordinates, or, more recently, in the ascendancy of Howard Geneen over his entourage in ITT.[20] The charismatic element is especially important in the early stages of an industrial organization's development, but is not confined to that period. The charisma of the founder becomes incorporated in the protective myths surrounding his successors: the Cadbury tradition.[21] Moreover, the simple fact of superordination and consequent social distance can lead to the attribution of extraordinary qualities, especially where the superordinate's roles are not clearly defined.[22]

In short, coercion, influence and authority are all important bases of power within management. But the most important is authority, especially legal rational authority – compliance willingly granted because superiors are legitimately appointed and are acting within their sphere of competence according to the rules. Capitalist enterprises are thus essentially bureaucratic. But bureaucratic structures are more varied and more flexible, their processes more ambiguous and less routinized, than the Weberian model suggests. Moreover, authority is not the exclusive basis of power. Coercion and influence can underpin, or undermine, authority relationships.

The amount of power in a given relation will vary with the goals of the parties, their respective structural locations, and the relative importance of different individual, group and collective goals. Middle-aged managers, who are unlikely to achieve further promotion and have decided that gardening is more important than office politics, will have a different hierarchy of goals from young managers hoping to rise: the one can minimize dependences vital to the other.[23] Similarly, there are likely to be different patterns of dependence between managers in production, marketing, finance and research and development, and according to the hierarchical level within any given department. All managers will be part of a hierarchy of authority, established by the organization's dominant coalition to achieve organizational goals and to sustain their own position, and a more fluid and ambiguous network of coercive and influence relations upon which they rely for the achievement of personal, group and, to a small extent, organizational goals.

Coalitions based upon these latter relations may be more or less institutionalized in cliques and cabals.[24]

Authority is distributed hierarchically within departments according to the principles of scientific management, human relations theory or whatever management philosophy happens to prevail at the time. The height and steepness of the slope of the pyramid depend upon the degree of closeness of control regarded by the dominant coalition as politically desirable and technologically feasible. Political desirability represents a compromise between the preservation of a particular predominance, the need to incorporate potentially hostile groups into 'responsible' decision-making positions, and the desire to raise morale by increasing participation. Technological feasibility depends upon the organization's primary work task, the men and material used to achieve it, and the dominant coalition's degree of willingness to sacrifice productivity for control. Research institutes are relatively flexible, large-batch mass-production technologies relatively inflexible – though the complexity of any large-scale manufacturing industry is now so great that no organization is completely inflexible.[25] The mixed pressures affecting the distribution of authority within departments are well illustrated by G. Dalton *et al.* in their study of organizational change in a large research and development organization, the Nampa Development Centre. The newly appointed director wished to establish his own distinctive position, and to increase productivity by making more efficient use of senior scientists and by raising morale. He therefore reduced the height of the hierarchy of authority by removing one level of supervisors, relieved a second level of responsibility for day to day operations, and established project-centred work-groups under relatively junior managers. The changes increased the authority of junior managers in the department, without changing the position of the director.[26]

Even within departments the formal distribution of authority is not conterminous with the actual distribution of power: coercion and influence are also present. Hence higher management might wish to rationalize their departments by using work-study techniques, or by computerizing accounting procedures, but be constrained from doing so by the fear of passive non-cooperation, increased labour turnover, or even strike action, and consequent dismissal following failure. Alternatively, fear of dismissal, as well as a feeling that union membership would be incompatible with white-collar status, may prevent lower managers from joining trade unions, as it did in the banking industry before the Second World War.[27] Influence arises within departments when the allocation of authority fails to accord with that required to achieve organizational goals, or when dependence arises based upon the need to achieve personal or group goals.

The distribution of influence usually broadly parallels, and supplements, the distribution of authority and power: superiors usually have more influence over inferiors than the reverse. This predominance is especially evident amongst managers, where future promotion is heavily dependent upon the direct superior's assessment of 'ability' – and evaluation of suitability for promotion is highly subjective: 'the higher you get the more your advancement depends upon impressions that your superiors have of you.'[28] However, influence also arises between managers with equal authority, or counter to the distribution of authority. Hence experienced managers can influence inexperienced ones because of their greater knowledge of operating short-cuts, even where formal authority is equal. Similarly, formal subordinates can influence their superiors through threatening to embarrass them by failure, or by disclosing information about dubiously legitimate but managerially convenient procedures.

The firm's dominant coalition allocates control over resources between as well as within departments in accordance with its perception of the firm's requirements. Hence authority is allocated to specific departments to enable them to achieve relevant subgoals; production departments are granted authority to requisition supplies from stores in accordance with specified procedures, etc. However, the formal allocation of authority between departments is an even less reliable index of the distribution of power than the formal distribution of authority within departments, for the more complex division of labour and the greater range of problems faced reduces the relevance of formal bureaucratic rules. Interdepartmental relations can be 'programmed' to only a limited degree. The lower the level of predictability, the greater the ambiguity, the greater the importance of non-authority power relations. The rate of organizational change is an additional reason for the importance of influence in interdepartmental relations:[29]

> The market changes, your personnel changes, relations with the union are always changing. [The central office] is always re-organizing the set-up. Staff people are always racking their brains for improvements of one kind or another. People are always fighting for promotions, and when they get them they all handle the same job differently – no two men do a job the same way. There are technological changes going on all the time. That always upsets planning.

The result of this process of influence bargaining – not of organizational necessity – is that marketing usually emerges as potentially the most important department: other departments are more dependent upon marketing for the continued provision of resources, especially those required to achieve group and organizational goals, than marketing is upon other departments. The total resources available for labour costs, including managerial salaries, is also ultimately determined by the success of marketing, although the responsibility for deciding individual salaries, and therefore for the achievement of personal goals, usually rests with the personnel function. However, the influence of personnel is often reduced by its distance from day to day operations (except for the industrial relations section) and by its reliance upon other departments for information. For example, personnel may establish the procedures for evaluating managers, but rely upon operating superiors for information about the performance of their own subordinates, effectively restricting personnel to initial recruitment and to attempts to establish interdepartmental comparability.

Patterns of dependence are determined by the distribution of control over resources required for the achievement of personal, group and collective goals. But actors can choose to increase or decrease the amount of power deriving from that dependence. Such choices may involve devising administrative structures to increase, or decrease, the exchange rate between dependence and power, the exercise of 'strategic choice': 'the exercise of strategic choice by the dominant coalition refers to a process the first stage of which is the coalition members' evaluation of their organization's position – what expectations are presented by resource providers such as business shareholders, what is the trend of events in the environment . . . and so on.'[30] Alternatively, such choices may be less institutionalized, as when individual managers decide to risk the penalties of non-compliance with the known wishes of a more powerful manager. The kinds of strategies followed by managers concerned to maintain their position are documented in Pettigrew's recent account of computer-programmers in a retail distribution firm. The computer-programmers were under attack from systems analysts, and gradually losing their monopoly over computing knowledge; in response they developed four major strategies designed to prevent the erosion of their knowledge monopoly by technological change and thus to avoid reduction in their domination over others. First, they denied the competence of outsiders to make decisions about computing. Second, they developed protective myths about the special attributes of their group, for example mathematical brilliance. Third, they withheld information that might have reduced the uncertainty or mystique of their task. Finally, they controlled the training and recruitment policies that protected their knowledge base.[31] At the same time the directors of the firm maintained control through the use of a number of strategies: 'By keeping distant from the scene of conflict, by giving the programmers some freedom from the system of bureaucratic rules, and by keeping job assignments uncertain, subject to change at any moment, they prevented the programmers from consolidating a stable power-base, and still managed to extract from them the knowledge and work necessary for the company's continued prosperity'.[32] Such strategies were possible and even necessary precisely because of the discrepancy between organizational, group and personal goals, and the looseness of the fit between organizational 'requirements' and member behaviour.

The basis and amount of power in managerial relations is not determined solely by internal factors: such relations are constantly influenced by changes in the firm's environment. The major environmental factor influencing the distribution of power is the firm's market position. Gross changes in the market situation of firms are likely to affect both the content of managers' goals and the relationship between different types of goals. During contraction the manager's interest in personal goals increases, at the expense of the individual's commitment to both group and organizational goals; as the inducements to contribute to the organization decline, search activity for alternative positions outside the organization increases. Whether the content of the actor's individual goals is likely to change or not is problematic. On the one hand, changes in the market may reduce the financial resources available for personal rewards, and thereby increase the reliance on intrinsic rewards. On the other hand, economic constraints may heighten experienced relative deprivation on all fronts.

Regardless of changes in the content of the goals of organization members, there will be changes in the relationship between the different categories of goals – personal, group and organizational – resulting from changes in the market situation. Under 'stable' market conditions individual, group and organizational goals may be satisfied simultaneously by a policy of growth. For the individual, growth provides greater opportunities for responsibility and thus self-actualization, as well as increased income. For the department, overall growth increases the total amount of resources available for use, demonstrates success to the outside world, and reduces the intensity of interdepartmental conflict. For the organization, growth may be justified as a demonstration of corporate prestige, an obvious indication of success, and as a way of maximizing the (long-run) rate of return on capital invested.

During periods of contraction this happy congruence between individual, group and organizational goals disintegrates. As time perspectives are shortened, the complicated system of 'side-payments' – to use Cyert and March's term – which sustains coalitions between organizational members becomes radically simplified:

'obligations cheques' are cashed as quickly as possible.[33] Individual, group and organizational goals can only be satisfied at the expense of each other; individual goals at the expense of those of other individuals, departments and the organization; departmental goals at the expense of individual, other departmental and organizational goals; and organizational goals at the expense of those of individuals and departments. In short, a positive-sum game has become a zero-sum game – with the sum continually diminishing.

The effects of changing market conditions upon the amount and distribution of resources available within the organization is obvious: they are reduced, and channelled into sectors most closely geared to acquiring resources required in the short run – especially finance and marketing. The consequences of this for power relations are obvious: other groups become more dependent upon such sectors, with consequent changes in the balance of power. Less obviously, the unpredictability of the situation places a premium upon reliable information, especially about personnel matters, for past experience ceases to be a reliable guide to the future. This may have the opposite effect to the preceding development, for it may 'flatten' dependence relations: the release of information is a 'costless' process, not involving non-self-regarding behaviour. This 'flattening' is all the more likely because individuals will be reluctant to miss opportunities for the exchange of information during periods of uncertainty, for they will not know what information others have to withhold or exchange. The extent to which required resources can be obtained by giving information, rather than by open-ended or specific commitments of other resources, is one factor in determining dependence and therefore power relationships.

Changes in the market situation also affect strategies of escape from dependence relations in the following general ways. First, any change in the supply of resources obviously affects the existence of alternative sources of supply. Second, the ability to offer exchanges in return without cost to oneself increases, because of the increased importance of information. Where previous individual experience ceases to be a reliable guide to the future, increased importance is attached to up-to-date information, with obvious consequences for dependence relations. Third, the squeeze upon resources makes combination between actors in similar dependence situations more difficult, for declining total resources obviously make competition fiercer for those who remain. The interaction between other environmental factors and the distribution of power can be examined in the same way.

Any realistic analysis of the distribution of power within management thus requires a multi-dimensional conceptualization of members' goals: it is inadequate to talk solely in terms of organizational goals and resources. A more complex picture emerges from this than from direct application of the Weberian theory of bureaucracy to management, whereby offices are arranged in an hierarchical line, according to expertise, and responsibility and resources are allocated to roles in accordance with the priorities of the organization, as determined by the head of the organization. According to Weber and classical managerial theory authority is regarded as in principle conterminous with power, any distortion being illegitimate. But this view is only partial because the exercise of something more than authority is necessary to obtain resources to satisfy even organizational goals and because of the multi-dimensional character of members' goals, all in some sense legitimate. The desire for promotion or salary increases is, in organizational terms, legitimate. But beyond the legitimate sense in which authority and power are not conterminous there is the obvious sense in which organizational resources can be 'misallocated' through the exercise of power. Such 'misallocations' are determined by the pattern of dependences illustrated above.

Hierarchical relations between different management groups can thus be analysed in terms of authority, coercion and influence. In terms of authority the Weberian model of bureaucracy, whilst problematic, provides an adequate basic model. Most authority is granted to the head of a pyramidal organization; this authority is based upon expertise, acquired partly through formal training and partly through experience. It is exercised through a formal system of communications and review of actions of subordinates, and by control over recruitment and promotion, albeit indirectly through the personnel function. Subordinates act according to the rules of the organization, and where these are inadequate because of unforeseen circumstances, problems are referred 'to higher authority'. But this picture of hierarchical relations is incomplete, for the distribution of power is not a direct reflection of the distribution of authority: it is also based upon the distribution of coercion and influence.

This discussion of managerial power relations has been illustrative rather than exhaustive: too little is known about hierarchical relations within management to answer even the most basic questions. It is therefore impossible to draw an accurate multi-dimensional picture of managerial power relations. However, I hope that the above framework at least suggests what information would be needed for such an analysis.

Power relations between management and workers

The distinction between management and workers adopted here is a conventional one, based upon Dahrendorf's usage, between those with and those without organizationally legitimated authority.[34] This distinction is obviously very crude, for the line between those with and those without such authority is very thin. Moreover, some roles – for example shop-steward – are authoritative and, especially where management agrees to the use of collective resources, organizationally legitimated; but the shop-steward cannot be regarded as belonging to management in the same way as the plant superintendent. Nevertheless, there are both 'objective' and subjective differences between management and workers, corresponding to the conventional usage of industrial-relations experts, despite blurring at the edges: the precise character of the blurring, and the ambiguities in the positions of marginal members of both groups, are irrelevant here. I will also assume in this section what the previous section has shown to be patently false: that management is united. For the alliances which develop between specific groups of managers and workers in attempts to influence the distribution and exercise of power are too complex to analyse here.[35] The aim is the already ambitious one of discussing the overall power differential between managers and workers, and the reasons for that differential. This involves examining coercion, authority and influence.

Coercion has been defined as the ability to obtain compliance by threatening to withdraw the means to sustain life. Superordinates in contemporary capitalism rarely possess such direct and overwhelming predominance that they can rely upon coercion: the individual can escape from particular dependences. Moreover, the extension of legal, political and social citizenship rights over the last hundred years has meant that labour market domination has been hedged around with political and social limitations: the provision of unemployment benefit and other forms of social welfare, and more recently legal restrictions upon dismissal, significantly limit the direct coercive power of management. In most circumstances coercion is neither a possible, nor a necessary, basis of management power· in contemporary capitalism. Nevertheless, there are coercive elements in managerial power: coercion remains an important ultimate threat in economic recession, and historic memories provide a legacy of fear to modify the balance of power based upon contemporary patterns of dependence. Moreover, coercion can operate indirectly and diffusely. Indirectly, threats to increase the overall level of unemployment have been used to improve labour discipline (although they have not proved very effective, for workers have not directly translated collective into individual threats). Coercion can operate diffusely through the imposition of managerial 'definitions of the situation' upon workers and by limiting the range of considerations regarded as relevant in contentious situations. Superordinates, through their greater influence upon socialization agencies, may secure the acceptance of definitions favourable to themselves. However, it is difficult to regard this 'mobilization of bias' as coercive, for the effectiveness of such mobilization depends upon subordinates granting consent, upon false premises. The relation is still one of authority rather than coercion regardless of the truth or falsity of the subordinates' understanding of the situation; the granting of consent, even when based upon a misunderstanding, transforms coercion into authority – although this authority is unlikely to be stable unless it can withstand the truth. Authority is fragile when it is based upon subordinates' systematically misinterpreting their dependence or failing to perceive means of escape.

In broad terms management has authority directly over workers, although the precise scope of this authority is controversial. In the nineteenth century 'managerial prerogatives' extended over both market and labour utilization aspects of the work situation; in the mid-twentieth century the authority of management over market factors has been successfully challenged by workers collectively, through the development of trade unions, and its authority over labour utilization is now being questioned.[36] Nevertheless, despite disagreement over the extent of managerial prerogatives, management retains authority over workers; at the very least, few would claim that workers have authority over management. This authority is legitimated primarily in legal rational terms, the workers' (usually taken-for-granted) acceptance of subordination because of the need to get things done, and recognition of the greater 'expertise' of management in supervisory skills, and occasionally in charismatic terms.[37] It is reinforced by extensive socialization outside the work setting, both formally in school and informally from parents and peers.[38]

Managers and workers have the ability to obtain compliance from each other without using either coercion or authority, through the use of influence. The debilitating results of relying upon coercion, and the need to act outside the specific rules agreed to authoritatively, lead to the frequent use of influence in everyday industrial life, especially in changing circumstances. This influence is based upon the dependence of each group upon reasonable behaviour by the other for the successful achievement of individual, group and organizational goals, and the consequent ability of both groups to make life difficult for each other. Management can make life difficult for workers by manipulating overtime and bonus payments, by allocating unpleasant work assignments, by disrupting established work groups, by failing to provide facilities for effective work performance (although this is a risky managerial tactic for it can easily be publicly criticized as 'mismanagement'), or by threatening to do any of these things. Similarly, workers – collectively and individually – can make life difficult for management. This is most obviously effective collectively, through strike action, the threat of strike action, work to rule or other forms of industrial action. (Strike action is sometimes regarded as coercive. But it rarely involves the deprivation, or threat of deprivation, of the means of existence, and is different in kind from the power exercised by the master over the slave.) Workers can also exercise influence individually, through 'skiving', pilfering or other forms of non-cooperation. In short, influence relations arise whenever management or workers obtain compliance with their wishes through withdrawal, or the threat of withdrawal, of the cooperation necessary for the mutual achievement of individual, group or organizational goals.

The overall distribution of power between management and workers results from a combination of the relative amounts of coercion, authority and influence. However, it is difficult to estimate the amount of power involved in such relationships, separately or together. The amount of power is measured by the scope, frequency and differential probability of the compliant actions performed by subordinates (above, p. 43). This involves a comparison between the compliant actions of management and workers. In general terms, managers are more powerful than workers, individually and collectively: they have more coercive power and more authority, although the distribution of influence is more nearly equal. Full demonstration of this tentative conclusion would involve a comprehensive examination of the scope, frequency and differential probability of non-self-regarding action by both managers and workers. In view of the impossibility of presenting such a comprehensive account here it is necessary to rely upon proximate indicators. The obvious proximate indicator is assessment of the results of open conflicts between the two, as in measures of 'bargaining power'.[39] However, there is no systematic evidence on the extent to which different sequences of conflict result in victory for one side or the other. Comprehensive studies of the results of industrial conflicts in these terms are rare, although there are spectacular occasions where rough measurement is easy – the postal workers lost the dispute with the Post Office in 1971, and the coal-miners won the disputes with the National Coal Board in 1972 and 1974. Such studies of conflict are rare largely because of the methodological problems involved in tracing the indirect costs of strike action. (The bad effects of the Post Office's 'victory' over the postal workers upon morale, productivity and labour turnover only revealed themselves slowly over the following years, but are obviously relevant to assessing the outcome of the conflict and thus the relative amount of power of the two parties.) Even if such comprehensive studies were available, concentration upon the outcome of manifest conflicts between management and workers would be seriously misleading, for power relations exist even where manifest conflict does not occur. Consideration of the results of open conflict alone would seriously distort the measurement of power, just as concentration upon specific outbreaks of violence seriously underestimates the amount of violence immanent in social relations. It is therefore necessary to rely upon indirect indicators of relative amounts of compliance, the amount of resources allocated to the two groups: at an aggregate level the extent to which the share of the gross national product devoted to wages or profits has increased, and the extent to which the earnings of managerial and supervisory groups have increased relative to the earnings of manual workers.

The interpretation of the statistics on the distribution of the gross national product and of earnings to different occupational groups is a complicated and controversial technical economic question. However, two general conclusions emerge. First, the share of the gross national product allocated to individual capitalists and managers is considerably greater than that allocated to individual workers; this conclusion is obvious from research into wealth, income and earnings. Second, there has been an increase in the collective (and to a lesser extent individual) workers' share of resources. The share of the gross national product allocated to profits and investment has been decreasing, although how far is a matter of controversy; the proportion of the gross national product allocated to earnings has increased. This does not, in itself, indicate that workers have been gaining at the expense of management, for official statistics on 'earnings' include the earnings of managers. However, statistics on the relative income levels of managers, supervisors and manual workers suggest that the share of manual workers has increased in the very recent past, although over the period since 1900 such an overall change has been small in the United Kingdom.[40]

Both sets of economic statistics indicate that there has been a shift in the distribution of power between management and workers. Additional evidence is provided by the success of 'unofficial' plant-level worker activity designed to increase the resources allocated to specific occupational groups, especially in the vehicle-building and other engineering industries. The effectiveness of these movements is indicated by the process of wage drift, in which piece-work rates have been ratcheted up within plants, mainly but not solely in engineering.[41] Frequent renegotiation of piece-work rates, whenever technology or the division of labour changes, has produced a rapid rise in earnings substantially above standard wage rates. Even in plants where rising piece-work rates do not provide a ready index of this power, as in the Ford Motor Company, a similar change in the distribution of power has occurred. For example, as Huw Beynon has shown, effective shop-steward organization at Ford's Halewood plant on Merseyside has encroached upon practices traditionally regarded as integral to the managerial prerogative, including regulation of the speed of the assembly line.[42] In short, there has been an 'irreversible devolution of bargaining power to the shop floor'.[43]

Why has this change in the balance of power between management and workers occurred? One common reason given is manifestly misleading – the increased power of the trade unions. For the trade unions have not grown more powerful since the Second World War. 'The only quantitative measure of trade union strength is density of organisation: the proportion of potential union members who are actually organised. Though total membership has increased a little over this period, overall density of organisation has declined between 1948 and 1967 from 45 to 42 per cent.'[44] The proportion of actual to potential union membership increased between 1948 and 1964 in declining industries, like coal-mining, agriculture and national government, but declined in expanding sectors such as education and business services.[45] Since 1967 this decline has been reversed, and by 1973 50 per cent of the labour force were union members. Despite this slight but perceptible increase in union density, union power has been weakened, paradoxically, by the developments which strengthened the power of the shop floor: national trade union leaders have been unable to 'control' the activities of work-groups, who have exerted pressure directly upon management at factory level: in this process trade union organization has proved irrelevant. The emergence of the 'unofficial' system of plant-level collective bargaining has undermined the position of the trade unions as the representatives of labour in the 'official' system.[46]

The shift away from management power has not been due to organizational changes amongst labour. Instead, at the most general level, the answer lies simply in the change in the balance of dependence between the two groups – management has become more dependent upon specific workers, whilst workers have become less dependent upon specific managements. This represents a simple change in market situation: the demand for labour has increased, the level of unemployment regarded as politically acceptable has dropped, and therefore the bargaining positions of the two groups have changed. This analysis is correct, but incomplete.[47] Even in its own terms this straightforward labour-market analysis is problematic: for example, there is little precise understanding of the determinants of labour demand. What explains variations in the politically acceptable level of unemployment? When do firms dismiss labour rather than pay increased wages? But, more importantly, simple economic analysis rests upon often unstated, unacceptably crude psychological and sociological assumptions and underestimates the importance of less readily identifiable and explicable changes in norms and values.

The primary motivation for working is of course economic and instrumental, the desire to obtain the means for material sustenance. This is true for both management and workers. Goldthorpe and Lockwood describe the 'instrumental orientation' to work in the following terms:[48]

> work is regarded as a means to an end, or ends, external to the work situation; that is, work is regarded as a means of acquiring the income necessary to support a valued way of life of which work itself is not an integral part . . . workers' involvement in the organization which employs them is primarily a *calculative* one; it will be maintained for so long as the economic return for effort is seen as the best available, but for no other reason.

The cash nexus is the tie binding both the manager and the worker to his work role. The difference lies in the fact that it is the only tie binding the worker; for the manager it is accompanied by other rewards, like prestige, or the opportunity for 'ego expansion', whilst for the worker it is the only compensation for the disutilities of work. This difference is not inherent in the motivational pattern of workers, in a congenital desire to minimize subjective involvement in work, but a simple result of the limitations of the rewards available. Preoccupation with what Maslow termed the 'lower' needs stems directly from an inability to satisfy the higher. When opportunities for fulfilling the 'motivating factors', to use Herzberg's terms, are available, as in experimental schemes for job-enrichment, they are grasped, provided they do not involve any sacrifice of satisfaction of hygiene factors (as they normally do not for managers).[49] Nevertheless, for whatever reason, the workers' tie to the organization is more single-stranded – and more fragile – than that of the manager. The labour-market analysis of the reasons for the change in the distribution of power between management and workers rests on this analysis of instrumentalism. The only tie binding the worker to his organization is the opportunity the organization provides for the satisfaction of personal goals and therefore that is the only pattern of dependence which matters. If the ability of the organization to satisfy those goals fluctuates, then his dependence upon that organization will fluctuate, and his power *vis-à-vis* management within it accordingly. Since such a change has occurred, over the period since the Second World War, the worker's relative power has changed accordingly. This interpretation is correct, as far as it goes. But it is only one-dimensional and neglects a crucial change in relations of domination and subordination, the fragmentation and progressive breakdown in normative regulation. Since the Second World War the norms governing relations of subordination between management and workers have been undermined, partly by the new labour-market position of workers, and, partly as an indirect consequence of this, by the elaboration of a multitude of different, only partially integrated systems of normative regulation, for example disrupting pre-existing relativities. As Fox and Flanders argue, in general terms:[50]

> In the typical situation a normative system covering a number of different groups comes under increasing tension for a variety of possible reasons. Perhaps anomalies and inconsistencies of regulation between groups within the system, or in relation to groups in other systems, are not resolved. In response to these failures of the system, those groups with sufficient power break through it and impose their own norms. Insofar as they serve as reference points for other groups, either in the same system or in others, their example is followed. Extreme frustration builds up among those groups who come under the same tensions but who lack power. Meanwhile, each normative system becomes either replaced or supplemented by a number of smaller systems. This increases the likelihood of disorder, since groups governed by different normative systems are clearly likely to behave in ways which frustrate each other's expectations. Besides making predictability and integration of action difficult this may create mutual frustration, jealousy, and rivalry, leading to severe inter-group conflict. Moreover, this fragmentation of normative systems is itself a factor making for tension between norms and aspirations. Disorder feeds upon disorder.

In this confused situation workers' attitudes towards the domination of management will change. At one level, the evident inconsistencies in the treatment of situations regarded as comparable are likely to undermine the legal rational basis of authority. Even if it remains clear what solutions should follow according to any specific rule, it becomes difficult to establish the relevant rule. At another level, the willingness to accept a given hierarchy without question is obviously undermined when other hierarchies are being disrupted – the aura of sanctity is tarnished. This is already revealing itself in changing attitudes towards managerial authority. For example, younger workers are more reluctant than older workers to defer to managerial authority: in a recent survey 45 per cent of manual workers aged under 25, compared with 78 per cent of workers aged 60 or more, agreed with the view that 'obedience and respect for authority are the most important characteristic of the good worker'.[51] Although the numbers involved were small the sample was drawn from a relatively deferential group of workers, and similar conclusions could be drawn from the analysis of other responses. Such normative changes are also apparent in the readiness to challenge managerial decisions directly in situations where previously they had been accepted, for example redundancy.[52]

Despite the weakness of such evidence – the unreliability of responses to attitude survey questionnaires and the unusual character of sit-ins – it does suggest a second, normative dimension complementary to the changes which have taken place within the labour market. Changes in the labour-market situation of workers have partly changed, and partly been changed by, changes in the structure of normative regulation. No future change in the labour market, for example an increase in the level of unemployment, will restore earlier patterns of domination unless it is accompanied by parallel normative changes. For the rules of the game have changed, not simply the strength of the participants in the game.

The combined effect of these market and normative changes has been to throw into disequilibrium the relationship between the distribution of authority and the distribution of power. The distribution of authority is changing slowly: management clearly retains some authority over workers, workers do not have authority over management. But the distribution of power has changed significantly. As a result it is difficult to assess the overall character of hierarchical relations between management and workers, and the outcome of any situation involving a conflict of interest between the two groups. In some situations workers will grant consent and subordination, based upon authority, will be accepted, in others not. In the long run it is likely that relations of authority will be re-aligned with power relations, as has happened in the past. But the extent of that long run is unknown. In the meantime the conflict between relations of authority and relations of power remains central to current industrial-relations problems.

Hierarchical relations between workers

Since I have defined workers as those lacking authority within the industrial enterprise, relations of authority do not exist, by definition, amongst workers. Moreover, the concept of coercion is scarcely relevant, for workers rarely possess the ability to deprive other workers of the means of existence (although marginal cases occur when native workers secure the initial dismissal of immigrant workers during economic recession). Nevertheless, relations of domination and subordination, based largely upon influence, do exist amongst workers. Workers, like management, do not constitute a coherent group. Although they share a common class position in Marxist terms, all depending solely upon their labour power, and share broadly similar patterns of earnings and life styles, their work relations and the pattern of social relations which emerge from them are very varied.[53] Power differentials are effected by the degree of skill associated with an occupation, and, related to this, the level of demand for workers in that occupation, the degree of unionization, the degree of informal work-group cohesion, the size of plant, and so on. But there is one fundamental difference in the character of power relations between workers compared with power relations between managers: the major defining characteristics of the workers' situation are provided by management. Thus the allocation of work roles, and decisions about the provision of resources for the performance of those roles, is primarily a management function. Power relations between workers thus take place in a context in which the major decisions about the allocation of resources required to satisfy personal, group and organizational goals are made by persons outside the conflict. Power relations between workers are thus less fateful than power relations between workers and management, or between different groups of managers. Nevertheless, power relations do exist between different groups of workers, even if they are often revealed indirectly, by way of relations through management.

Evidence suggesting the existence of power differentials between workers can be found in the dispersal of earnings amongst different occupational groups, the differential distribution of other rewards derived from labour, and the differential control exerted over work situation, although of course these differences derive from different power positions *vis-à-vis* management as much as *vis-à-vis* other workers. In addition, in specific industries, for example the docks, the existence of a form of indirect labour system has in the past given direct power to one work group over another. In general terms, the earnings of skilled manual workers, expressed as a percentage of the earnings of all occupational groups, in 1960 were 117 per cent, of semi-skilled workers 85 per cent, and of unskilled workers 79 per cent.[54] Such dispersal in earnings existed in specific industries or groups of industries, not simply as a statistical artefact. For example, in the engineering industry, the earnings of fitters as a percentage of the earnings of tool-room fitters was 90·2 per cent, of semi-skilled turners and machinemen 81·8 per cent and of labourers 74·5 per cent.[55] Differences are also evident in the distribution of non-financial benefits, for example holidays and sick pay. There are marked differences between clerical and other workers in both areas;[56] there are also significant differences between different groups of manual workers. Finally, there are obvious differences in the degree to which different workers control their own work situation, ranging from the relative autonomy of workers in the printing industry to the regimented activity of workers on the motor-car assembly line.[57]

The major explanation for such differences in rewards relates to differences in ability to exert pressure upon management, and as such cannot be explained directly by the character of hierarchical relations between different groups of workers; the major decisions about the allocation of resources to satisfy personal goals are made by management. However, the balance of dependences between workers is relevant indirectly, in two senses. Obviously management is not normally directly involved in the process of production, and therefore the determinant of its willingness to increase the allocation of rewards is in practice the extent to which one group of workers is capable of preventing others from getting on with their jobs. But, more directly, some strategic groups of workers are in a better position to exert pressure upon management for increased rewards, whether for themselves or for other people. Hence strategic groups of workers, whether organized into their own union or organized as a special section of an industrial or general union, are less dispensable than others in negotiation. Thus the engine-drivers have, until recently, been able to exert a disproportionate influence upon the formulation of wage demands on the railways, because their support is necessary to give immediate 'bite' in the case of an industrial dispute. This motivation was evident in the negotiations which led up to the formation of the Triple Alliance in 1921, which collapsed on 'Black Friday', 15 April 1921: the railways would immensely increase the leverage available to the coal-miners in their dispute with the coal-owners, but the miners could not similarly assist the railwaymen. The significance of such dependence is evident when a key occupational group fails to support the actions of a related group, as happened in the postal dispute in 1971. The failure of the telephone-operators to support the Union of Postal Workers was an important element in the failure of the strike.[58] Similar differences are evident in grievance activity at plant level, as Sayles has convincingly shown.

Workers are thus differentially dependent upon each other for the achievement of their personal goals. They are also differentially dependent upon each other for the achievement of group and organizational goals. The significance of dependency for the achievement of group goals is evident from the dynamics of relations between skilled men and their mates; the ability of mates to achieve

123

their group goal of collective aggrandizement is more dependent upon the craftsmen than the reverse is the case. (Recognition of this dependence helped to keep semi-skilled engineering workers subordinate to craftsmen for many years in the AEU.) But more interesting is the extent to which power differentials emerge from differential dependences deriving from the need to achieve organizational goals. For workers are differentially dependent upon each other for the achievement of organizational goals, just as managers are differentially dependent upon each other. The significance of this dependence, and its consequences for the distribution of power, are evident in Crozier's classic study of the French tobacco monopoly.

The critical relationship in the tobacco monopoly was that between production workers and maintenance men, and focused around machine stoppages.[59] These were frequent, because of the difficulty of conditioning the raw material. Production workers disliked such disruptions because of the need to work harder to catch up on lost production, and the fear of being displaced if the stoppage lasted long enough. Maintenance workers were the only personnel able to deal with stoppages, because of their technical skill, a skill monopoly which they strenuously sought to maintain. The result was an uncomfortable dependence by production workers upon maintenance men: maintenance men were necessary for the satisfactory performance of production workers, but, except in an absolute sense, the reverse was not the case:[60]

> Production workers resent their dependence, but cannot express their hostility openly, because they need the maintenance men's help and good will individually at the shop, and because, collectively, they know that they can keep their privileges only by maintaining a common front with the other workers' group. Union solidarity and working class unity are the values in the name of which production workers accept the maintenance workers' leadership.

Such leadership was accepted in the name of solidarity, but not because of it; more important was the dependence relationship. Such relationships are especially likely to emerge – and especially likely to cause conflict – where the technology of production requires cooperation between workers but where payment is by piece-work, as in garment workshops.[61]

All workers are, by definition, devoid of authority; but it would be a mistake to conclude that the only differentiation between workers is horizontal, reflecting the different interests stemming from employment in different industries. Vertical differentiation is evident in the conventional allocation of occupational prestige –

although the ability of respondents to order occupations hierarchically does not indicate the distance between the top and bottom of the hierarchy – and in the standard Census categorization into skilled, semi-skilled and unskilled. Such differentiation reflects differences in the power of different groups, both with regard to management and with regard to each other, differences in the ability to persuade management of indispensability, differences in the ability to prevent other work groups from encroaching upon one's 'mandate', and differences in the ability to persuade other work groups to support one's claim.[62] Differences in such abilities rest upon differences in the balance of dependences between groups and in the extent to which groups need each other to achieve personal, group and organizational goals.

In this chapter I have attempted to analyse relations of domination and subordination within industry under capitalism, focusing upon relations between different groups of managers, between management and workers, and between different groups of workers. Authority is seen in Weberian terms, as the agreed distribution of control over resources, including personnel, legitimated as the necessary means of achieving organizational goals. But examination of the distribution of authority is only of limited value, revealing only the narrowly formal aspects of hierarchical relations. Equally important are coercion and influence. The overall distribution of power is the result of the balance of dependences between groups, and the means available to escape from them. Such dependences derive from the possession of resources required to achieve the personal, group and organizational goals of others. The distribution of such resources is not simply an artefact of the distribution of authority, for there are significant differences in the power of groups possessing the same degree of authority, or even in reversal of the distribution of authority. For example, sales managers were found to be more powerful than production managers (in most circumstances), for they controlled more crucial resources than other managers of the same formal rank. Moreover, the allocation of authority between management and workers is not paralleled by a similar distribution of power: in contemporary capitalism work groups have more power than authority.

Examination of the distribution of power within industry is the first step towards understanding the structure and processes of domination and subordination under capitalism, for capitalism, like slavery, is essentially a system of labour exploitation. However, unlike the plantation, the capitalist industrial enterprise is not a total institution; the distribution of power within other institutional orders is only partially determined by relations within the industrial enterprise. In chapter 9 I examine the distribution of power within political organizations, before looking at the links between industry and politics.

9 Power relations within capitalism: political organizations

According to classical democratic theory power within political organizations belongs to the majority of organizational members: power is seen as conterminous with authority, and authority is based upon the will of the majority as expressed through the electoral process. In the current theory of representation political leaders act according to the expressed preferences of their supporters, when mandated, or according to their conception of members' interests when not.[1] An alternative, élitist tradition in political theory views such analyses as ideological mystification: rank-and-file members of political organizations are primarily the passive objects of leadership manoeuvring not the active sponsors of leadership action. Pareto, Mosca, Michels, Duverger, and in a different form C. Wright Mills, have popularized this more sceptical view.[2] Michels has provided the most elaborate application of this perspective to the study of the internal power structure of political organizations, arguing that minority domination of political organizations is inevitable, due to the technical demands of organization, but is assisted by contingent political and psychological tendencies:[3]

> if we leave out of consideration the tendency of the leaders to organize themselves and to consolidate their interests, and if we also leave out of consideration the gratitude of the led towards their leaders, and the general immobility and passivity of the masses, we are led to conclude that the principle cause of oligarchy in the democratic parties is to be found in the technical indispensability of leadership.

The role of followers is restricted to agreeing (usually) or disagreeing (occasionally) with leadership initiatives.

Neither the formal theory of representation nor the alternative Michelsian theory provides an adequate comprehensive explanation for the distribution of power in political organizations. The theory of representation ignores the ability of leaders to mould follower preferences and to disregard expressed preferences, and the practical difficulties followers encounter in attempting to exercise effective surveillance – much less control – over leaders. Élitist theory under-emphasizes the significance of divisions amongst leaders and – in the case of Michels – confuses the inevitability of revolutionary betrayal with the inevitability of organizational oligarchy. Political organizations are variably oligarchic – how far, and why, is the concern of this chapter. The first part deals with political parties, the second with trade unions.

Michels, and other writers in the élitist tradition, distinguish sharply between the political élite with a common background, common interests and common attitudes, and the mass. Élite members are recruited from similar backgrounds (usually middle-class), have a common interest in maintaining the current distribution of in-equality, and adopt conservative attitudes towards social change. Hence Michels documented carefully the social background and present interests and attitudes of the leaders of the Social Demo-cratic Party, showing how they had become incorporated into the established capitalist political élite. SDP leaders, and lesser officials, acquired the interests and perspectives of the petit-bourgeoisie, and lost whatever identification they may have had with the rank-and-file membership. Parliamentary and bureaucratic leaders, even of proletarian parties, were drawn disproportionately from middle- and upper-middle-class backgrounds; and leaders 'with proletarian backgrounds lost their identity on obtaining office:[4]

> the manual worker of former days becomes a petit-bourgeois
> or even a bourgeois. In addition to this metamorphosis, and
> despite his frequent contact with the mass of workers, he
> undergoes a profound psychological transformation. The paid
> official, living at a higher social level, will not always possess the
> moral strength to resist the seductions of his new environment.
> His political and moral education will seldom suffice to
> immunize him against the new influences.

For Michels, bourgeois life-styles and attitudes begat common interests and led to the distortion of organizational democracy.

Michels's conclusions about the limited social backgrounds of political leaders are largely confirmed by recent research in Britain, the United States and Canada, but not in Australia. In Britain, leading positions within both the Conservative and Labour parties are held mainly by politicians drawn from middle-class backgrounds

– and the higher the position, the greater the predominance of middle-class officials.[5] In the 1970 Parliament 36·1 per cent of Conservative MPs came from professional backgrounds, 32·4 per cent from commerce and industry, 12·1 per cent from politics and journalism, 9·4 per cent farming, 7·2 per cent military, and 0·9 per cent white- or blue-collar working class; during the period 1955–70 79 per cent of Conservative Cabinet ministers belonged to the middle class, 21 per cent to the aristocracy, none to the working class.[6] The proportion of leaders from working-class backgrounds has declined sharply in the British Labour Party in recent years, from 36·7 per cent in 1955 to 27·5 per cent in 1970 (including routine white-collar workers). In 1970 45·6 per cent of Labour MPs were drawn from the professions, 27·5 per cent from the working class, 13·2 per cent from politics and journalism, 11·8 per cent from commerce and industry and 0·3 per cent from farming. Over the period 1955–70 35 per cent of Labour Cabinet ministers were drawn from the working class, 62 per cent from the middle class, and 3·0 per cent from the aristocracy: in 1970 only one Labour Minister (Callaghan) remained of the original working-class group in the 1964 Cabinet; and he had been a white-collar worker.[7]

A similar pattern of occupational representation has been evident in North America. Although American parties are more fragmented and less directly hierarchical than British political parties, there is a similar tendency towards selective recruitment to higher positions. At the apex of the legislative process, in the Senate, children of fathers in professional, entrepreneurial, and farming occupations are heavily overrepresented, industrial wage-earners underrepresented. Matthews's survey showed that 24 per cent of Senators were children of professional men, 35 per cent of proprietors and officials, 32 per cent of farmers; only 5 per cent were children of industrial wage-earners (although 39 per cent of the labour force in 1900 were industrial wage-earners), and 2 per cent of low-salaried workers. Although the personnel of the Senate has changed since Matthews's figures were collected, there is no reason to believe that the underrepresentation of wage-earners has changed: the proportion of professionals has probably risen, of farmers declined. (By citing the occupational background of fathers, rather than of the Senators themselves before election, I have exaggerated the occupational heterogeneity of the Senate: about half the Senators were lawyers.)[8]

In Canada there has been virtually no working-class representation in the Federal political élite: before 1960 only one Cabinet minister was recruited from a working-class background, and he (Humphrey Mitchell) was explicitly recruited by the Liberals to represent the interests of Labour during the Second World War.

Canadian political leaders have been recruited mainly from the middle class – not the upper middle or working class.[9]

The occupational background of Australian political leaders has been more varied than that of British, American or Canadian leaders: the occupational background of Federal MPs, although not of Cabinet ministers, reflects the occupational distribution of support for the parties. Hence in 1958–61 the previous occupations of Federal Labour MPs included trade union officials (20), white-collar employees (17), teachers (10), manual workers (9) and only 3 former lawyers; the previous occupations of non-Labour Federal MPs included business and administration (24), pastoralists (22), other rural proprietors (18), lawyers (18), commercial and clerical (15) with no trade union officials or manual workers.[10] A survey of Federal and State Cabinet ministers showed a similar, but less sharp, contrast: on the Labour side 15 ministers had fathers in commercial and clerical occupations, 12 in manual work, 11 professionals, and 11 rural proprietors; on the non-Labour side 29 were the children of rural proprietors, 22 of professional and semi-professional fathers, 18 administrative and business, 10 commercial and clerical, and 8 manual workers.[11] The occupations of Australian Labour Prime Ministers (until Whitlam) have been very different from those of their British counterparts: a compositor (Watson), a coal-miner (Fisher), two trade union organizers (Hughes, Curtin), a grocer (Scullin), an electrician (Forde) and an engine-driver (Chifley).[12]

Broad similarities in social background – social origins, education and occupational experience – are likely to lead to broadly similar orientations towards politics, especially towards the importance of maintaining the conventional rules of the game. John Porter, for example, has argued that:[13]

> From the point of view of political power what is more important than interest representation is the range of social perspectives which are brought to bear on public issues. If we accept Mannheim's persuasive argument that a person's beliefs about social reality are shaped by the social milieu to which he has been exposed, we can see that the definitions of reality which provide the framework for making political decisions depend much on the social background and life experiences of politicians. The predominance of some occupational groups and people of one class background means that limited perspectives are brought to bear on public issues.

At the most general level this view has considerable plausibility, and is returned to below (p. 147); however, it is easy to exaggerate the importance of common background, and it does not provide a satisfactory basis for cohesion amongst dominant groups within political parties. The broad similarity in background amongst British political leaders conceals important differences: although both Conservative and Labour leaders are drawn from the middle class, they are drawn from different sectors of the middle class – teachers and journalists on the Labour side, independent professionals and businessmen on the Conservative side.[14] (The British Communist Party, like the Labour Party, has a very large proportion of middle-class members, mainly teachers and social workers.)[15] In the United States more Democrats than Republicans are drawn from professional backgrounds, but more Republicans than Democrats from business backgrounds.[16] Nor does similar education necessarily produce similar orientations: amongst prominent contemporary British politicians Michael Foot, Anthony Wedgwood Benn, Barbara Castle, Harold Wilson, Jeremy Thorpe, Edward Heath and Margaret Thatcher were all educated at Oxford; as were the present leader of the Australian Liberal Party, Malcolm Fraser, and the current President of both the Australian Labour Party and the Australian Confederation of Trade Unions, Bob Hawke. Different backgrounds can produce similar policies. Porter attributes the conservatism of Canadian politics to the limited social background of Canadian politicians; but the Australian Labour Party has followed broadly conservative policies (except towards trade unions) despite recruiting its leaders from a broad social background. In short, the influence of background upon attitudes is diffuse and difficult to trace: leaders with similar backgrounds have adopted different orientations, and leaders with different backgrounds similar orientations (see below, p. 147).

Past social background is less important than present institutionalized interest for the development of common interests amongst political leaders which set them apart from rank-and-file party members. Office-holders within political parties possess an obvious interest in remaining in office, or acquiring higher office, and in enhancing the material rewards of office and security of tenure. However, the potential for unity upon such institutional issues is limited by the competitiveness required for individual occupational success: office-holders are in competition with each other for higher office, and under attack from aspirants for their own offices. Accordingly, attempts to cement unity by suggesting a reduction in the frequency of elections rarely materialize, and attempts to restrict political activity founder. The ability of political leaders to increase the material rewards of party office is limited by the customary poverty of political parties (with the partial and occasional exception of American Republican Presidential parties during election campaigns) and by popular disapproval: the material rewards of political activity are derived primarily from elective office outside the party, which can only be acquired after intraparty competition.[17] Limited financial resources have forestalled the development of dominant full-time party bureaucrats in Britain, the United States, Canada and Australia (although this poverty has not, of course, necessarily limited the power of parliamentarians).

Similar occupational and educational backgrounds do not lead to similar interests and policies: the assumption of the iron law of oligarchy that the differences amongst leaders, and amongst groups of followers, are necessarily less important than the differences between leaders and led is not justified. As Hindess commented, in perhaps unnecessarily metaphysical terms, 'we cannot talk in terms of "the leader" and "the masses" without introducing elements of mystification and reification into the discussion.'[18] Leaders and followers are social beings, with individual interests and aspirations, not metaphysical essences. These individual interests and aspirations, and competition over the resources required to satisfy them, lead to conflict among leaders and among followers, and to differences of power within each group, as much as between leaders and followers. Hence, although there may be overall stability in the membership of the leadership cadre, there is instability within it.

In Britain there have been successful revolts against the leadership in both the Conservative and the Labour parties throughout this century: in the Conservative Party against Balfour in 1911, against the coalition government in 1922, against Neville Chamberlain in 1940, against Eden in 1951, against Heath in 1974, and possibly against Macmillan in 1963; in the Labour Party against MacDonald in 1931. In the United States the fragmentation of the leadership cadre is institutionalized in the separation of powers between the President and Congress, with neither group able to dominate the other. Presidential control over the executive branch, including the armed services, is constrained by Congressional control over funding and right of veto over major appointments. Such fragmentation and conflict is especially evident when the President and the Congressional majorities belong to different parties, as now: but they also occur when the same party is in control of both the White House and Capitol Hill. In Australia the recent history of the Liberal and Labour parties has been characterized by revolts, most recently the successful revolt in the Liberal Party by Fraser, the present Prime Minister, against the then Liberal leader Snedden, and the, as yet unsuccessful, revolt against Whitlam following Labour's defeat in the 1975 election.

Political leaders are obliged to attempt to win over their supporters within the élite, as well as outside the élite, on controversial matters: hence, in Britain, the Labour government's nationalization of the steel industry in 1965-6, or the Conservative government's complex manoeuvring over tariff reform in 1903–5. Occasionally apparently dominant groups within the leadership fail to achieve their objectives: the reform of the Conservative Party in 1947–8 was carried through by Lord Woolton and R. A. Butler in the face of the hostile sufferance of their leader Winston Churchill; Harold Wilson failed to carry his colleagues with him over Mrs Castle's Industrial Relations Bill in 1969. President Nixon failed to win Congressional support for his Cambodian policy, just as President Ford has failed to win support for his Angolan policy.

Conflict within the leadership, not parliamentarianism, is the main threat to oligarchy, despite the arguments put forward by Robert Mackenzie: 'a crude application of Michels' theories would ignore ... the division of labour within British political parties. It would ignore the fact that the primary function of the mass organization is to sustain competing teams of potential leaders in the House of Commons in order that the electorate as a whole may choose between them.'[19] Members of Parliament should hold themselves responsible to the mass of the electorate, not to rank-and-file members of their parties; the availability of electoral choice to the mass electorate is seen as the guarantee of democracy. Similarly in the United States: the restricted role of rank-and-file party members is insignificant, compared with the importance of maintaining effective two-party competition through the organization of effective electoral campaign machinery. However, as Michels himself originally argued, dual representation provides one basis for oligarchic domination by parliamentarians, not a limitation upon it.[20] From the perspective of the subordinate member of political parties the party remains oligarchic, even where the reason for that oligarchy is responsiveness to himself *qua* voter rather than *qua* party member. Dual responsibility provides ample opportunities for playing one responsibility off against another, especially in conditions of limited knowledge. In short, the political division of labour between the party rank-and-file membership, as the electoral provider, and the mass electorate, as the selector, does not itself undermine the tendency to oligarchy within political parties.

Some defenders of the oligarchic thesis have argued that divisions within the leadership cadre are insignificant, having no decisive impact upon the basic structure of oligarchy. Hence Duverger:[21]

the development [of conflict groups] is not a sign of the liberty of members and of a weakening of the authority of the leaders. . . . Splitting does not take place at the level of the masses but at the level of the leaders: generally it is the result of an attempt by subordinate leaders to oust leaders of higher rank, or of certain higher ranking officials to obtain the majority in collective executive bodies.

This seriously underestimates the significance for the overall distribution of power of divisions within dominant groups. For such divisions inevitably weaken the power of the leadership group as a whole *vis-à-vis* the led, if only because different sides seek to mobilize support from below for their point of view: such political mobilization inevitably increases mutual interdependence, as the history of intraparty factionalism amply demonstrates. The result is the fragmentation of the oligarchy into a plurality of sometimes competing groups, a form of political system appropriately termed 'democratic elitism'.[22]

Relations of domination and subordination in political parties are thus not the result of an automatic working out of the 'iron law' of oligarchy, the artefact of common background, attitudes and interests. Instead, it is necessary 'to look for the differential pattern of relationships between leaders and led, for differences in political expectation and concern, and for the social structuring of returns and satisfactions to be gained from [such relationships]'.[23] In some circumstances leaders will be subject to tight constraints from their followers, and presented with little alternative but to accede to their pressure, for example during election campaigns, when delivering the vote depends upon the enthusiastic participation of rank-and-file activists. More frequently, leaders will be able to ignore pressure, or to manipulate conflicting pressures; followers may fail to exert pressure out of apathy, pessimism or satisfaction with the existing level of performance. Leadership groups may also 'manage' the pressure exerted upon them by appearing to favour different policies at different times, or simply by disseminating information widely about some policies, and keeping quiet about others. Similarly, some potential demands upon the leadership group may be defined as 'non-political', and discussion stifled.

Analysis of the distribution of power within political parties thus cannot be reduced to the application of an axiomatic principle of organization: the basic distinction involved in Michels's thesis, the dichotomy between the élite and the masses, is inadequate. There are significant differences between leaders, and between different groups of followers, corresponding to both vertical and horizontal alignments. Different patterns of dependence develop amongst political leaders, based upon personal, group and organization goals: competitive desires for office or promotion, different orientations to interest groups, divergences over policy issues, lead to imbalances in dependence and thus to power relations. Such patterns are perhaps clearest in the American Senate, where the complexity of interpersonal political dependences is only slowly being simplified – or driven underground – by the development of party ideology and discipline. Similar differences exist amongst follower groups, although less keenly felt because of the lower salience of politics.

Political activity consists of groups, and individuals, whether leaders or followers, with similar or complementary goals attempting to obtain compliance with their wishes through use of their control over desired resources. These alignments cut across the line between the élite and the mass. Hence, within the British Conservative Party leadership groups wishing to direct the party towards a more explicitly Tory policy attempted to rouse back-bench and rank-and-file opinion in 1974; left-wing leaders in the Labour Party have similarly organized back-bench MPs into a self-conscious faction (the 'Tribune' group), canvassed for support at Annual Conference, and generally mobilized support amongst party activists. This is not simply a one-way process, especially within the Labour Party – rank-and-file activists working with a minority of leaders have changed party policy, over nuclear disarmament, nationalization and trade union legislation. Political leaders, with their greater involvement in politics, obviously play a more active role than followers: but the latter are not simply an inert mass.

In short, power within political parties is not distributed according to the formal theory of representation, nor according to the iron law of oligarchy. Instead, its distribution depends upon the differing goals of organization members, the distribution of resources required to achieve them, and the possibilities of escape from the dependences thereby created. Political leaders rely upon rank-and-file party members for unpaid work during campaigns for election to office, and for votes; rank-and-file party members depend upon their leaders for expert guidance in formulating policies, winning public office and implementing agreed policies. The balance of dependences is weighted individually in favour of leaders, collectively in favour of the rank and file. The marginal utility of one leader in the achievement of organizational goals is greater than the marginal utility of a single rank-and-file member, but leaders cannot function without the rank and file collectively, whilst the rank and file can evolve new leaders. In direct conflicts between a united leadership and a united rank and file the rank and file would predominate. However, such direct confrontations of united blocs are rare: in practice leadership groups prevail in the normal run of political life and leadership groups obtain more non-self-regarding action from rank-and-file members than the opposite. The amount of this will depend upon the constraints exercised upon the leadership by external factors (especially the degree of dependence upon voluntary activists for electoral mobilization), by the internal structure of the party (especially the formal distribution of responsibility for policy formulation, the degree of participation of professional advisers in internal politics, the overall accessibility of élites to membership pressure), and by shared ideology. These constraints will obviously vary from party to party, and according to circumstances within parties. Where political campaigning is professionalized the role of the voluntary activist is obviously reduced. Similarly, constraints upon executive action are clearly limited where political parties are organized on principles of democratic centralism. Where full-time advisers are able to participate in internal politics, and their communication skills are placed at the service of leadership groups, manipulation of the preferences of rank-and-file members is facilitated (and is comparatively easy on relatively technical subjects, where few alternative sources of information are available). Élite responsiveness is partly the result of such factors, and partly the result of party ideology; the *Führerprinzip* and direct democracy obviously point in different directions, regardless of environmental or structural factors.

This disaggregated approach to power relations in political parties obviously limits the possibilities of generalization – it becomes impossible to short-circuit empirical research by talismanic recourse to classical democratic or élitist theory. Environmental, structural and ideological variations clearly alter the distribution of power in political parties, in the manner suggested. This limited conclusion is reinforced by consideration of similar issues in the distribution of power in the other form of political organization discussed, trade unions.

Like the leaders of democratic political parties, trade union leaders derive their authority from the support of their rank-and-file members: leaders are held to be responsive to the wishes of their members, and subject to electoral recall. As in political parties, the power of union leaders exceeds their authority – trade unions show the same oligarchical tendencies as political parties. Union leaders develop specific interests, distinct from those of their members, and can satisfy those interests regardless of the wishes of their members in some circumstances. At the simplest level, these differences arise from union leaders wishing to retain office, and to increase their material rewards: more fundamentally, differences derive from divergent attitudes towards due process. The degree to which dominant coalitions of leaders are able to satisfy their own interests and to disregard those of their members depends upon the interests themselves and on the ability of opposition groups within the leadership cadre and/or the rank and file to exert pressure. This section deals with such interests and the factors which influence the success of external pressure.

Union office provides significant material and status rewards for union leaders. Although the salaries of union leaders vary considerably – there is no 'rate for the job' – the rewards comfortably exceed those of union members, even where the ideology of relating salaries to the average earnings of the union members survives. There are no generally available published figures. However, the salaries of British union leaders in 1973–4 ranged from £11,000 for the General Secretary of the National Association of Local Government Officers to £4,200 for the General Secretary of the Union of Construction, Allied Trades and Technicians, with salaries of white-collar union leaders exceeding those of leaders of blue-collar unions. In the United States union leaders' salaries are considerably higher, ranging from £52,000 in the Teamsters to £16,000 in the Automobile Workers, with proportionately generous expense allowances.[24] Canadian and Australian union salaries are considerably lower than American – in Canada the unions are largely outgrowths of American unions, while trade unions are relatively small – but powerful – in Australia. There are also significant indirect financial rewards for union leaders, deriving from co-optation on to government and party-political bodies and public corporations, from journalism and lectures, and from career openings as industrial relations experts. Union leadership also provides less tangible rewards – the interest and satisfaction derived from varied and responsible work, the feeling of self-importance fostered by the deference of politicians, mediamen, businessmen and others, pleasant in itself and useful in reminding rank-and-file members of one's own importance. But the conflicts of interest deriving from personal stakes in office are probably less important than those deriving from different attitudes towards due process: union leaders are more committed to maintaining procedures negotiated with management (and government) than members, for their survival depends upon the maintenance of orderly relations. The arbitrary exercise of work-group power in defiance of executive policy, even when in accord with the long-term aims of the union, undermines the authority of union leaders directly and indirectly, by increasing the chances of similar arbitrary actions by employers when circumstances change. (Hence the willingness of even the British AEU to contemplate outlawing unofficial strikes in exchange for the closed shop.)[25] Union leaders thus develop specific economic and status interests, and their occupational role requires specific attitudes: union members, at least *qua* union member, have more limited goals – the protection and improvement of their standard of living.[26] These differences of interest do not always result in conflict between leaders and followers, for union leaders recognize that retaining office requires at least minimal satisfaction of their members' conceptions of their interests – but the interests of leaders and led are interdependent, not identical.

Union leaders depend upon their members for the achievement of personal, group and organizational goals. At a personal level they hope for re-election, or election to higher office; at a group level for the provision of resources to sustain their collective level of material reward and bureaucratic facilities; and at an organizational level for acceptance of properly formulated collective-bargaining tactics and strategies.[27] Rank-and-file members depend upon leaders for expertise and coordination in using collective strength to maintain or improve their standard of living. Members grant leaders authority to perform generally specified tasks, and in return accept organizational discipline: both sides agree to perform non-self-regarding actions in specified circumstances. When conflicts based upon different interests and power bases arise, they are likely to be between one leadership group and another, the 'out-group' amongst the leaders taking the initiative in attempting to mobilize support amongst the rank and file. The extent to which such opposition tactics succeed depends upon the issues involved, the environment within which the union operates, the institutional structure of the union, and the motivations and abilities of both leaders and rank and file in using the resources available to them. The major relevant environmental factors may be classified into economic, political and normative; the major institutional factors are the structure of collective bargaining, the degree of bureaucratization, and the formal political system; the major personal attributes involved are organizational commitment, educational level and political skill. As I have written about these issues elsewhere I will only discuss each factor briefly in general terms.[28]

The dominant coalition is likely to prevail during periods of prosperity, and during periods of economic difficulty; it is less likely to prevail during periods of mild prosperity, or mild difficulty; and it is least likely to prevail during periods of mild economic difficulty following periods of relative prosperity. The ability to secure compliance rests upon different bases during periods of prosperity and depression. In prosperity union leaders can satisfy members' interests, as well as their own, through compromise according to agreed procedures with comparatively limited difficulty: employers are willing to concede increases with minimal resistance, confident that profits can be sustained by passing on increased costs in increased prices; and the majority of union members are ready to endorse, or passively acquiesce in, leadership action, satisfied with increases in real earnings. Such favourable circumstances are rare, but are likely where the demand for products produced is inelastic, the establishment of new firms, or the development of alternative products difficult, the size of the product market comparatively small (or comprising other manufacturers, thus reducing the political visibility of joint exploitation of consumers) and entry into the relevant occupation limited. Unfavourable economic conditions foster executive domination for opposite reasons. When union members are preoccupied with economic pressures, they are likely to have few resources or little energy to devote to union activities, and union membership declines; at the same time, union leaders are able to stress the importance of unity and loyalty as necessary means of preventing employers exploiting their labour market position, and thereby preserving earnings. Unions organizing workers in very tight product markets will thus tend to be oligarchic, other things being equal. The economic circumstances most likely to produce conflict between executive and rank and file occur when a period of rising prosperity is followed by sharp but not catastrophic decline – the familiar inverted-J curve of political sociologists.

The political environment within which unions are operating influences the ability to obtain compliance directly and indirectly. Directly, it can increase or decrease the resources available to different groups, and increase or decrease their liabilities. Government policies may favour those of union leaders, or may encourage the media exposure of union leaders, enhancing their prestige within the union as well as within society at large; or government policies may force union leaders to assume 'responsible' attitudes towards social and economic problems, occasionally placing leaders at odds with their members.[29] Similarly, external political groups, especially the Communist Party, may provide resources for anti-leadership groups within the union and thus increase the effectiveness of their political activities. Finally, the disintegrating pattern of normative regulation which has directly affected the distribution of power between management and workers in industry has also affected the distribution of power within trade unions, leading to increased power in non-leadership groups.[30]

The major institutional factors relevant to the distribution of power are the system of collective bargaining, the degree of bureaucratization in administration, and the political constitution. Where collective bargaining is centralized, the administration highly bureaucratic, little scope permitted for the development of substructural autonomy, full-time officials permitted to participate actively in authoritative policy-making processes, and limitations placed upon the organization of unofficial political activity, union leaders are likely to be able to prevail without difficulty. Where bargaining is decentralized, administration personalized, full-time officials banned from active participation in general policy-making decisions, and no limitations placed upon the organization of unofficial political activity, rank-and-file union members are more likely to be able to ensure leadership responsiveness.

Variations in the administrative and political structures of unions, and the environments within which they operate, condition but do not determine the distribution of power: they can make it more or less difficult for union leaders to 'control' their members, or the reverse. However, there is no inevitable link between such institutional and environmental factors and non-self-regarding action: such action depends upon the motivations and abilities of the respective parties to use the resources and opportunities available. Union leaders can fail to predominate over their rank and file even where the environment and the organizational structure appear to favour them; rank-and-file members can effectively abrogate their influence even when the environment and the structure facilitate it. Part of the explanation for such patterns lies simply in the individual abilities of union leaders and activists; part lies in the degree of organizational commitment of the union member, his readiness to translate that commitment into political terms, and his possession of the skills required to translate political belief into action effectively. Organizational commitment depends upon the importance of the union to the member as a social or economic institution. In some occupations the link between occupational communities and the union provides a basis for commitment, for example in printing; in others the union may be essential as a means of exercising economic power, as in electrical contracting.[31] Whether this commitment is interpreted in politically relevant terms depends upon the extent to which members' expectations of the union can be fully met locally, without involving the union above shop-floor level: the motivation to participate politically is limited when the union is in practice identified with shop-level organization. The ability to translate political interest into effective action depends partly upon the factors discussed earlier, and partly upon the general political awareness of the membership, likely to be conditioned by the educational level required for the occupation, and partly upon the effort made by the union to increase membership awareness.

The interaction between environmental, institutional and personal factors is evident in the British AUEW, whose politics exemplify a distinctive form of democratic élitism. The influence of the external economic situation upon the union is relatively low, because of a very wide diversity of product-markets and shop conditions. Ownership within particular industries is dispersed, and national agreements are supplemented by district and, more importantly, workshop agreements. A sound basis for consensus and cleavage is provided by the occupational distribution of union members – power remains mainly in the hands of skilled men, spread over a wide range of industries. External pressure for centralization and unanimity within the union is comparatively low, whilst the workshop power of union members is comparatively high. Internal factors, reflecting external pressures, membership traditions, and the functional needs of the organization, act in a similar fashion. Membership commitment to craft 'custom and practice' is combined with 'an almost fanatical attachment to local autonomy'.[32] The shop-steward system, the plethora of branch offices, and the District Committee system provide a training ground for lay members, increasing their political awareness, and a chance to build up independent power bases, whilst the paucity of appointed officials further limits executive initiative. These constraints are mediated through an almost excessively democratic political structure. A high degree of branch and district autonomy is accompanied by effective provision for lay oversight over full-time officials, the National Committee 'instructing' the executive, whilst the system of indirect election of delegates to the annual conference reduces the advantage the executive gains from its control of the union publicity machine.[33]

The distribution of power in trade unions is thus not the inevitable consequence of the iron law of oligarchy. But Michels's analysis is probably more relevant to relations of domination and subordination in trade unions than in political parties, for two reasons. First, trade union members are less involved than rank-and-file political party members in the activities of their organizations: the level of attendance at union branch meetings and the level of participation in union elections are low. Average attendance at trade union branch meetings is below 10 per cent; the poll in union elections usually approximates the same level, although some unions, like the National Union of Mineworkers, which conduct elections at the work-place rather than the branch, achieve significantly higher levels – in the NUM 60 per cent.[34] For the majority of trade unionists membership is a function of the requirements of the job, rather than political commitment; indeed, about four-fifths of British trade union members are covered by closed-shop agreements, including nearly all printing workers, ship-building workers, miners and time-served craftsmen in the engineering industry, and have no choice in whether they belong to a union or not.[35] Moreover, a significant number of the voluntary joiners regard their union as a service organization, a form of crisis insurance in case of difficulties with employers: their disposition to intervene politically is thus normally low. Membership of a political party involves a purposive act by the individual, and the major rewards to be derived from it relate to the individual's conception of policy; membership of a trade union need involve neither. The disposition to intervene in the activities of political parties is thus greater. Moreover (second) trade unions are self-evidently conflict organizations, engaged in conflict with employers: a premium is therefore placed upon loyalty and unity to avoid weakness in the bargaining process. The union's 'power to' depends partly upon the union leadership's 'power over'. Political parties, especially radical political parties, draw upon the same sentiments, but to a lesser degree. Trade unions are thus more likely to be at the 'oligarchy' end of the 'oligarchy–democracy' continuum than political parties.

In both political parties and trade unions the distribution of power is not conterminous with the distribution of authority: the few have more power than the mass in both types of organizations. Leaders have greater control over the means of communication within the organization than the rank and file, possess more political skills, and can draw upon the prestige which is normally associated with responsible office. Yet the relations between leaders and led are more complex than the iron law of oligarchy would suggest. Neither the leaders nor the led constitute a homogeneous group; each can be regarded as unified only in very general terms. There are thus closer links between some groups of leaders and their followers than between different groups of leaders (for example, the alliance between the 'Tribune' group of MPs in the Parliamentary Labour Party in the 1950s and their supporters in the constituency parties was closer than the link between the Tribunites and some of their parliamentary colleagues on some contentious issues). Nor is this always a case of leaders seeking to mobilize sympathetic supporters. In trade unions, for example, communist rank-and-file activists lend their support to non-communist left-wing candidates for office without any initiative being taken by the candidate himself (and occasionally in the face of attempts by the candidate to reject their support). Moreover, in the last resort, the leader depends upon his followers for their votes; without votes the leader perishes.

Power relations, as I have argued earlier, are essentially exchange relations; the power derives from imbalances in exchanges. In political organizations leaders make authoritative decisions about the allocation of resources and provide guidance, in exchange for votes and support. To adopt the terminology of systems theory, leaders transform demands into decisions, in exchange for supports. Unfortunately, determination of the balance of dependences and therefore of overall power relations in political organizations is problematic. In general terms, the contribution of the leader to the led exceeds the contribution of the led to the leader; the value of

Harold Wilson's decision-making or electioneering abilities to the rank-and-file Labour Party member should exceed the value of the rank and file's vote to the party leader, and in one sense it does. Leadership incapacity does more damage to the party than the loss of individual votes. But the significance of loss of office to Mr Wilson exceeds the significance of the loss of Mr Wilson to the voter. In this sense Mr Wilson is more dependent upon the rank-and-file party members collectively than the individual rank-and-file party member is upon Mr Wilson. Thus, paradoxically, the imbalance in the distribution of power in political organizations is not as great as it seems at first sight for, in the last analysis, office means more to the politician than his vote means to the voter.

10 Élite theory: relations between economy and polity within capitalism

In the preceding two chapters I explored the factors which influence the distribution of power within industrial and political institutions separately, largely in isolation from each other. This separation into industrial and political institutions was only an analytical convenience. I do not agree with Dahrendorf's view that the separation between industry and politics is a major characteristic of contemporary industrial society, distinguishing it from the monolithic political economy of nineteenth-century capitalism: 'in post-capitalist [industrial] society industry and society have, by contrast to capitalist society, been dissociated. . . . In post-capitalist society, the industrial enterprise is no longer the model after which all other relations are fashioned.'[1] Nor do I agree with the Marxist-derived view that political institutions are epiphenomena whose role is ultimately determined by economic class relations: 'the State in [capitalist] societies is primarily and inevitably the guardian and protector of the economic interests which are dominant in them. Its "real" purpose and mission is to ensure their continued predominance.'[2] The relationship is rather one of symbiosis, in which political institutions are partially autonomous, and influence, as well as being influenced by economic institutions. The distribution of power within political organizations affects the distribution of power in industrial organizations, and vice versa: political and industrial goals are formulated in the light of each other, power resources are often transferable, and power acquired in one arena may be increased – or lost – in the other. The interrelations between industrial and political organizations, in so far as they influence the distribution of power within and between them, are examined in this chapter. This necessarily involves a more comprehensive review of élite theory, in both its Marxist and its non-Marxist forms, than was necessary in chapter 9, where élite theory was considered only in so far as it was directly relevant to the distribution of power within political organizations.[3]

Élite theorists analyse society in dichotomous terms, with a more or less cohesive minority dominating an amorphous majority. This domination may be achieved directly, through a monopoly of the means of violence and/or subsistence, or indirectly, through the control of 'middle-men' with specific authority in limited areas, or through 'hegemonic' control over the formulation of social values.[4] Members of the élite are bound to each other by ties of family, class origin, education, occupational experience and institutional interest, and develop a consciousness of kind and of common interests; the dispersed and oppressed mass possess neither the knowledge nor the resources to transcend their limited horizons and to realize their common interest in opposing élite domination. Although the terms used to describe the minority differ, the boundaries of the élite are vague and the connecting links between élite members change, élite theorists share a common belief in the predominance of a more-or-less cohesive minority.[5] This minority, which derives its power from private property, according to Miliband, or from organizational position, according to Wright Mills, dominates both economic and political organizations. For élite theorists the issue of the relation between the distribution of power in political and industrial organizations is thus secondary to that of the basic division of society: industry and politics are simply two arenas in which the élite exercises its dominance. Before considering the interrelation between the distribution of power in industrial and political institutions it is thus necessary to examine élite theory in general more closely.

Leadership groups in both industrial and political organizations are recruited from only a limited range of occupational backgrounds, educated at a limited number of schools, and exposed to only limited work and cultural environments. These conclusions have been documented extensively in most Western capitalist countries – for example, by Giddens, Crewe, and others in Britain, Wright Mills and Domhoff in the United States, Porter and Presthus in Canada, and Encel in Australia.[6] At the apex of society the links between members of the élite are genealogical – what Simon Haxey in the 1930s called 'the cousinhood'; lower down, the initial links are provided by parental acquaintance, residential proximity and shared education.[7] Such education – at the 'Clarendon' public schools and Oxbridge in Britain, at élite private schools like Groton and St Paul's

145

and the Ivy League universities in the United States, Upper Canada College and the University of Toronto in Canada, the nine 'prestige' private schools and the Universities of Sydney, Melbourne and Adelaide in Australia – reinforces informal socialization within the family, furnishes peer-group contacts, and facilitates the acquisition of generally legitimated educational qualifications. In Britain both leading businessmen and top civil servants, as well as party political leaders discussed earlier, are drawn from a limited social group and educated at a small number of schools. Only 1 per cent of company chairmen over the period 1900–72 were from working-class backgrounds, 3 per cent from small business, and 66 per cent from the 'upper class' (industrialists, land-owners, significant wealth-holders).[8] The proportion of high-ranking civil servants (under-secretary and above in current rankings) with manual working-class backgrounds increased from 7 per cent in 1929 to 9 per cent in 1939, 20 per cent in 1950, and 17 per cent in 1967.[9] As in business, the highest-ranking personnel have been drawn from the wealthiest backgrounds. Similarly, a disproportionate number of senior businessmen and civil servants are privately educated – 65 per cent of company chairmen attended public schools, whilst 64 per cent of senior civil servants in 1966–7 did not attend local authority schools.[10] Research in the United States, Canada and Australia has revealed a similar picture. Intragenerational occupational mobility between industrial and political roles increases the pressure towards élite conformity, as well as providing further useful personal contacts. In Ralph Miliband's words: 'the world of administration and the world of large-scale enterprise are now increasingly linked in terms of an almost interchanging personnel ... more and more businessmen find their way into one part or other of the state system at both political and administrative levels ... higher civil servants ever more regularly find their way into corporate enterprise.'[11]

Élite theorists pay close attention to the social background and personal attributes of members of the élite because they believe that such factors significantly influence the distribution of power:[12]

the major reason for focusing on the social antecedents of élite personnel is the implicit assumption that if we know who they are, and were, and how they came to be such, then we already have a reliable guide to what they believe and do ... [they justify] their focus by arguing that social background is a useful indicator of the following characteristics of an élite: (1) its cohesion (2) its self-interest (3) its values (4) its representativeness of the general public (or special publics with which it deals), and therefore (5) its responsiveness to the needs and demands of the general public (6) its performance –

usually in terms of efficiency and professionalism and (7) the smoothness of its relationships with other élites.

The influence of social background may be pervasive, but it is not specific. Studies of the relationship between social background and specific policy preferences have not revealed a very close fit: adult political attitudes and interests have proved more accurate indicators of policy preferences, as shown by Edinger and Searing's study of French and German political élites, and Farlie and Budge's more wide-ranging study: 'the definite conclusion [is] that no set of background characteristics can be isolated which acts as an invariant – or even relatively invariant – predictor of issue-preferences.'[13] Precise connections between social background and specific policy preferences are perhaps less likely than a more general association between social background and fundamental political attitudes: but even this modified thesis is not sustained:[14]

we have not found a peculiarly pronounced élite consensus on issues related to a fundamental restructuring of the economy, nor on issues which might be regarded as fundamental by other criteria. . . . The attitudinal effects of social background vary so much even between British cities that general inferences can hardly be drawn from the exclusive characteristics shared by all élites . . . the import of our findings is generally against the thesis of concurrent élite action in defence of the *status quo*, even in its fundamental aspects.

The direct influence of social background upon policy preferences is thus probably low. But social background influences political action in two other ways: directly, through its effect upon political recruitment, and indirectly, through socialization. Social background and experience is important in élite recruitment, whether recruitment is formalized in examination qualifications or through informal connections. Formally, the close association between social-class background and educational achievement – demonstrated exhaustively in outline for all capitalist countries, if not understood precisely in any – limits the range of candidates for élite positions.[15] Moreover, in a world in which the number of important élite positions is fewer than the number of candidates formally qualified to fill them, social background may furnish decisive informal qualifications. The following journalist's account of an interview with Lord Rothschild on the recruitment of members of the Central Policy Review Staff illustrates this graphically:[16]

we looked around. I sometimes go to the Barbados, and since Dick Ross [a member of CPRS] told me he knew a very good man on one of these sugar boards called Hector Hawkins, I

147

made it my business to have a rum punch with him – perhaps
two – and I thought Hector was very nice and very good. . . .
Well, then Peter Bowcock was recommended to me by Lord
Jellicoe. Kate Mortimer I knew because she was a contemporary
of my daughter Emma's at Oxford. . . . I think I got hold of
William Plowden because his father's rather a friend of mine
and I asked his father if he might like it.

(A minor irony illustrating the limitations of the social background
approach is that one of Kate Mortimer's acquaintances at
Oxford was a leading British supporter of Castro's Cuba.)
Reliance upon such informal contacts derives as much from a
psychological tendency to 'satisfice' as it does from a desire to
maintain the ideological unity of a ruling élite – although the
end-result may be the same.

Shared social background and experience exercises a more
diffuse, but equally significant influence upon the distribution of
power through its importance for the socialization process. At the
most general level, common background eases the acquisition of a
common language, enabling political and industrial actors to
'understand one another' (to use a stock phrase): inflexion and
intonation, as well as words, are important in fostering understanding. Moreover, shared experience helps to create agreement
upon legitimate 'vocabularies of motive', limiting public discussion
to acceptable justifications for action. More specifically, primary and
secondary socialization determines attitudes towards authority in
general, and towards political authority in particular. For example,
Melvin Kohn has shown how experience within the family, education
system, and work-place fosters conformity; others have traced the
process of acquisition of political values during adolescence.[17]
However, the process of socialization does not produce uniformity,
even amongst actors from similar social backgrounds: the political
élite agrees upon only very diffuse political values, whilst subordinate
groups appear to possess at least two layers of political values.[18]
Moreover, it is easy to attach too much importance to shared values
as the basis for political action, as earlier discussion has shown.

Examination of social-class origins, education experience and
personal acquaintances thus cannot be used as a short-cut to understanding power relationships within and between industrial and
political organizations. However, this does not necessarily disprove
a 'power élite' theory, for the most plausible form of élite theory
relates domination to current institutional interests, not to social
or cultural homogeneity. For Wright Mills the domination of the
military–industrial complex is based upon the institutional interests
of corporate executives, military leaders and politicians in defining

political issues in military terms and in maintaining the level of military expenditure necessary to achieve militarily defined strategic interests:

> The idea of the power élite rests upon . . . the several coincidences of objective interests between economic, military, and political institutions; the social similarities and the psychological affinities of the men who occupy the command posts of these structures . . . [and] the ramifications, to the point of virtual totality, of the kind of decisions that are made at the top.

Similarly Domhoff concludes:[19]

> the income, wealth, and institutional leadership of . . . the 'American business aristocracy' are more than sufficient to earn it the designation 'governing class'. . . . This 'ruling class' is based upon the national corporate economy and the institutions that economy nourishes. It manifests itself through . . . the power élite.

Both Miliband and Westergaard in Britain see the power élite as based on institutional interests – those of the directors and senior managers of large industrial corporations, whose power is derived ultimately from the private ownership of capital. Although economic élites compete, their competition is subordinated to the need to preserve the fundamental structure of privately owned corporate capitalism. Hence Miliband:

> it may readily be granted that there does exist a plurality of economic élites in advanced capitalist societies; and that despite the integrating tendencies of advanced capitalism these élites constitute distinct groupings and interests, whose competition greatly affects the political process. This 'élite pluralism' does not, however, prevent the separate élites in capitalist society from constituting a dominant economic class, possessed of a high degree of cohesion and solidarity, with common interests and common purposes which far transcend their specific differences and disagreements.

In short:[20]

> the most important political fact about advanced capitalist societies . . . is the continued existence in them of private and ever more concentrated economic power. As a result of that power the men – owners and controllers – in whose hands it lies enjoy a massive preponderance in society, in the political system, and in the determination of the state's policies and actions.

The military–industrial complex, or the owners of private capital, clearly have an interest in the preservation of the basic structure of the society within which they prosper: this is neither surprising nor interesting. More controversial is evaluation of the extent to which such groups are able to dominate society – or, more narrowly, the extent to which dominant groups in industrial life can determine the outcome of political action. C. J. Hewitt's study of the influence of different types of organizations upon national political issues indicated that very few organizations or types of organization exerted influence over more than one issue (out of 24) in Britain during the period 1944–64, measuring influence by the minimal criterion of taking a position on the subject – 86 per cent of organizations were involved in only one issue, and only 23 organizations (4 per cent) were involved in four or more issues.[21] The overall numbers of organizations involved, and their apparent lack of general interest, is not convincing in itself, for the 581 organizations considered could be grouped into four nearly homogeneous groupings – business organizations, religious organizations, blue-collar unions and white-collar occupations. However, none of the four blocs were uniformly successful in securing compliance with their wishes – business groups secured favourable policy outcomes on the use of sanctions against Iran, the emasculation of steel nationalization (pre-1965), railway nationalization, rent decontrol and the motorway programme; were defeated over the independent nuclear deterrent, nationalization of road haulage, abolition of Resale Price Maintenance, initial entry into the Common Market and the Town and Country Planning Act; and obtained some of their objectives on commercial television and the Clean Air Act.[22]

Such conclusions are similar to those of Arnold Rose, S. Keller, Grant McConnell and E. M. Epstein in their earlier work in the United States: '[Economic élites] do not "rate" in the sense of commanding the entire nation. Quite the contrary, they tend to pursue a policy of non-involvement in the large issues of statesmanship.'[23] 'Corporations appear to have greater national political power when pursuing narrow interests than when engaging in broader policy issues.'[24] Economic groups, whether business or trade union, attempt to use their economic power in the political arena in pursuit of their goals within the area of their major interest, economic life, just as political groups attempt to mobilize economic allies for political purposes: they are most likely to intervene, and most likely to be successful, where their specific interests are involved.[25]

In general terms, thus, the extent of the influence of economic groups depends upon their motivation to intervene in political activities, the resources available to them to carry out their wishes, their access to the political hierarchy, and the balance of dependences between dominant political groupings and dominant or subordinate industrial groupings.

The motivation of industrial groups to intervene politically is largely determined by the likelihood of success, itself mainly influenced by the relative willingness of political groups to intervene in industrial life to assist specific groups within it: where political actors are willing and able to intervene, there will be a disposition by industrial groups to secure political intervention. Hence, to the extent that political organizations attempt to regulate industrial activity, whether through safety regulations, tariffs or restrictions upon profits and earnings, different industrial groups will be motivated to intervene. Dominant groups have attempted to reinforce their collective position by securing material and ideological support, or to improve their individual positions through tariffs, investment grants or other selective benefits. Subordinate groups have been even more willing to intervene, to introduce a balancing influence against dominant groups. Hence British trade unions in the late nineteenth century attempted to stimulate political concern, for example over safety questions, and eventually supported socialist attempts to form an independent labour party as an explicit means of using political influence to shift the balance of power within industry.

In general terms the major determinant of the disposition of industrial groups to intervene politically is the likely response of political actors to that intervention. A second major factor is the legitimacy of intervention in politics: both dominant and subordinate groups within industry have had reservations about the legitimacy of seeking political support, at different historical periods. In the nineteenth century many British entrepreneurs were committed to *laissez-faire* conceptions of economics (although the extent of this commitment can be easily exaggerated) and were reluctant to attempt to seek political assistance; they were therefore slower to seek protective tariffs against foreign competition in the late nineteenth century than their American contemporaries. Similarly, the persistence of deferential attitudes amongst substantial sectors of the working class has led to reservations about the legitimacy of a purely working-class political party, committed to intervention in industry on behalf of sectional rather than national interests. Although there is little systematic evidence on the distribution of deferential attitudes amongst subordinate groups, inarticulate legitimation of hierarchy remains significant, although probably declining.[26] In my own research, for example, carried out in 1968–9, a quarter of manual and routine non-manual workers possessed what could be described as a deferential world-view.[27] To the extent that deference is generally accorded to higher social groups there will be little attempt to use political means to overturn the industrial hierarchy, and the attitudes in the one will simply mirror the attitudes in the other; political hierarchy will reflect and reinforce industrial hierarchy. However, reservations about the legitimacy of such intervention have now largely broken down. The traditional interest of dominant business groups in limiting foreign competition by erecting tariff barriers has been widened to include obtaining direct government financial assistance in major investment programmes (ship-building, aerospace), in mitigating the economic consequences of recession, and in attempting to increase worker-productivity.[28] In Britain, the erosion of 'free collective bargaining' in the 1960s and early 1970s was partly the result of attempts by dominant industrial groups to re-assert their control, especially over wages; the Industrial Relations Act (1971) was explicitly designed to limit 'A Giant's Strength', the Inns of Court Conservative Lawyers' Association's term for the power of the trade unions.[29] Similarly in the United States, where the Taft-Hartley Act (1947) was explicitly designed to use political power to restrict the industrial power of trade unionism.

The major resources available to industrial groups to mobilize political support are material and votes. In terms of material resources dominant groups within industry are better placed than subordinate groups, with greater individual capital resources and higher incomes, and with control over the expenditure of organizational resources. This is most obvious in industrial contributions to political parties. For example, in Britain, between the autumn of 1967 and the spring of 1969 the Conservative Party's special National Appeal raised £2¼ millions, including approximately £1½ millions from business contributions. (In a normal non-election year the party's income in the late 1960s was approximately £850,000, an unknown proportion being contributed by business organizations.) This compared with a Labour Party income of only £366,620 in 1969, including £272,145 in trade union affiliation fees.[30] In the United States the material resources normally available to Republican parties – before the 1974 Federal Election Campaign Funds Act came into force – comfortably exceeded those available to the Democratic Party, and were drawn mainly from business sources, both individual and collective. The reported gross receipts of the Republican National Campaign Committees in 1968 were $29,020,000, of the Democratic National Campaign Committees $20,723,000: 'the most impressive part of recent Republican Presidential campaigns has been in their financing'. In 1968 the Republican Party received $7,658,160 from contributors of $10,000 or more, compared with the Democratic Party's $4,290,561: the largest single occupational grouping contributing to the Republicans was 'family and inherited wealth' ($2,135,804), to the Democrats 'investment banking and brokerage' ($862,686).[31]

The ability of subordinate groups to mobilize votes as a counter-vailing influence in the political arena depends upon the readiness of the members of such groups to accept the decisions of their industrial leaders. But the voting behaviour of subordinates is only partially determined by industrial leadership: in Britain, the United States, Canada and Australia, religious, regional and ethnic loyalties also influence political behaviour, reducing the leverage of subordinate industrial groups.[32] Moreover, although the majority of members of the working class support non-conservative parties, this is due to their general experience of deprivation, not to any direct acceptance of industrial direction, and does not provide a reliable basis for concerted action. Although the majority of trade unionists in Britain vote Labour (73 per cent of union families voted Labour, compared with 42 per cent of non-union families in 1964), this is probably due to the greater tendency of Labour supporters than non-Labour supporters to join trade unions, rather than to the influence of trade unionism.[33] The majority of respondents in the Butler and Stokes survey of political attitudes in Britain thought that the trade unions should stay out of politics (74 per cent in 1966, 72 per cent in 1970), including a majority of trade union members (65 per cent in 1966, no figures published for 1970).[34] This is not to suggest that work experiences do not influence political attitudes and behaviour – they clearly do; it is to suggest that the ability of subordinate groups in industry to compensate for lack of material resources by mobilizing numbers is severely limited. The direct political influence of subordinate workers' organizations is thus limited even in the country with the highest association between social-class background and voting behaviour in the English-speaking world; it is more limited in the U.S.A., Canada and Australia.

Resources, whether of material or votes, are likely to be more effectively mobilized by dominant than subordinate industrial groups because of the former's greater knowledge of the workings of the political system, acquired during pressure-group activity, and the receptivity of political organizations to the conception of the national interest represented by dominant industrial hierarchies: in Veblen's words, 'the chief – virtually sole – concern of the constituted authorities in any democratic nation is a concern about the profitable business of the nation's substantial citizens'.[35]

The third factor influencing the ability of industrial groupings to mobilize political support to change the distribution of power within industry is their degree of access to political organizations. In capitalist societies business has obvious access to conservative

153

parties (whether Conservative in Britain, Republican in the United States, or Liberal in Canada and Australia), trade unions and the organized working class to labour parties: such access may be formalized, as in the British and Australian Labour Parties, semiformal, as in the Political Action Committee of the AFL–CIO, or informal, as in the links between business groups and conservative parties.[36] In the last resort the value of this access can only be judged by examining the electoral fortunes of the respective political parties in the countries concerned, a subject beyond the scope of this study. However, even where Labour parties are electorally successful, many decisions relevant to the distribution of industrial power are detailed administrative decisions, taken by civil servants rather than politicians, and where issues do raise political considerations politicians will ask the advice of their civil servants. Dominant industrial groups have more access to civil servants than their subordinates partly because of their knowledge of where to exert pressure, derived from extensive working in cooperation, and partly because of their greater similarity of social background. It is obviously easier for civil servants to regard people like themselves as trustworthy and reliable, and thus likely to have a proper regard for the public interest, than people they meet only in formal confrontations: in this context the background social attributes of élite members discussed earlier acquire direct political significance.

The goals of industrial groups, the resources available to achieve them, and access to the political system are not in themselves decisive: success is determined by the reciprocal dependences of political organizations. The specific resources available to industrial groups, especially material and votes, have been discussed briefly earlier: political actors clearly require money and votes for the achievement of their individual and organizational goals, and will be influenced directly by the ability of industrial groups to provide either. However, it is not enough to analyse the relationship between political actors and industrial groups as a direct exchange of political decisions for support, whether money or votes, as implied by the more enthusiastic advocates of an economic approach to political science: a more complex approach is required. This issue has been analysed by systems theorists, who have devoted considerable attention to sub-system exchanges. For example, Parsons characterizes the double exchange between the polity and the economy in the following terms:[37]

In to G	Control of productivity
In to A	Opportunity for effectiveness
Out to G	Commitment of services to collectivity
Out to A	Allocation of fluid resources (financial)

However, this is unsatisfactory: the exchange is not – as Parsons implies – truly bilateral. For the products of the economy are defined politically, but not vice versa: hence the opportunity for effectiveness is a political product, which can be transformed into economic activity (productivity) if the opportunity is seized. Moreover, structural functional systems theory is only one-dimensional, involving a transfer of the normative conceptions of the democratic theory of sovereignty into the analysis.[38] There is no conceptualization of the individual and group goals of political actors, which influence 'systemic' objectives; nor is there any assessment of the substantial problems involved in implementing the allegedly authoritative 'will of the majority'. A change of plan and a more complex approach is necessary.

In general terms, economic actors provide the goods and resources indispensable to the operation of the political system, whilst political actors perform boundary-maintaining functions, provide ideological justifications for social arrangements, and act as brokers in conflicts between different economic groups. In addition to these political analogues of organizational goals political actors possess individual and group goals, for office and material reward. The balance of dependences which emerges from exchanges between political and economic actors depends partly upon the individual and group goals discussed earlier, and partly upon the overall needs of each system for the resources provided by the other. These will depend largely upon the extent to which the overall survival of the political system, and its dominant institutions, is dependent upon the maximization of economic growth. In some circumstances, the commitment of the population to the achievement of economic growth will increase the power of economic actors at the expense of political actors, although it will not obliterate the power of the latter completely: in other circumstances the commitment of members of the social system to group expansion through military aggression will increase the power of the polity at the expense of the economy, although again it will not completely destroy the power of the economy. But in contemporary society the most important decisions relate to the priority given to economic growth, the type of institutions developed to achieve that growth, and the distribution of the rewards resulting from that growth.

Functionalist theories of industrialization have focused attention upon the universal 'logic of industrialization' – although less so than their critics have maintained – and the concomitant changes required in the social and political systems.[39] To the extent that economic growth is accorded priority, universalistic achievement values and political pluralism are likely to predominate. However, decisions about the priority to be accorded to economic growth are political decisions, although political decisions taken within the constraints of economic aspirations and also, once taken, of the economic logic of those decisions. Moreover, there are several methods of achieving economic growth, according different weight to the respective roles of the state and the individual entrepreneur. There are at least seven decisions about economic growth with implications for relations between the polity and the economy which require resolution: the speed; the major sources of capital; the allocation of priorities to different sectors of the economy; the pressures placed on managers; the role of the educational system as transmitter of traditional values or teacher of technical skills; the degree of integration within the world economy; and the attitude taken towards population expansion.[40] None of these decisions can be taken on narrow, technical economic grounds; each has obvious implications for relations between the polity and the economy. For example, the attitude taken to the population problem: if an attempt is made to control population growth the domestic market grows only slowly, hence making developing industries dependent upon world export markets; there is the possibility of private capital accumulation; and the problem of the maintenance of public order is relatively easy. The first may be expected to increase the power of the polity at the expense of the economy, because of the importance of tariffs, etc., whilst the second and third may be expected to increase the power of the economy. But especially fateful are decisions about the pace of economic growth and the source of capital accumulation.

Decisions about the pace of economic growth and the source of capital accumulation are related – the faster the rate of growth desired, the less accumulation can be left to the autonomous activities of individual entrepreneurs, the greater the role of 'forced' accumulation through taxation.[41] The prerequisite for economic growth is capital accumulation, either by the concentration of wealth in the hands of individuals with 'low time preferences', or by the forced removal of resources from individuals who would, if permitted, consume their resources immediately. In Britain in the nineteenth century economic growth occurred largely through the former process, through the use of resources accumulated by individuals with low time preferences. The role of the state in capital accumulation was therefore minimal, and the power of the polity vis-à-vis the economy relatively small. On the other hand, in Germany and Russia in the late nineteenth century, and even more in developing countries in the twentieth, capital accumulation has been largely through the state, either in the form of the direct investment of state resources derived from central government property (or central government concessions to foreign enterprises, as in nineteenth-century Russia), or through expropriation, or indirectly through heavy taxation. In such circumstances the role of the state in capital accumulation is obviously greater, and the role of the polity *vis-à-vis* the economy greater.

Even in societies attaching primary importance to economic growth, there is thus a substantial difference depending upon whether the growth is predominantly through capital accumulation by entrepreneurs, acting autonomously, or through capital accumulation by the state. There is, of course, an even greater difference between societies committed to economic growth, in which the logic of industrialization operates, however tenuously, and societies in which questions of distribution rather than accumulation are accorded priority. The polity is obviously more powerful in societies preoccupied with questions of distribution rather than accumulation.[42] Whether, as critics of state socialism allege, political intervention in the operation of the distribution of rewards in Eastern Europe distorts the rate of economic growth or not remains an open question. But there is undoubtedly a connection between allocating priority to questions of distribution, whether in the name of social justice or some other ultimate end, and maintaining the supremacy of the polity.[43] In the state socialist societies of Eastern Europe the polity has undoubtedly retained its supremacy over the economy.

The response of political organizations to industrial intervention thus differs according to the priority accorded to economic growth, and according to the predominant means of capital accumulation. The final determinant of this response is the industrial structure of the relevant society, for relations between the polity and economy are obviously affected by the extent to which the success of specific industries depends upon favourable treatment by governments, either in the form of contracts, for example in the aerospace and defence industries, or for protection against foreign competition, as in the cotton-textile industry in Britain in the 1950s and 1960s. To the extent that the prosperity of a given industry is dependent upon such assistance, the power of political organizations *vis-à-vis* the economy will be increased. In the United States in the 1950s and early 1960s aircraft firms relied on the Department of Defence for 80 per cent of their sales, and were at the mercy of changes in government defence policy.[44] Similarly, British industry in the early 1930s was highly dependent upon the government for protection against foreign competition. The Import Duties Act of 1932 provided for a general 10 per cent ad valorem import duty, and for additional duties in cases where the government thought they were required. In exchange the government, through the Import Duties Advisory Committee, was able to insist on the internal reorganization of industry, for example in the iron and steel industry.[45] Such interdependence between government and industry is a commonplace in contemporary capitalist society.

The interrelationship between the distribution of power in industrial and in political organizations is thus highly complex, dependent upon the goals – personal, group and organizational – of actors within each arena, and the extent to which the resources required to satisfy them are controlled by industrial or political actors. The distribution of power within political organizations cannot be seen as a direct result of the attitudes and activities of industrial actors, or of the institutional interests of industrial organizations. Political actors depend upon industrial groups for assistance in achieving individual goals, especially office, group goals, improved material living standards, and 'organizational' goals, especially the survival of the political system. In societies which accord primary importance to economic growth economically dominant groups will be more important to politically dominant groups than in societies committed to political expansion, where economic demands may be sacrificed to strategic needs. In contemporary developing countries, where priority is accorded to economic growth, dominant political groups are obliged to pursue policies designed to develop social and political institutions congruent with the demands of the specific character of the economy. Yet, even here, the relationship between political and economic groups is one of interdependence, not complete domination and subordination. There are controversies over the best means of achieving economic growth which are not resolvable in economic terms – over the rate of economic growth desired, or over the respective roles of public and private capital accumulation. Such judgments can only be made by political groups, in the light of their judgments of value. The significance of such political autonomy is even greater where there is no willingness to accord primacy to economic growth. Although the National Socialist regime in the 1930s temporized with dominant industrial groups, especially when their assistance became necessary to achieve the rearmament programme, the Nazi Party dominated the economy, as well as the military and the state.[46] The coalition between big business, the military, the Nazi Party and the SS was a highly complex quadripartite structure, documented extensively by Arthur Schweitzer in *Big Business in the Third Reich*, in which the Nazi Party played the leading role.[47]

The major power-holders in capitalist society are thus less united than élitist theory suggests; their behaviour is not an automatic response to the pressures of social-class background or group interest. More particularly, the actions of political actors are not determined solely by the requirements of capitalist industry. According to Miliband:[48]

the business and propertied interests of advanced capitalist countries have generally been able to rely on the positive and

158

active good will of their governments; and also that where, occasionally, governments have come into being whose members, or some of whose members, could not, in terms of the ultimate purpose and official rhetoric of their parties, be relied on, their *actual* approach to affairs has greatly reduced or altogether nullified the dangers which these interests were deemed to face.

But this exaggerates the degree of unity between the political and business élite, and within the business élite itself. For the fact that both the political and business élites are drawn from the same social background, and may even have been to the same schools and universities, does not necessarily imply that they share the same interests (or that their interests are congruent with each other). Such élites may speak the same language, but use different words. Each élite has an obvious interest in maximizing the share of the gross national product allocated to itself; the political élite will not share the business élite's attitude to company taxation, or to the public ownership of the means of production, distribution and exchange. Moreover, the analysis exaggerates the degree of unity within each élite, as well as between élites. In Britain, both Conservative and Labour MPs are drawn disproportionately from the middle class (although the sector of the middle class from which they are drawn differs, the Conservatives being drawn more from business, Labour from academic life). But there are significant differences in attitudes taken by the parties over questions fundamental to relations of domination and subordination, including education, taxation and public control over economic life.

The Marxist analysis exaggerates the degree of unity between the political élite and the industrial élite, and of unity within each élite. But it retains more plausibility than the opposing market interpretation, stressing the autonomy of political actors. For there are a multitude of links between business and politics which make the view of the polity as the supreme autonomous power seriously misleading. The polity is dependent upon the economy for resources both of men and material, as the discussion of political recruitment and political expenditure showed. This dependence inevitably involves a balance of power between the two sets of institutions, with the balance often tilted in the direction of the economy, especially where the ability of dominant political groups to retain their electoral position depends upon the economy's ability to perform its role of satisfying material aspirations. Moreover, the ability of dominant political groups within capitalism to use their political resources to undermine the position of industrial groups is severely limited by the concepts of legitimacy current among dominant and subordinate groups in both sectors. Attempts to use political means to support or undermine industrial hierarchies may be inhibited by limited definitions of appropriate action; such definitions are the result of socialization experiences, especially within the family, the school and the work-place. Assessing the importance of such inhibitions involves examining the significance of ideology, which mediates the effects of capitalism as a system of labour exploitation upon the distribution of power within political organizations, and between political and industrial institutions.

In short, contemporary capitalism is not dominated by a small, cohesive power élite. But neither is it ruled by the popular will, as understood in the doctrine of popular sovereignty. The characteristic political structure of contemporary capitalism is rather one of democratic élitism.

11 Conclusion: the sociology of power

In this book I have adopted a synoptic, comparative approach to the study of power, examining relations of domination and subordination in different types of society, defined in terms of systems of labour exploitation. Different systems of labour exploitation – slavery, feudalism and capitalism – develop characteristic patterns of dependence relations, and thereby characteristic relations of domination and subordination. Domination may be based upon coercion, authority or influence; although they are not mutually exclusive, any given hierarchical relation is likely to be predominantly coercive, authoritarian or influential. In general, coercion is a successful means of obtaining compliance only in highly asymmetric dependence relations; authority and influence are the major bases of compliance where dependence is relatively balanced.

In the broadest sense, power relations, of whatever kind, arise out of interdependence – alter possessing resources which ego requires in order to achieve his own goals, and which ego can only obtain by performing non-self-regarding actions. The distribution of power results directly from the multiple and varying goals of actors, the resources required to achieve them, and the means available to escape from the dependences thereby created. Power relations may result from the goal of increased wealth, prestige, affection, 'ego expansion' or whatever. However, my concern has been with the patterns of dependence which emerge out of the methods used to obtain the basic necessities of life, for they have been the most fateful for hierarchical relations. Dependence derives from differential control over access to the resources required to sustain life. This differential control is based partly upon inheritance and partly upon the differential 'criticalness' of specific resources at a particular time. 'Criticalness' is determined primarily by the prevailing forces of production, especially technology, and scarcity. In summary terms, technology and scarcity lead to 'criticalness'; criticalness and inheritance lead to control over desired resources; control over resources and goals lead to dependence; dependence and limited escape potential lead to power relations. The major part of this book develops this basic view.

Power relations are thus the result of a complex network of factors. Different conditions influence each set of factors, and a comprehensive theory of power relations would include propositions about the conditions relevant for each set, and their implications for hierarchical relations. However, such a comprehensive theory is beyond the scope of this study, and the present state of sociological knowledge. Instead, I have examined the configurations characteristic of different 'ideal-types' of systems of labour exploitation – slavery, feudalism and capitalism.

Slavery represents the extreme form of asymmetric dependence relation, where the slave is dependent upon the master for his very existence: the slave is literally his master's creature. This dependence is based upon the slave's complete lack of any access to the resources required to maintain his existence, and subordination to the master's effective monopoly over the means of violence. This system originates in the seizure of the slave during conflict, and persists to the extent that it constitutes a profitable form of labour exploitation for superordinates. This profitability depends upon both supply and demand factors: the easy replenishment of captives, and a plantation economy based upon a relatively simple level of technology, where the machinery of production is proof against carelessness. However, slavery is not the characteristic relation of production in all primitive societies, being rare in pre-Roman Europe north of the Alps, for it is not suitable to hunting and gathering societies, where constant mobility makes escape relatively easy: Marx, and his followers, have exaggerated the significance of slavery in the ancient world.[1]

Feudalism is also based upon asymmetric dependence relations, in which the lord has a monopoly over the primary means of sustenance – the land. But, once granted tenure of the land, the peasant has a socially recognized personality and rights which the lord cannot revoke. Moreover, although the lord has an effective monopoly of the means of physical violence, the peasant has an effective monopoly over the means of working the land, an especially effective monopoly during periods of labour shortage. There is thus some balance in the dependence between lord and peasant. Feudalism can accommodate a more sophisticated form of technology than slavery, for the danger of sabotage is less: productivity is in the interests of the peasant as well as the lord. But the fragmentation of jurisdiction over individual holdings leads to such complexity that only a relatively simple division of labour is possible, and the rate of implementation of technological change even slower than the rate of technological innovation. Moreover, feudalism fosters an even more inelastic labour market than slavery, for the peasant is tied to his unit of production, a given piece of land. In effect, there is no labour market. It is therefore difficult to accommodate any change in the relation between population and available land within feudalism: the landless labourer constitutes at best a permanent source of embarrassment, at worst a revolutionary danger, to the feudal order.

Under capitalism exchange relations are more symmetrical than under either slavery or feudalism, and power relations are based less upon coercion – although coercive elements continue to exist. The subordinate is dependent upon the superordinate for access to the means of sustenance, but there are a number of alternative superordinates, with differing resources. Moreover, capital equipment is useless without labour, just as labour is of only limited productivity without capital equipment. Control over resources is more dispersed than under slavery or feudalism. Similarly the goals of both dominant and subordinate are more diversified, partly because of the diversity of resources made possible by the abundance created by efficient technology, and partly because of the diversity of interests created by the elaborate division of labour required by that technology. Complexity, and the elaboration of the concept of contract, facilitated the development of the labour market as a means of adjusting to market and technological change. In this more 'balanced' situation coercion is supplemented by authority, especially legal rational authority, and influence as alternative bases of compliance.

These very brief sketches of power relations under slavery, feudalism and capitalism are, of course, only illustrations of the general features characteristic of each mode of labour exploitation, and there is considerable variability within each genus: more detailed discussions are presented in earlier chapters. But they indicate how each system hangs together, to form a more or less coherent, dynamic whole. This whole is an unstable network of interdependent, unequal and conflictual individuals and groups, not the homeostatic organism or machine of systems theory. Changes in patterns of dependence, deriving from the discovery of new natural resources, technological innovation, the evolution of inheritance rules, or simply from different priorities, or changes in the means available for escape from dependence, lead to new patterns of power relations.

By tracing the thread of causation backwards from power relations to technology I do not want to suggest that technology is 'basic', a substructure moulding the superstructure of power relations to its own requirements – the view caricatured in Marx's aphorism 'The hand-mill gives you society with the feudal lord; the steam-mill society with the industrial capitalist'. For each stage in the process is 'basic', the process is circular; hence Lenski's recent ambitious attempt to construct a general theory of social stratification based upon laws of individual and social development founders upon his technological evolutionary determinism.[3] Power relations themselves affect technology, for dominant groups attempt to restrict the development of new technologies which might undermine their power based upon a given distribution of control over resources. The diffusion and adoption of new technologies are socially conditioned processes, and there may be considerable time-lags between the invention of a particular technique and its general use. Moreover, the fatefulness of specific developments depends upon timing, the simultaneous occurrence of parallel changes. Hence, changes in the technology of war in Europe in the early Middle Ages, and the development of primogeniture, facilitated the development of the manorial economy, with consequential effects upon the distribution of power under feudalism. The outcome of this process depended upon particular combinations of circumstances, and would have been different if the *timing* of identical developments had been different. In short, in cybernetic terms, any general model must allow both for feedback and for additive interaction effects.[4]

The general concepts used in this study are Marxist, involving a dialectic between the forces of production, especially technology, and the relations of production. I have similarly attached primary importance to the system of labour exploitation, the patterns of interdependence (or in Marxist terms exploitation) derived from this system, and the resulting relations of domination and subordination. However, there are obvious and significant differences between this study and contemporary Marxist approaches to the study of power, both in theoretical terms and in empirical conclusions: it is less determinist, and the conclusions, as indicated in the preceding chapters, more pluralist. Not surprisingly, my approach is less ambitious and self-confident than Marx's, for it is grounded in historical sociology not in Hegelian philosophy of history, and is not intended to fulfil a political mobilization role. The argument is couched in contingent rather than necessary terms. Moreover, the conclusions reached are more equivocal than those of contemporary Marxists, society being seen as less monolithic than in the works of, for example, Poulantzas or even Miliband.[5] The present study can be theoretically located within the broad tradition of humanist Marxism and Weberian theory, but outside the contemporary mainstream of Marxist theory. The significance of this position becomes evident through examination of the related concepts of 'consciousness' and 'interests'.

Following the social action tradition, compliance is seen as a conscious act – subordinates are performing subjectively meaningful non-self-regarding action. However, action may *in fact* be non-self-regarding, but not recognized as such by the actors involved: subordinates may act out of incomplete knowledge or out of an unthinking acceptance of routine, of 'the way things are done here', without understanding its non-self-regarding significance. Hence Westergaard and Resler comment:[6]

> power derives more from the routine application of effectively unchallenged assumptions than from the manifest dominance of one faction, group, interest or policy over others in open conflict . . . the institutionalization of conflict involves just that kind of unspoken adoption of lay assumptions, behind which there is pragmatically dictated agreement but no legitimation through positive consensus. The effect is to restrict the policy alternatives about which there is practical dispute to a much narrower range than would otherwise be the case. So, many decisions are not 'made' because they are built in from the start. Power lies closest to the interests that benefit most from this predetermination of the boundaries of conflict.

The routine operation of social institutions is thus a major source of power for dominant groups, reinforcing domination by rendering subordinates unaware of their subordination. This ignorance has both general and specific roots. At the most general and diffuse level subordinate understanding is inhibited by the process of linguistic development. Hence Claus Mueller (whose interesting recent work has been largely neglected by British writers) has developed Bernstein's ideas to show how the restricted speech code of the poor inhibits the development of political consciousness:[7]

> The language of the hard-core poor is a restricted speech code in the extreme. . . . Since it cannot be used in an instrumental, reflective way, the language itself, spoken by a person living in starkly deprived conditions, reinforces his social location. The individual's language, cast in the immediacy of his environment, conditions his perception. The categories of his language allow for a grasp of the here and now, but they do not permit an analysis, hence a transcendence, of his social context. . . . The individual's language becomes his internal plausibility structure. In narrowing his ability to discriminate, to conceptualize, and to analyse, it renders his condition more acceptable to him.

At the most general level, subordinates can perceive their situation experientially, but are unable to translate their specific experiences into general terms and thus unable to define their own position adequately. This inadequacy has direct implications for power relations, for it inhibits political consciousness and thus united action. Its effects are reinforced by the specific routines of politics, which conventionally define the scope of politics in limited terms, restrict the range of problems – and solutions – considered by political actors, and restrict access to the political system through a systematic 'mobilization of bias'. This mobilization may be conscious; but it is probably more effective when unconscious.[8] In short, linguistic deprivation and the mobilization of bias are two manifestations of the process whereby the hegemonic bourgeois culture of contemporary capitalism hinders the development of subordinate consciousness and reinforces the position of specific dominant groups.[9]

At one level, this emphasis upon the cultural conditioning of subordinate groups is a valuable antidote to the naïve behaviouralism of some pluralist political scientists. It is necessary to examine the influences upon the values of actors, and to avoid simply accepting stated values as final, independent causes-of-action. The effects of linguistic deprivation are reinforced by the total experience of socialization within the family, the education system, and the workplace, as well as by the more directly political mobilization of bias. Yet such an analysis easily attaches both too little, and too much importance to the role of subjective attitudes in power relations: too little because it neglects the possibility of individual 'resistance' to such values, too much because it surprisingly follows functionalist theory in stressing the role of value-consensus in maintaining stable social relations. (The relevant sentence in Westergaard and Resler's book on this issue quoted above, p. 165, is opaque, but appears to support this conclusion, with its antithesis between the stability of 'positive consensus' and the instability of 'pragmatically dictated' agreement. These are not the only alternatives and pragmatic agreement can be stable.) Power relations will be stable without positive consensus where patterns of dependence and the means available to escape from them do not change.

Moreover, it is easy to exaggerate the cultural hegemony of any one group in contemporary capitalism. As Frank Parkin has argued:[10]

the subordinate class has two distinct levels of normative reference; the dominant value system and a 'stretched' or 'negotiated' version of it . . . which of the two frames of reference is actually drawn upon will be situationally determined; more specifically, . . . in situations where purely abstract evaluations are called for, the dominant value system will provide the moral frame of reference; but in concrete social situations involving choice and action, the negotiated version – or the subordinate value system – will provide the moral framework.

Hence, subordinates may answer abstract opinion-poll questions on trade unions in terms of the 'dominant value system' (using the term in the narrow sense, to refer to the value system of the dominant group) but act very differently in day to day work-place activity. Normative ambivalence and pragmatic acceptance of the values of dominant groups – especially when such values do not matter – are probably more characteristic of subordinate groups in contemporary capitalism than incorporation into a one-dimensional bourgeois culture. Exactly how far they are is an empirical question to be analysed in specific power relations, in which subordinate interpretations are evaluated in the light of personal biography and the available stock of ideas. Compliance is a conscious act, but consciousness is neither fully conditioned nor purely idiosyncratic.

The first difficulty posed by contemporary Marxist analyses of power is the tangled empirical question of the determinants of consciousness, especially subordinate consciousness. A second and more fundamental difficulty is presented by the concept of 'interests'. Lukes has argued that 'any view of power rests on some normatively specific conception of interests', and classified such definitions into liberal, reformist and radical (in ascending order of virtue): his own, radical view is that men's definitions of their wants may be (are?) determined by a system which works against their interests, 'and, in such cases [I relate] the latter to what they would want and prefer, were they able to make the choice'.[11] Similarly, Westergaard and Resler state:[12]

We take . . . a 'sociological' conception of interests – i.e. we see interests as the possibilities and potential objectives of action which are inherent in economic positions regardless of whether the incumbents of those positions in fact so define their objectives at any given time. To define interests in 'psychological' terms – to confine labour 'interests' to those objectives which workers in fact recognise and act upon at any given time, for example – would be to ignore the point that part of the power of capital rests precisely on its routine capacity to rule out certain potential labour objectives as impracticable. Our conception of interests – a Marxist conception – is ostensibly open to the objection that it leaves the specification of interests 'arbitrarily' to the observer. But the 'arbitrariness' involved is no more than that involved in any specification of concepts and categories by social scientists.

All three authors look back to Lukács's 'objective possibilities', and beyond him to Marx himself.[13]

Neither definition of interests provides a satisfactory basis for sociological investigation – 'possibilities and potential objectives' are infinite, and it is impossible to decide which, out of a range of possibilities, are relevant, unless one specifically links 'interests' to the revolutionary potential of the proletariat (as Lukács does, but neither Westergaard and Resler nor Lukes do). Comparison between events and probable courses-of-action is necessary to obtain any measure of power, to assess the difference made by alter to ego's actions. But such courses-of-action should be based upon previous action in similar circumstances, or action in comparable circumstances, or the intentions of both super- and subordinates, not upon limitless potentialities. Nor is this emphasis upon probable courses-of-action necessarily 'psychological', unless sociology is identified with one strand of Marxism and all alternative conceptualizations made 'psychological' by definition.

The absolutist concept of interests adopted by Westergaard and Resler parallels one strand in contemporary continental European Marxism, the structuralism currently associated with Althusser and Poulantzas (although Westergaard and Resler do not mention Althusser and Poulantzas is dismissed, with some justice, as 'abstract and obscure').[14] For Althusser men are not autonomous actors but agents of an historical process, whose logic operates according to laws independent of the goals and aspirations of individual actors – '[for Althusser] history . . . is not based on man. . . . Men do not constitute a unit of analysis, only relations of production . . . relations and structures are the unit for analysis, rather than man's lived and subjective experience, and these are to be explained by impersonal structural forces.'[15] Hence ideology is the product of structural requirements:[16]

Dans le mode de production théorique de l'idéologie . . . la formulation d'un problème, n'est que l'expression théorique des conditions permettant à une *solution*, déjà produite en dehors du processus de connaissance, parce qu'imposée par des instances et exigences extra-théorique (par des 'intérêts' religieux, moraux, politiques ou autres), de se reconnaître dans un problème artificiel, fabriqué pour lui servir tout à la fois de miroir théorique et de justification pratique.

Such views can be traced back to the later works of Marx, and, more especially, to those of Engels: hence Engels's 1880 discussion of historical materialism:[17]

> The materialist conception of history starts from the proposition that the production of the means to support human life – and, next to production, the exchange of things produced – is the basis of all social structure. . . . From this point of view the final causes of all social changes and political revolutions are to be sought not in men's brains, not in man's better insight into eternal truth and justice, but in changes in the modes of production and exchange.

However, this 'old intuitive mechanistic materialism' is only one strand in the Marxist tradition, and the least fruitful sociologically.[18] As Marx commented succinctly: 'So-called *objective* historiography just consists in treating the historical conditions independent of activity. Reactionary character.'[19] For Marxism is neither necessarily materialist nor necessarily determinist.

History is the story of the *'unceasing overthrow of the objective forms that shape the life of man'* (original emphasis), not the story of his subservience to those forms.[20] 'The objective economic evolution could do no more than create the position of the proletariat in the production process . . . the objective position could only give the proletariat the opportunity and the necessity to change society. Any transformation can only come about as the product of the – free – action of the proletariat.'[21] Man, whether bourgeois or proletarian, is an active social being, not simply the passive instrument of system-logic. This activity is conditioned by the natural environment and the social structure within which man acts, but is not determined by them.

It is thus impossible to explain social action by the logic of economic development, whether Marxist or functionalist, and to see deviations from that logic as simply the product of phases of transition, irrelevant hangovers from earlier systems. Nor is it possible to see consciousness – whether directly experiential or mediated through ideology – as the product of material interest. Instead, consciousness is as real as the interests which figure in that consciousness, and requires investigation if sociology is to become more than a bastardized, and deceitfully depoliticized, form of historical materialism. Weber's pupil, Otto Hintze, summarized the views of both of them when he wrote:[22]

> All human action arises from a common source. . . . Everywhere the first impulse to social action is given as a rule by real interests, i.e., by political and economic interests. But ideal

169

interests lend wings to these real interests, give them a spiritual meaning, and serve to justify them. . . . Interests without such 'spiritual wings' are lame; but on the other hand, ideas can win out in history only if and insofar as they are associated with real interests. . . an. . . . image is that of a polar coordination of interests and ideas. In the long run, neither of the two can survive without the other, historically speaking; each requires the other as a supplementation. Whenever interests are vigorously pursued, an ideology tends to be developed also to give meaning, re-enforcement and justification to these interests. And this ideology is as 'real' as the real interests themselves, for ideology is an indispensable part of the life process which is expressed in action. And conversely: wherever ideas are to conquer the world, they require the leverage of real interests, although frequently ideas will more or less detract these interests from their original aim.

I hope that this study has shown how ideas and interests, or goals and resources, interact in relations of domination and subordination, and by doing so to have written squarely within the Weberian tradition, a tradition closer to the humanistic strand of Marxism than historians of sociology anxious to see Weber as a reaction against Marx appear ready to admit.[23]

Notes

Preface

1 For a standard survey see R. E. Dowse and J. Hughes, *Political Sociology* (New York: John Wiley, 1972).
2 This disquiet is not unique, as P. Abrams's review of Dowse and Hughes, *op. cit.*, indicates: 'Is This a Time for Anyone but Historians to be Studying Text-books?', *Sociology*, 1974, p. 329.
3 For a review of the field as it appeared in the early 1960s see L. A. Coser (ed.), *Political Sociology: Selected Essays*, especially the 'authoritative' first paper by R. Bendix and S. M. Lipset (New York: Harper Torchbooks, 1967).
4 P. M. Blau, *Exchange and Power in Social Life* (New York: John Wiley, 1964).
5 See also R. D. Jessop, 'Exchange and Power in Social Life', *Sociological Review*, 1969, pp. 415–30.
6 For an excellent if pessimistic account of these problems see J. G. March, 'The Power of Power,' in D. Easton (ed.), *Varieties of Political Theory* (Englewood Cliffs: Prentice-Hall, 1966).
7 For a useful collection of papers see R. Bell, D. V. Edwards, R. H. Wagner, *Political Power: a Reader in Theory and Research* (New York: Free Press, 1969).

1 Systems theory

1 For a brief uncritical survey of the literature see M. R. Davies and V. A. Lewis, *Models of Political Systems* (London: Pall Mall, 1971), or for a longer, confusing, but still uncritical survey see H. V. Wiseman, *Political Systems: some Sociological Approaches* (London: Routledge & Kegan Paul, 1966).
2 C. E. Russett, *The Concept of Equilibrium in American Social Thought* (New Haven: Yale University Press, 1966), p. 145; H. J. Spiro in J. C. Charlesworth (ed.), *Contemporary Political Analysis* (New York: Free Press, 1967), p. 165.

3 Bertram Gross in a review of D. Easton, *A Systems Analysis of Political Life* (New York: John Wiley, 1965), *APSR*, 1967, pp. 155–8.
4 A. J. Gregor, 'Political Science and Functional Analysis', *APSR*, 1968, p. 438.
5 S. E. Finer, 'Almond's Concept of Political System', *Government and Opposition*, 1970, p. 4.
6 See, for example, D. Katz and R. L. Kahn, *The Social Psychology of Organizations* (New York: John Wiley, 1966); for a critique see D. Silverman, *The Theory of Organizations* (London: Heinemann, 1970).
7 There is no history of systems theory, but W. J. Buckley, *Sociology and Modern Systems Theory* (Englewood Cliffs: Prentice-Hall, 1967), and Russett, *op. cit.*, contain useful historical surveys. For a contemporary survey see F. E. Emery, *Systems Thinking* (Harmondsworth: Penguin Books, 1969).
8 D. Easton, *A Framework for Political Analysis* (Englewood Cliffs: Prentice-Hall, 1965), p. 25.
9 P. Nettl, 'The Concept of System in Political Science', *Political Studies*, 1966, p. 324.
10 The major works considered are: D. Easton, *The Political System* (New York: Knopf, 1953); *A Framework for Political Analysis*; and *A Systems Analysis of Political Life*; T. Parsons, *The Social System* (London: Routledge & Kegan Paul, 1951); G. A. Almond and G. B. Powell, *Comparative Politics: a developmental approach* (Boston: Little, Brown, 1966); K. Deutsch, *The Nerves of Government* (New York: Free Press, 1966 ed.).
11 Easton, *A Framework for Political Analysis*, p. 27.
12 Easton, *The Political System*, p. 146.
13 H. Stretton, *The Political Sciences* (London: Routledge & Kegan Paul, 1969), has summarized Easton's theory in the following terms: 'Politics is an exchange of services for support. People support politicians and systems who do most for them, and make the least (or the least resistible) demands upon them. If people demand too much service and supply too little support, systems are in trouble. Then politicians may increase the services, use the services to reorganize the support and change the system, or see it break down' (p. 386). Readers must consult the original to assess the justice of this Wright-Millsian parody.
14 See, for example, J. F. Scott, 'The Changing Foundations of the Parsonian Action Scheme', *American Sociological Review*, 1963; M. H. Lessnoff, 'Parsons' System Problems', *Sociological Review*, 1968.
15 There are, of course, two long essays – 'On the Concept of Political Power', *Proceedings of the American Philosophical Society*, 1963, and 'The Political Aspect of Structure and Process' in D. Easton (ed.), *Varieties of Political Theory* (Englewood Cliffs: Prentice-Hall, 1966) and an attempt by W. C. Mitchell to apply Parsonian theory to politics – *Sociological Analysis and Politics: the Theories of Talcott Parsons* (Englewood Cliffs: Prentice-Hall, 1967), as well as a number of

shorter pieces. But there is no political equivalent to T. Parsons and N. Smelser, *Economy and Society* (London: Routledge & Kegan Paul, 1956).

16 M. Levy, *The Structure of Society* (Princeton University Press, 1952).

17 For summaries and a critical survey see M. Black (ed.), *The Social Theories of Talcott Parsons* (Englewood Cliffs: Prentice-Hall, 1961).

18 Parsons and Smelser, *op. cit.*, p. 59.

19 From S. M. Lipset and S. Rokkan, 'Cleavage Structures, Party Systems, and Voter Alignments', in S. M. Lipset and S. Rokkan (eds), *Party Systems and Voter Alignments* (New York: Free Press, 1967), p. 7.

20 G. A. Almond, 'Introduction: a Functional Approach to Comparative Politics', in G. A. Almond and J. S. Coleman (eds), *The Politics of the Developing Areas* (Princeton University Press, 1960), p. 7.

21 This summary is based mainly upon Almond and Powell, *Comparative Politics*, chap. 2.

22 N. Wiener, *Cybernetics* (Cambridge, New York: MIT-Wiley, 1961).

23 Deutsch, *The Nerves of Government*, p. 77.

24 *Ibid.*, p. xxvii.

25 *Ibid.*, pp. 186–7.

26 See especially *ibid.*, p. 80. Interestingly, the analogy between society and the nervous system was also used by Durkheim (S. M. Lukes, *Émile Durkheim*, London: Allen Lane, 1973, p. 269).

27 Black, *op. cit.*, p. 283.

28 Stretton, *op. cit.*, pp. 393–4.

29 R. K. Merton, *Social Theory and Social Structure* (Chicago: Free Press, 1957), pp. 87–8; cf. R. Dahrendorf, *Essays in the Theory of Society* (London: Routledge & Kegan Paul, 1968), p. viii.

30 T. Parsons, review of Pareto, *Treatise on General Sociology*, *American Sociological Review*, vol. 1, p. 141.

31 This involves omitting consideration of the possibly ideological character of systems theory, which has been described as 'blatant ideology' (A. Brittan, *Meanings and Situations*, London: Routledge & Kegan Paul, 1973, p. 10). Systems theories, like other theoretical models, are not ideologies, i.e. more or less consistent sets of ideas designed to legitimate, or discredit, a given social order; instead, they are intended to comprise a set of selected propositions not contradicted by empirical evidence. As such they may be more or less useful means of legitimating given social orders. But all statements about society are ideological in this sense, and the ideological character of systems theories is thus a less interesting question than some critics of systems theories assume.

32 A. Rapoport, 'General Systems Theory', *International Encyclopaedia of the Social Sciences* (New York: Macmillan/Free Press, 1968), vol. 15, p. 453; A. L. Stinchcombe, *Constructing Social Theories* (New York: Harcourt, Brace & World, 1968), chap. 3.

33 To name only a few: whereas Parsons is primarily concerned with the 'super-structure' of values, Marx focuses upon the sub-structure of interests; whereas Parsons is primarily concerned with the conditions of social order, Marx is primarily concerned with the dynamics

of social change; whereas Parsons is primarily concerned with the cohesive functions of norms and values, Marx is primarily concerned with the divisive consequences of social interests; and so on. (Cf. D. Lockwood, 'Some Remarks on The Social System', *British Journal of Sociology*, 1956, pp. 134–46.)

34 Almond and Powell, *op. cit.*, p. 19.

35 A. W. Gouldner, *The Coming Crisis of Western Sociology* (London: Heinemann, 1971), p. 214: '[Parsons] tells us what his *social* system is, but not what his social *system* is. In short, he has given only the most primitive analysis to the formal concept of a system, allowing matters to rest very largely with the affirmation that it has the unexamined attributes of interdependence and self-maintenance.' Gouldner's criticism is largely justified.

36 T. Parsons, E. Shils, K. Naegle, *et al.*, *Towards a General Theory of Action* (New York: Harper Torchbooks, 1962 ed.), p. 5, n.5.

37 Mitchell, *op. cit.*, p. 51; cf. T. Parsons, 'An Outline of the Social System', in T. Parsons, E. Shils, *et al.*, *Theories of Society* (New York: Free Press, 1961), p. 36: 'The concept of an open system . . . implies *boundaries* and their maintenance. . . . A boundary means simply that a theoretically and empirically significant difference between structures and processes internal to the system and those external to it exists and tends to be maintained. In so far as boundaries in this sense do not exist, it is not possible to identify a set of interdependent phenomena as a system.'

38 Cf. Finer, *op. cit.*, p. 11.

39 This confusion is exemplified in Almond and Powell's identification of boundary shifts with boundary crossing (*Comparative Politics*, p. 20).

40 See G. H. Sabine, *A History of Political Theory* (3rd ed.) (London: Harrap, 1951), chaps 2 and 3; see also S. S. Wolin, *Politics and Vision* (London: George Allen & Unwin, 1961), chap. 2.

41 Easton, *A Framework for Political Analysis*, p. 21.

42 Deutsch, *op. cit.*, p. 124.

43 Cf. Parsons, *The Social System*, p. 126, with Parsons, *Societies: Evolutionary and Comparative Perspectives* (Englewood Cliffs: Prentice-Hall, 1966), p. 25. See also M. H. Lessnoff, *op. cit.*, p. 200.

44 Stinchcombe, *op. cit.*, pp. 98–9.

45 K. Popper, *The Poverty of Historicism* (London: Routledge & Kegan Paul, 1957), p. 123. For a more extended discussion of the logic of functionalism see C. G. Hemple, 'The Logic of Functionalism', in L. Gross (ed.), *Symposium on Sociological Theory* (Evanston: Row, Peterson, 1959), pp. 271–307; and R. Dore, 'Function and Cause', *American Sociological Review*, 1961, pp. 843–53. For an (almost) comprehensive collection of papers on functionalism see N. J. Demercth III and R. A. Peterson, *System, Change, and Conflict* (New York: Free Press, 1967).

46 Stinchcombe, *op. cit.*, p. 99.

47 For example, Parsons, in T. Parsons, E. Shils, *et al.* (eds), *op. cit.*, p. 53; cf. Lessnoff, *op. cit.*, p. 188.

48 Merton, *op. cit.*, pp. 33–6, 52.

49 L. Mair, *Primitive Government* (Harmondsworth: Penguin Books, 1962), chap. 3.
50 Merton, *op. cit.*, pp. 51, 53.
51 *Ibid.*, pp. 71–82.
52 See p. 90.
53 For small-group studies see A. P. Hare, E. F. Borgatta and R. F. Bales (eds), *Small Groups: Studies in Social Interaction* (New York: Knopf, 1955).
54 Buckley, *op. cit.*, p. 30.
55 Parsons, in Parsons, *et al.* (eds), *Theories of Society*, p. 37.
56 Summary based upon Parsons, *ibid.*, pp. 73–9; cf. Parsons, *Societies: Evolutionary and Comparative Perspectives*, pp. 21–2 for a similar, but simpler and less helpful account.
57 C. Johnson, *Revolutionary Change* (University of London Press, 1968).
58 *Ibid.*, p. 13.
59 One of the very rare references in Parsons's work to the influence of other authors on his thinking.
60 Deutsch, *op. cit.*, p. 88.
61 *Ibid.*, p. 97.
62 Easton, *Systems Analysis*, p. 32.
63 *Ibid.*, p. 21.
64 *Ibid.*, p. 121.
65 Deutsch, *op. cit.*, p. 111.
66 Deutsch, *op. cit.*, p. 124.
67 Easton, *Systems Analysis*, p. 474n.; March, 'The Power of Power', in D. Easton (ed.), *Varieties of Political Theory*.
68 Easton, *Systems Analysis*, pp. 474–5.
69 Parsons, 'On the Concept of Political Power', in T. Parsons (ed.), *Politics and Social Structure* (New York: Free Press, 1969).
70 Interestingly, Deutsch also uses the analogy between power and money (*The Nerves of Government*, pp. 120–2).
71 For a fuller discussion see R. Martin, 'The Concept of Power: a Critical Defence', *British Journal of Sociology*, 1971, pp. 244–5.
72 See pp. 36–7.
73 A. Giddens, 'Power in the Recent Writings of Talcott Parsons', *Sociology*, 1968, p. 264.
74 Easton, *Systems Analysis*, p. xiii.
75 K. Marx, *Economic and Philosophical Manuscripts of 1844*, in T. Bottomore (ed.), *Karl Marx: Early Writings* (New York: C. A. Watts, 1963), p. 158; cf. D. Silverman, *The Theory of Organizations*, *passim*.
76 Role theory is an enormous topic, beyond the scope of this study. For an important discussion see R. Dahrendorf, 'Homo Sociologus', in R. Dahrendorf, *Essays in the Theory of Society* (London: Routledge & Kegan Paul, 1968), for an important collection of papers see B. J. Biddle and E. J. Thomas (eds), *Role Theory: Concept and Research* (New York: John Wiley, 1966).
77 D. Wrong, 'The Oversocialized Conception of Man in Modern Sociology', *American Sociological Review*, 1961, pp. 183–93.

78 For 'conflict' and 'ambiguity' see R. L. Kahn, *et al.*, *Organizational Stress* (New York: John Wiley, 1964); and N. Gross, *et al.*, *Explorations in Role Analysis* (New York: John Wiley, 1958).

2 Social action theory

1 For a valuable collection of papers on symbolic interactionism see A. M. Rose, *Human Behaviour and Social Processes* (London: Routledge & Kegan Paul, 1962); for ethnomethodology see D. Sudnow, *Studies in Social Interaction* (New York: Free Press, 1972).

2 Rose's comment is still valid: '[In interactionist theory] there is a neglect of power relations between persons or groups, and while these are generally assumed to exist, they are seldom given due weight' (p. x).

3 As in J. Douglas, *The Sociology of Everyday Life* (London: Routledge & Kegan Paul, 1972). Cf. I. Taylor, P. Walton, J. Young, *The New Criminology: for a social theory of deviance* (London: Routledge & Kegan Paul, 1973), p. 206: 'If we take the phenomenological import of ethnomethodology seriously, then it would seem to be committed either to the arbitrary and endless task of demonstrating how everyday life is constructed, or to revealing rules of interpretation necessary for its maintenance (something denied to them if they are to be consistent).' For a recent attempt to develop an ethnomethodologically informed theory of power, which does not fully resolve this problem, see S. Clegg, *Power, Rule and Domination* (London: Routledge & Kegan Paul, 1975).

4 M. Weber, *Methodology of the Social Sciences* (Chicago: Free Press, 1949), p. 74.

5 M. Weber (eds, G. Roth and C. Wittich), *Economy and Society* (New York: Bedminster Press, 1968), vol. 1, p. 4.

6 A. Brittan, *Meanings and Situations* (London: Routledge & Kegan Paul, 1973), p. 25.

7 Weber, *Economy and Society*, *op. cit.*, vol. 1, p. 4.

8 There are a large number of discussions of this key definition. See, for example, T. Parsons, *The Structure of Social Action* (Chicago: Free Press, 1949), p. 641, and A. Giddens, *Capitalism and Modern Social Theory: an analysis of the writings of Marx, Durkheim and Weber* (Cambridge University Press, 1971), p. 146.

9 Parsons, *The Structure of Social Action*, p. 642.

10 *Ibid.*, pp. 732–3. There are differences between this statement and the definition of social action adopted by Parsons in his later work, which have important implications for his sociological theory in general (cf. T. Parsons, and E. Shils, *et al.* (eds), *Towards a General Theory of Action*, New York: Harper Torchbooks, 1962 ed., p. 53). But the differences are not significant in the present context. See J. F. Scott, 'The Changing Foundations of the Parsonian Action Scheme', in W. L. Wallace (ed.), *Sociological Theory* (London: Heinemann, 1969), pp. 252–8.

11 J. Rex, *Key Problems in Sociological Theory* (London: Routledge & Kegan Paul, 1961), p. 86.

12 Parsons and Shils (eds), *op. cit.*, p. 53; J. Rex, *op. cit.*, p. 88.

13 Cf. Runciman's parallel discussion of the limited reference groups chosen by the British working class (W. G. Runciman, *Relative Deprivation and Social Justice*, London: Routledge & Kegan Paul, 1966, p. 27): 'whatever the relative magnitudes of relative deprivation, those near the bottom are likely, even in a society with an egalitarian ideology, to choose reference groups nearer the bottom than self-conscious egalitarianism would imply. Or to phrase it more carefully, they are likely to modify their reference groups in such a way that their aspirations are diverted from those goals which the rags-to-riches myth misleadingly holds out for them.'

14 Cf. R. Martin and R. H. Fryer, *Redundancy and Paternalist Capitalism* (London: George Allen & Unwin, 1973), chap. 7.

15 G. Allport, *Personality* (New York: Holt, 1937), chap. 7 for psychological mechanisms involved.

16 R. K. Merton, *Social Theory and Social Structure* (Chicago: Free Press, 1957), pp. 199–200.

17 A. Giddens, 'Power in the Recent Writings of Talcott Parsons', *Sociology*, 1968, p. 139.

18 For an easily accessible and useful account of Weber's intellectual development see R. Bendix, *Max Weber: An Intellectual Portrait* (London: Heinemann, 1960).

19 Cf. D. Martindale, 'Sociological Theory and the Ideal Type', in L. Gross (ed.), *Symposium on Sociological Theory* (New York: Harper & Row, 1959), p. 88: 'ideal types will continue to be employed as long as sociology or any science relies upon the comparative method.'

20 Giddens, *op. cit.*, pp. 141–2.

21 Although the use of ideal-types can be justified in its own right, independently of the complexity of the social world, this complexity is one of the reasons for the use of ideal-types: 'in the sociological field as elsewhere, averages, and hence average types, can be formulated with a relative degree of precision only where they are concerned with differences of degree in respect to action which remains qualitatively the same. Such uses do occur, but in the majority of cases of action important to history or sociology the motives which determine it are qualitatively heterogeneous. Then it is quite impossible to speak of an "average" in the true sense' (*Economy and Society*, pp. 20–1). It is thus the mixed character of motives which necessitates ideal-types rather than averages.

22 Parsons, *The Structure of Social Action*, *op. cit.*, pp. 603–4.

23 C. J. Friedrich, 'Some Observations on Weber's Analysis of Bureaucracy', in R. K. Merton, A. P. Gray, B. Hockey, H. C. Selvin (eds), *Reader in Bureaucracy* (Chicago: Free Press, 1952), pp. 28–9.

24 Weber, *Economy and Society*, p. 21.

25 J. Rex, *Sociology and the De-mystification of the Modern World* (London: Routledge & Kegan Paul, 1974), chaps 3 and 4. See also Schutz's discussion of 'homunculi' in A. Schutz, 'Concept and Theory

Formation in the Social Sciences', in M. Natanson (ed.), *A. Schutz: Collected Papers: I, The Problem of Social Reality* (The Hague: Martinus Nijhoff, 1971), pp. 63–4: 'How does the social scientist proceed? He observes certain facts and events within social reality which refer to human action and he constructs typical behaviour or course-of-action patterns from what he has observed. Thereupon he coordinates to these typical course-of-action patterns models of an ideal actor or actors, whom he imagines as being gifted with consciousness. . . . He thus ascribes to this fictitious consciousness a set of typical notions, purposes, goals, which are assumed to be invariant in the specious consciousness of the imaginary actor-model. . . . Among these homunculi with which the social scientist populates his model of the social world of everyday life, sets of motives, goals, roles – in general systems of relevances – are distributed in such a way as the scientific problems under scrutiny require. Yet – and this is the main point – these constructs are by no means arbitrary. They are subject to the postulate of logical consistency and to the postulate of adequacy. The latter means that each term in such a scientific model of human action must be constructed in such a way that a human act performed within the real world by an individual actor as indicated by the typical construct would be understandable to the actor himself as well as to his fellow-men in terms of common-sense interpretation of everyday life.'

26 Weber, *Economy and Society*, p. 85.
27 For example, A. Downs, *An Economic Theory of Democracy* (New York: Harper, 1957).
28 B. M. Barry, *Sociologists, Economists, and Democracy* (London: Collier-Macmillan, 1970), p. 21. For a useful general discussion see *ibid.*, especially chaps 2 and 5.
29 Weber, *Economy and Society*, p. 85.
30 S. E. Finer (ed.), *Pareto's Sociological Writings* (London: Pall Mall, 1966).
31 V. Pareto (ed., A. Livingstone), *The Mind and Society*, 4 vols (New York: Harcourt Brace, 1935), vol. 1, pp. 480–1.
32 For a severe critique of Pareto see I. Zeitlin, *Ideology and the Development of Sociological Theory* (Englewood Cliffs: Prentice-Hall, 1968), chap. 12.
33 H. Lasswell, *Psychopathology and Politics*, in *The Political Writings of Harold D. Lasswell* (Chicago: Free Press, 1951).
34 There is, of course, an extensive literature on the appeals of fascism and communism to neurotic personalities: see, for example, G. A. Almond, *The Appeals of Communism* (Princeton University Press, 1954) where a minority of ex-communists showed psychological weakness.
35 R. E. Lane, *Political Ideology* (New York: Free Press, 1962), p. 43.
36 M. Brewster Smith, 'Opinions, Personality, and Political Behaviour', in N. W. Polsby, R. A. Dentler, P. A. Smith (eds), *Politics and Social Life* (Boston: Houghton-Mifflin, 1963), p. 213.
37 The psychological mechanisms involved have been explained clearly

by B. Bettelheim and M. Janowitz, *Dynamics of Prejudice* (New York: Harper, 1950): '[Prejudice] is a projection of unacceptable inner strivings onto a minority group. Projection is a mechanism by means of which one tries to solve a conflict within oneself by ascribing to another person emotions, motives, and behaviour which actually belong to oneself. For instance, if we hate another person without justification, that creates a conflict within us if our conscience does not approve of the emotion of hatred. Instead of solving this conflict by overcoming our hatred, we may try to get rid of it through projection. We project our hatred into the other person so that it appears to us not as if we hate him, but that he hates us. Thus in a devious way we not only try to get rid of an emotion which is not acceptable to our conscience (super ego), we are also now justified in hating the other person if we so desire, because we think he is hating us' (p. 42).

38 In one sense, of course, psychological differences are the result of a trick of perspective: apparently flat surfaces look bumpy under the microscope.

39 H. A. Simon, *Administrative Behaviour* (New York: Free Press, 1965).

40 D. Matza, *Becoming Deviant* (Englewood Cliffs: Prentice-Hall, 1969), p. 8. Matza associates Weber, Mead and MacIver with this 'naturalist' perspective.

41 K. Marx and F. Engels (ed., C. J. Arthur), *The German Ideology* (London: Lawrence & Wishart, 1970), p. 47.

42 T. Kynaston-Reeves, 'Constrained and Facilitated Behaviour: a Typology of Behaviour in Organizations', *British Journal of Industrial Relations*, 1967, p. 145 *et seq.*

43 Marx and Engels, *op. cit.*, pp. 47-8.

44 P. S. Cohen, *Modern Social Theory* (London: Heinemann, 1968), p. 94.

3 The sociology of power: problems of definition and measurement

1 R. A. Dahl, 'Power', *International Encyclopaedia of the Social Sciences* (New York: Collier-Macmillan, 1968), vol. 12, p. 407.

2 H. A. Simon, *Models of Man* (New York: John Wiley, 1957), p. 5.

3 M. Weber, *The Theory of Social and Economic Organization*, trans., A. M. Henderson and T. Parsons (Chicago: Free Press, 1947), p. 152.

4 R. A. Dahl, 'On the Concept of Power', *Behavioural Science*, 1957, pp. 202-3.

5 J. R. P. French and B. Raven, 'The Bases of Social Power', in D. Cartwright and A. Zander (eds), *Group Dynamics: Research and Theory* (2nd ed.) (London: Tavistock, 1960), p. 609.

6 R. Dahrendorf, *Class and Class Conflict in Industrial Society* (Palo Alto: Stanford University Press, 1959), p. 166.

7 *Ibid.*, p. 176.

8 P. M. Blau, *Exchange and Power in Social Life* (New York: John Wiley, 1967), p. 117.

9 *Ibid.*, p. 117, n.4.

10 'On the Concept of Political Power', in T. Parsons, *Sociological Theory and Modern Society* (New York: Free Press, 1967).

11 *Ibid.*, p. 308.
12 Dahl, 'Concept of Power', p. 202.
13 W. J. Buckley, *Sociology and Modern Systems Theory* (Englewood Cliffs: Prentice-Hall, 1967), pp. 50, 47.
14 A. W. Gouldner, *The Coming Crisis of Western Sociology*, p. 293.
15 S. Lukes, *Power: A Radical View* (London: Macmillan, 1974); J. H. Westergaard, 'Some Aspects of the Study of Modern British Society' in J. Rex (ed.), *Approaches to Sociology* (London: Routledge & Kegan Paul, 1974); R. H. Elliott, 'A Case Study of Management and Worker Attitudes to Managerial Authority and Prerogatives' (unpub. Ph.D. thesis, University of London, 1976).
16 Lukes, *op. cit.*, p. 34.
17 Westergaard, *op. cit.*, p. 31; see also J. H. Westergaard and H. Resler, *Class in a Capitalist Society* (London: Heinemann, 1975), esp. part III, chap. 1.
18 A. Etzioni, *A Comparative Analysis of Complex Organizations* (rev. ed.) (New York: Free Press, 1975), p. 3.
19 *Ibid.*, p. 5.
20 M. Tumin, *Caste in a Peasant Society* (Princeton University Press, 1952).
21 For a more elaborate theoretical discussion of authority see C. J. Friedrich (ed.), *Authority* (Cambridge, Mass.: Harvard University Press, 1958).
22 A. Fox, *A Sociology of Work in Industry* (New York: Collier-Macmillan, 1971), p. 34.
23 T. Parsons, 'A Revised Analytical Approach to Theory of Social Stratification', in T. Parsons, *Essays in Sociological Theory* (rev. ed.) (Chicago: Free Press, 1954), p. 409.
24 Dahl, 'Concept of Power', p. 205; see also E. Dahlestrom, 'Exchange, Influence, and Power', *Acta Sociologica*, 1966, pp. 265–6.
25 R. Lippitt, *et al.*, 'The Dynamics of Power', in E. E. Maccoby, T. M. Newcomb and E. L. Hartley (eds), *Readings in Social Psychology* (3rd ed.) (London: Methuen, 1959), pp. 252–4.
26 A. Bandura, *et al.*, 'A Comparative Test of the Status Envy, Social Power, and Secondary Reinforcement Theories of Identificatory Learning', in R. S. Lazarus and E. M. Opton (eds), *Personality* (Harmondsworth: Penguin Books, 1969), pp. 433–7. For a useful review of the social psychological literature on power see J. Schopter, 'Social Power', in L. Berkowitz (ed.), *Advances in Experimental Social Psychology*, Vol. 2 (New York: Academic Press, 1965), pp. 177–218.
27 F. Hunter, *Community Power Structure* (Chapel Hill: University of North Carolina Press, 1953). For a full and more recent survey see T. N. Clark, *Community Power Structures* (San Francisco: Chandler, 1969).
28 Cf. N. W. Polsby's uncharitable critique of reputationalist methodology: *Community Power and Political Theory* (New Haven: Yale University Press, 1963).
29 R. Dahl, *Who Governs?* (New Haven: Yale University Press, 1961), appendix b.

30 *Ibid.*, p. 332.

31 P. Bachrach and M. S. Baratz, *Power and Poverty: Theory and Practice* (New York: Oxford University Press, 1971), chap. 1.

32 I have concentrated upon the two 'basic' works produced by the community-power debate because they encapsulate the major problems involved; there is of course an enormous derivative literature. See, for example, C. M. Bonjean, T. N. Clark and R. L. Lineberry, *Community Politics: A Behavioral Approach* (New York: Free Press, 1971).

4 Power relations and dependence

1 For an extended discussion of definitions of technology see M. Meissner, *Technology and the Worker* (San Francisco: Chandler, 1969), pp. 13–42.

2 G. Lenski, *Power and Privilege* (New York: McGraw-Hill, 1966).

3 D. Dickson, *Alternative Technology* (London: Fontana, 1974).

4 For example in P. Halmos, *The Development of Industrial Societies*, Sociological Review Monographs, no. 8; A. W. Gouldner and R. Peterson, *Notes on Technology and the Moral Order* (New York: Bobbs-Merrill, 1962), p. 51.

5 M. Meissner, *op. cit.*

6 This classification is adapted from Lenski, *op. cit.*, pp. 46–50, 91–3. The distinction between simple and advanced horticultural societies has been criticized by Fallers, *ASR*, 1966, p. 718.

7 G. C. Homans, *English Villagers of the Thirteenth Century* (Cambridge, Mass.: Harvard University Press, 1942).

8 For slavery see E. D. Genovese, *Roll, Jordan, Roll* (André Deutsch, 1975); for prison labour see S. Dawson, 'Power and influence in Prison Workshops', in P. Abell (ed.), *Organizations as Bargaining and Influence Systems* (Heinemann, 1975).

5 Total power: the sociology of slavery

1 *Aristotle's Politics* (trans., B. Jowett) (Oxford: Clarendon Press, 1905), p. 32.

2 D. B. Davis, *The Problem of Slavery in Western Culture* (Ithaca: Cornell University Press, 1966), p. 35.

3 Pseudo-Aristotle's *Oeconomica*, quoted in M. I. Finley, 'Was Greek Civilization Based on Slave Labour?', in M. I. Finley (ed.), *Slavery in Classical Antiquity* (Cambridge: William Heffer, 1960), p. 54.

4 Cf. S. Elkins, *Slavery* (2nd ed.) (Chicago University Press, 1969), p. 52.

5 Quoted in O. Patterson, *The Sociology of Slavery* (London: Mac-Gibbon & Kee, 1967), p. 80.

6 Davis, *op. cit.*, p. 60.

7 Quoted in Elkins, *op. cit.*, p. 59.

8 W. L. Westermann, *Slave Systems of Greek and Roman Antiquity* (Philadelphia: American Philosophical Society, 1955), p. 20, n. 152.

9 K. Stampp, *The Peculiar Institution* (New York: Knopf, 1956), p. 34;

see also K. Marx (ed., E. J. Hobsbawm), *Pre-Capitalist Economic Formations* (London: Lawrence & Wishart, 1964).

10 *Aristotle's Politics, op. cit.*, pp. 32–4.

11 G. Fitzhugh, *Sociology for the South: or the Failure of Free Society* (Richmond, Va.: A. Morris, 1854). In view of the title of the present study Fitzhugh's apology for his title is worth quoting at length: 'We hesitated some time in selecting the title of our work. We did not like to employ the newly coined word Sociology. We could, however, find none other in the whole range of the English language, that would even faintly convey the idea which we wished to express. We looked to the history of the term. We found that within the last half century, disease, long lurking in the system of free society, had broken out into a hundred manifestations. . . . Society had never been in such a state before. New exigencies in its situation had given rise to new ideas, and to a new philosophy. This new philosophy must have a name, and as none could be found ready-made to suit the occasion, the term Sociology was compounded, of hybrid birth, half Greek and half Latin, as the technical appelation of the new science. . . . It grates harshly, as yet, on Southern ears, because to us it is new and super-fluous – the disease of which it treats being unknown amongst us. But as our book is intended to prove that we are indebted to domestic slavery for our happy exemption from the social afflictions that have originated this philosophy, it became necessary and appropriate that we should employ this new word in our title. The fact that, before the institution of Free Society, there was no such term, and that it is not in use in slave countries now, shows pretty clearly that Slave Society, ancient and modern, has ever been in so happy a condition, so exempt from ailments, that no doctors have arisen to treat it of its complaints, or to propose remedies for their cure. The term, therefore, is not only appropriate to the subject and the occasion, but pregnantly suggestive of facts and arguments that sustain our theory' (pp. v–vi). For Fitzhugh the development of sociology was a regrettable sign of the times. For an extended discussion of similar works see W. S. Jenkins, *Pro-Slavery Thought in the Old South* (Chapel Hill: University of North Carolina Press, 1935).

12 U. B. Phillips, *American Negro Slavery* (New York: Appleton, 1929), p. 501.

13 Quoted in *ibid.*, p. 270.

14 Quoted in Stampp, *op. cit.*, p. 208.

15 *De Bow's Review*, 1853, quoted in Elkins, *op. cit.*, p. 56. The writer obviously regarded this as the most efficient way of administering law.

16 Quoted in R. Wade, *Slavery in the Cities 1820–60* (New York: Oxford University Press, 1964), p. 190.

17 See further below, pp. 70–2.

18 Strabo quoted in Westermann, *op. cit.*, p. 72, n.65; Phillips, *op. cit.*, p. 339.

19 Quoted in Stampp, *op. cit.*, p. 102.

20 Quoted in *ibid.*, p. 418.

21 *Ibid.*, pp. 66–7.

22 S. Walker, a Louisiana planter, quoted in Wade, *op. cit.*, pp. 3–4.
23 Quoted in *ibid.*, p. 51.
24 *Ibid.*, p. 243.
25 Olmsted, quoted in *ibid.*, p. 4.
26 R. W. Fogel and S. L. Engerman, *Time on the Cross: The Economics of American Negro Slavery* (Boston: Little-Brown, 1974); see also C. V. Woodward, 'The Jolly Institution', *New York Review of Books*, May, 1974, pp. 3–6.
27 Stampp, *op. cit.*, pp. 32–3.
28 For Quashee see Patterson, *op. cit.*, p. 176; for Sambo see Elkins, *op. cit.*, p. 82, and E. D. Genovese, 'Rebelliousness and Docility in the Slave', in E. D. Genovese, *In Red and Black: Marxian Explorations in Southern and Afro-American History* (New York: Vintage Books, 1968), pp. 73–101.
29 Genovese, *op. cit.*, pp. 77–8.
30 Quoted in *ibid.*, p. 76.
31 Phillips, *op. cit.*, p. 291.
32 Patterson, *op. cit.*, p. 150.
33 Quoted in Stampp, *op. cit.*, p. 99.
34 Quoted in Phillips, *op. cit.*, p. 302.
35 Patterson, *op. cit.*, pp. 264–5; but see comments by E. D. Genovese, *Roll, Jordan, Roll* (London: André Deutsch, 1975), pp. 639–40.
36 A. Smith, *The Wealth of Nations* (London: Ward, Lock, n.d.), p. 308.
37 Quoted in Phillips, *op. cit.*, pp. 255–6.
38 W. C. Adams, 1857, quoted in Stampp, *op. cit.*, p. 100.
39 Wade, *op. cit.*, p. 91.
40 Jenkins, *op. cit.*, p. 295.
41 Quoted in *ibid.*, p. 297.
42 Quoted in Stampp, *op. cit.*, p. 90.
43 Sandra Dawson, 'Power and Influence in Prison Workshops', paper given at a conference on Power in Organizations at Imperial College, London, September 1974, p. 4.

6 Authority

1 A. Fox, *A Sociology of Work in Industry* (New York: Collier-Macmillan, 1971), p. 35.
2 One writer has gone so far as to argue that 'only at the beginning of the nineteenth century does legitimacy appear as a problem' (O. Brunner, 'Feudalism: the History of a Concept', in F. Cheyette (ed.), *Lordship and Community in Mediaeval Europe* (New York: Holt, Rinehart & Winston, 1968), p. 53.
3 M. Weber (eds G. Roth and C. Wittich), *Economy and Society* (New York: Bedminster Press, 1968), vol. 1, p. 215.
4 Cf. Parsons's discussion, *The Structure of Social Action* (Chicago: Free Press, 1949), pp. 646–7.
5 Weber, *op. cit.*, vol. 1, p. 326.
6 *Ibid.*, vol. 1, p. 241.
7 *Ibid.*, vol. 1, p. 244.

8 *Ibid.*, vol. 1, p. 242.
9 *Ibid.*, vol. 3, pp. 1116–17.
10 J. V. Downton, *Rebel Leadership: Commitment and Charisma in the Revolutionary Process* (New York: Free Press, 1973), p. 272.
11 P. Worsley, *The Trumpet Shall Sound* (London: Paladin, 1970), pp. 285–97.
12 W. H. Friedland, 'For a Sociological Concept of Charisma', *Social Forces*, vol. 43, 1964, pp. 18–26.
13 Downton, *op. cit.*, p. 234.
14 Friedland, *op. cit.*, pp. 24–5.
15 A. W. Singham, *The Hero and the Crowd in a Colonial Polity* (New Haven: Yale University Press, 1968).
16 W. G. Runciman, Charismatic Legitimacy and One-Party Rule in Ghana', *Arch. Europ. Sociol.*, 1963.
17 S. N. Eisenstadt, 'Introduction' to S. N. Eisenstadt (ed.), *Max Weber: On Charisma and Institution Building* (Chicago University Press, 1968); E. Shils, 'Charisma, Order, and Status', *American Sociological Review*, 1965, p. 205.
18 A. Giddens, *Capitalism and Modern Social Theory: an analysis of the writings of Marx, Durkheim and Weber* (Cambridge University Press, 1971), pp. 157–8, summarizing *Economy and Society*, vol. 1, pp. 217–18.
19 Although rules do, of course, perform several additional functions, including the specification of a minimum level of performance. See A. W. Gouldner's sensitive discussion in *Patterns of Industrial Bureaucracy* (Chicago: Free Press, 1954), chap. ix. For a fuller discussion of bureaucracy see below, p. 106.
20 Parsons, *op. cit.*, pp. 655–8.
21 Cf. R. Bendix and G. Roth, *Scholarship and Partisanship: Essays on Max Weber* (Berkeley: University of California Press, 1971), p. 126.
22 Weber, *op. cit.*, vol. 1, p. 216.
23 *Ibid.*, vol. 1, p. 263.

7 Power relations under feudalism

1 For a full discussion of the history of the concept see O. Brunner, 'Feudalism: the History of a Concept', in F. Cheyette (ed.), *Lordship and Community in Mediaeval Europe* (New York: Holt, Rhinehart & Winston, 1968), pp. 32–61.
2 F. L. Ganshof, *Feudalism* (London: Longmans, 1952), p. xv.
3 M. Bloch, 'The Rise of Dependent Cultivation and Seignorial Institutions', in M. M. Postan (ed.), *The Cambridge Economic History of Europe, Vol. 1, The Agrarian Life of the Middle Ages* (2nd ed.) (Cambridge University Press, 1966), p. 266.
4 Ganshof, *op. cit.*, p. xvi.
5 Bloch, *op. cit.*, pp. 235–6.
6 Quoted in M. Bloch, *Feudal Society* (trans., L. A. Manyon) (London: Routledge & Kegan Paul, 1961), pp. 232–3.
7 J. R. Strayer, 'Feudalism in Western Europe', in Cheyette (ed.),

op. cit., p. 13. This fragmentation is also found in other societies, and cannot itself be regarded as the defining characteristic of feudalism.

8 Bloch, *Feudal Society*, p. 279.
9 Quoted in R. W. Southern, *The Making of the Middle Ages* (London: Hutchinsons University Library, 1953), p. 104; see further, pp. 98–107.
10 C. D. Kernig (ed.), *Marxism, Communism, and Western Society: a Comparative Encyclopaedia* (New York: Herder & Herder, 1972), vol. 3, pp. 328–34.
11 Bloch, 'Dependent Cultivation', pp. 250–1.
12 *Ibid.*, p. 264.
13 *Ibid.*, pp. 261–2.
14 Bloch, *Feudal Society*, p. 142.
15 L. White, *Mediaeval Technology and Social Change* (Oxford: Clarendon Press, 1962), pp. 27–8.
16 *Ibid.*, p. 38.
17 Bloch, 'Dependent Cultivation', p. 284.
18 Quoted in Bloch, *Feudal Society*, p. 296.
19 Quoted in *ibid.*, pp. 411–12.
20 F. M. Stenton, *The First Century of English Feudalism, 1066–1166* (Oxford: Clarendon Press, 1932), chap. 7.
21 For feudalism and the 'natural economy' see B. H. Slicher Van Bath, *The Agrarian History of Western Europe, A.D. 500–1850* (London: Edward Arnold, 1963), chap. 1.
22 K. Marx, *The Eighteenth Brumaire of Louis Bonaparte*, in L. Feuer (ed.), *Marx and Engels: Basic Writings* (London: Fontana, 1969), pp. 377–8.
23 Quoted in Southern, *op. cit.*, pp. 99–100.

8 Power relations under capitalism: industry

1 R. Dahrendorf, *Essays in the Theory of Society* (London: Routledge & Kegan Paul, 1968), p. 219.
2 'Between a half and two-thirds of those who left £100,000 or more in the 1950s and 1960s [in the UK] were preceded by fathers leaving at least £25,000', C. D. Harbury and P. C. McMahon, 'Intergenerational Wealth Transmission', in P. Stanworth and A. Giddens (eds), *Elites and Power in British Society* (Cambridge University Press, 1974), p. 142.
3 Table 16, Long term trends in the distribution of private property, J. Westergaard and H. Resler, *op. cit.*, p. 112.
4 R. Dahrendorf, *Class and Class Conflict in Industrial Society* (Palo Alto: Stanford University Press, 1959), p. 268; see the whole discussion, pp. 267–76.
5 I have not examined power relations within the family, the education system, or religious institutions, as would be required by a fully comprehensive study. However, my major concern is with systems of labour exploitation, and the character of dependence relations within these other three areas is significantly different from that discussed here.
6 For a clear statement of the 'cash nexus' argument within the main-

stream of Marxist theory see J. H. Westergaard, 'The Rediscovery of the Cash Nexus', in R. Miliband and J. Savile (eds), *The Socialist Register 1970* (New York: Merlin Press, 1970).

7 Although most of the evidence used is derived from Anglo-American sources, and there are significant differences between Atlantic and other capitalist cultures (as well as differences between Britain and the United States), I hope the arguments have more general relevance. For the contrast between Britain and Japan see R. Dore, *British Factory – Japanese Factory* (London: George Allen & Unwin, 1973); but for significant similarities in management thinking see M. Haire, *et al.*, *Managerial Thinking* (New York: John Wiley, 1966).

8 D. J. Hickson, C. R. Hinings, R. E. Schneck, N. M. Pennings, 'A Strategic Contingencies Theory of Intraorganizational Power', *Administrative Science Quarterly*, vol. 16, 1971, pp. 219–22.

9 C. Perrow, 'Departmental Power and Perspective in Industrial Firms', in M. N. Zald (ed.), *Power in Organizations* (Nashville: Vanderbilt University Press, 1970), p. 63.

10 *Ibid.*, p. 65.

11 Hickson, *et al.*, *op. cit.*, p. 227.

12 See O. E. Williamson, *Corporate Control and Business Behavior* (Englewood Cliffs: Prentice-Hall, 1970).

13 C. Fletcher, 'The End of Management', in J. Child (ed.), *Man and Organization* (London: George Allen & Unwin, 1973), p. 138.

14 M. Weber (eds, G. Roth and C. Wittich), *Economy and Society* (New York: Bedminster Press, 1968), vol. 1, p. 225.

15 For 'size' see G. K. Ingham, *Size of Industrial Organization and Worker Behaviour* (Cambridge University Press, 1970), chap. 2 and references; for 'task' see, e.g., A. K. Rice, *The Enterprise and its Environment* (London: Tavistock, 1963), chap. 2; for 'technology' see J. Woodward's classic, *Industrial Organization: Theory and Practice* (Oxford University Press, 1965), and H. Aldrich's review of an extensive literature, 'Technology and Structure', *Administrative Science Quarterly*, 1972, pp. 26 *et seq.*

16 D. S. Pugh, D. J. Hickson, C. R. Hinings, 'An Empirical Taxonomy of Structure of Work Organizations', *Administrative Science Quarterly*, 1969, pp. 115 *et seq.*; P. M. Blau and R. A. Schoenherr, *The Structure of Organizations* (New York: Basic Books, 1971).

17 T. Burns and G. M. Stalker, *The Management of Innovation* (London: Tavistock, 1961).

18 T. Parsons, 'Introduction to M. Weber', *Theory of Economic and Social Organization* (Chicago: Free Press/Falcon's Wing Press, 1947), pp. 58–60, n.4; P. M. Blau and W. R. Scott, *Formal Organizations* (London: Routledge & Kegan Paul, 1963).

19 W. Kornhauser, *Scientists in Industry* (Berkeley: University of California Press, 1962).

20 A. Sampson, *The Sovereign State; the secret history of I.T.T.* (London: Hodder & Stoughton, 1973).

21 J. Child, 'Quaker Employers and Industrial Relations', *Sociological Review*, 1964, pp. 293–315.

22 R. Presthus, *The Organizational Society* (New York: Vintage Books, 1962), p. 32.
23 C. Sofer, *Men in Mid-Career* (Cambridge University Press, 1970).
24 For extensive discussions of cliques and cabals see M. Dalton, *Men who Manage* (New York: John Wiley, 1959), and T. Burns, Micro-Politics, *ASQ*, 1961–2, pp. 25 *et seq.*: J. Woodward, *Industrial Organization: Behaviour and Control* (Oxford University Press, 1970), esp. chap. 3.
25 Complexity favours flexibility in at least two important ways: first at a simple mechanical level, by increasing the number of available alternative routes to a given destination; and, second, by increasing the difficulty of external surveillance and control.
26 G. W. Dalton, L. B. Barnes, A. Zaleznik, *The Distribution of Authority in Formal Organizations* (Cambridge, Mass.: MIT Press, 1968). There is of course an extensive prescriptive literature on 'democratic' managerial styles. See for example F. Heller, *Managerial Decision Making* (London: Tavistock, 1971).
27 R. M. Blackburn, *Union Character and Social Class* (London: Batsford, 1967).
28 Quoted in Dalton, *op. cit.*, p. 156.
29 Quoted in *ibid.*, p. 220.
30 J. Child, 'Organizational Structure, Environment and Performance', *Sociology*, vol. 6, no. 1, 1972, p. 17.
31 A. Pettigrew, *The Politics of Organizational Decision-Making* (London: Tavistock, 1973), pp. 150–3.
32 *Ibid.*, p. 145.
33 R. M. Cyert and J. G. March, *A Behavioral Theory of the Firm* (Englewood Cliffs: Prentice-Hall, 1963), p. 29.
34 R. Dahrendorf, *Class and Class Conflict*, chap. 5.
35 For an account of shared interests between industrial-relations officials and union leaders see F. H. Goldner, 'The Division of Labour: Process and Power', in M. Zald (ed.), *Power in Organizations* (Nashville: Vanderbilt University Press, 1970), chap. 3.
36 A. Fox, *A Sociology of Work in Industry* (New York: Collier-Macmillan, 1971), pp. 157–9.
37 For extensive evidence see R. Martin and R. H. Fryer, 'The Deferential Worker?', in Martin Bulmer (ed.), *Working Class Images of Society* (London: Routledge & Kegan Paul, 1975), pp. 72–8.
38 For a discussion of socialization into inequality in general see F. Parkin, *Class, Inequality, and Political Order* (London: MacGibbon & Kee, 1971), esp. chap. 2.
39 K. G. J. Alexander, 'Bargaining Power', unpublished paper presented to the 25th Annual Conference of the British Universities Industrial Relations Association, University of Stirling, 1974.
40 A. Glyn and B. Sutcliffe, *British Capitalism, Workers and the Profits Squeeze* (Harmondsworth: Penguin Books, 1972); A. B. Atkinson (ed.), *Wealth, Income and Inequality* (Harmondsworth: Penguin Books, 1973).
41 W. Brown, *Piecework Bargaining* (London: Heinemann Educational, 1973).

42 H. Beynon, *Working for Ford* (Harmondsworth: Penguin Books, 1973).
43 W. E. J. McCarthy and N. D. Ellis, *Management by Agreement* (London: Hutchinson, 1973), p. 3.
44 A. Fox and A. Flanders, 'Collective Bargaining – from Donovan to Durkheim', in A. Flanders, *Management and Workers* (Faber and Faber, 1970), p. 244.
45 H. A. Clegg, *The System of Industrial Relations in Britain* (Oxford: Basil Blackwell & Mott, 1970), p. 64.
46 *Report of the Royal Commission on Trade Unions and Employers' Associations* (Donovan Report) (London: HMSO, 1968).
47 See, for example, W. E. J. McCarthy and N. D. Ellis, *op. cit.*
48 J. H. Goldthorpe, D. Lockwood, F. Bechofer, J. Platt, *The Affluent Worker: Industrial Attitudes and Behaviour* (Cambridge University Press, 1968), pp. 38–9.
49 There is an enormous literature on worker motivation. For two relevant studies see F. Herzberg, *Work and the Nature of Man* (St Albans: Staples Press, 1968), W. W. Daniel, *Beyond the Wage Work Bargain* (London: Allen & Unwin, 1970).
50 Fox and Flanders, *op. cit.*, pp. 253–4.
51 Martin and Fryer, *op. cit.*, p. 90.
52 The number of redundancy sit-ins increased from 5 in the first six months of 1972 to 12 in the first six months of 1975, and of industrial relations sit-ins from 4 (excluding the special case of the Manchester district work-ins stimulated by the AUEW) to 15. Although small, the numbers are significant. (J. Hemingway and W. Keyser, *Who's in Charge? Worker Sit-Ins in Britain To-day*, Oxford: Metra Oxford Consulting, 1975.)
53 There is no adequate synoptic account of the British working class. For three different groups see N. Dennis, F. Henriques and D. Slaughter, *Coal is Our Life* (2nd ed.) (London: Tavistock, 1969); J. Goldthorpe, D. Lockwood, F. Bechofer, J. Platt, *The Affluent Worker in the Class Structure* (Cambridge University Press, 1970); and R. K. Brown and P. Brannen, 'Social Relations and Social Perspectives amongst Shipbuilding Workers', *Sociology*, 1970, pp. 71–84, 197–211.
54 G. Routh, *Occupation and Pay in Great Britain, 1906–60* (Cambridge University Press, 1965), p. 107.
55 *Ibid.*, p. 129.
56 D. Wedderburn, 'The Conditions of Employment of Manual Workers', in J. H. Goldthorpe and M. J. Mann (eds), *Proceedings of an S.S.R.C. Conference, Social Stratification and Industrial Relations* (Cambridge University Press, 1969).
57 See R. Blauner's classic account, *Alienation and Freedom* (Chicago University Press, 1964); K. Sisson, *Industrial Relations in Fleet Street* (Oxford: Basil Blackwell, 1975), chap. 5.
58 L. Sayles, *The Behaviour of Industrial Work Groups* (London: Chapman & Hall, 1958).
59 M. Crozier, *The Bureaucratic Phenomenon* (London: Tavistock, 1964), pp. 108–10.

60 *Ibid.*, p. 107.
61 S. Cunnison, *Wages and Work Allocation* (London: Tavistock, 1966), p. 140.
62 For 'mandate' see E. C. Hughes, *Men and Their Work* (Chicago: Free Press, 1958), p. 159; for the use of the concept in the electrical industry see D. R. Lewis, 'The Electrical Trades Union and the Growth of the Electrical Industry to 1926' (unpub. D.Phil. thesis, University of Oxford, 1970), esp. pp. 438–46.

9 Power relations within capitalism: political organizations

1 For a comprehensive analysis of the theory of representation see H. Pitkin, *The Concept of Representation* (Berkeley and Los Angeles: University of California Press, 1967).
2 G. Parry, *Political Élites* (London: George Allen & Unwin, 1969) contains a useful summary of classical and contemporary élitist theory.
3 R. Michels, *Political Parties* (New York: Dover Publications, 1959), p. 400.
4 *Ibid.*, p. 278.
5 For the social background of local political leaders see J. Blondel, *Voters, Parties, and Leaders: the Social Fabric of British Politics* (Harmondsworth: Penguin Books, 1963), pp. 97–103.
6 W. L. Guttsman, 'The British Political Élite and the Class Structure', in P. Stanworth and A. Giddens (eds), *Élites and Power in British Society* (Cambridge University Press, 1974), pp. 34, 36.
7 R. W. Johnson, 'The British Political Élite', *Archiv. europ. sociol.*, vol. XIV, 1973, p. 50.
8 D. R. Matthews, *U.S. Senators and their World* (Chapel Hill: University of North Carolina Press, 1960), pp. 20, 33.
9 J. Porter, *The Vertical Mosaic: an Analysis of Social Class and Power in Canada* (University of Toronto Press, 1965), pp. 394–8.
10 S. Encel, *Equality and Authority: a study of Class, Status and Power in Australia* (London: Tavistock, 1970), pp. 230–1.
11 *Ibid.*, p. 236.
12 *Ibid.*, pp. 239–40.
13 Porter, *op. cit.*, p. 391.
14 Guttsman, *op. cit.*, p. 34.
15 K. Newton, *The Sociology of British Communism* (London: Allen Lane/The Penguin Press, 1969), pp. 164–5 (although the value of the figures is limited as they are drawn from only one Party District).
16 Matthews, *op. cit.*, p. 21.
17 For financial data on British parties see D. E. Butler and A. Sloman, *British Political Facts* (London: Macmillan, 1975); for the United States the various works of H. E. Alexander, including *Financing the 1968 Election* (Lexington: Heath Lexington, 1971), and D. W. Adamany and G. E. Ayree, *Political Money: a strategy for campaign financing in America* (Baltimore: Johns Hopkins University Press, 1975).
18 B. Hindess, *The Decline of Working Class Politics* (London: Mac-Gibbon & Kee, 1971), p. 38.

19 R. Mackenzie, *British Political Parties* (New York: F. A. Praeger, 1965), pp. 644–5.

20 See also R. Miliband, *Parliamentary Socialism: A Study in the Politics of Labour* (London: George Allen & Unwin, 1961).

21 M. Duverger, *Political Parties* (London: Methuen, 1964), p. 124.

22 For material on factionalism in the British Labour Party see M. Foot, *Aneurin Bevan, 1945–60* (Davis-Poynter, 1973). For a general discussion of democratic élitism see P. Bachrach, *The Theory of Democratic Élitism: a critique* (University of London Press, 1969).

23 Hindess, *op. cit.*, p. 38.

24 I am grateful to Mr K. Rosewell, of St Edmund Hall, Oxford, for information on union officers' salaries.

25 *Minutes of Evidence to the Royal Commission on Trade Unions and Employers' Associations (Donovan)*, no. 24, p. 936. I owe this reference to Dr C. J. Crouch.

26 There is of course a large literature on union members' attitudes towards their unions: see especially M. van de Vall, *Labour Organizations* (Cambridge University Press, 1970), Part II.

27 The personal and organizational goals are probably more important for British (if not American) union leaders, for the levels of material reward and bureaucratic facilities are relatively low: the leaders of Britain's largest unions receive only an average middle management salary.

28 R. Martin, 'Union Democracy: an Explanatory Framework', *Sociology*, 1968, pp. 205–20; see also 'The Effects of Recent Changes in Industrial Conflict upon the Internal Politics of Trade Unions', in C. Crouch and A. Pizzorno (eds), *The Resurgence of Industrial Conflict in Western Europe*, vol. 2 (London: Macmillan, forthcoming).

29 Especially, of course, when governments attempt to use trade unions in implementing incomes policies: for a discussion of one such attempt see J. G. Corina, 'Wage Restraint 1948–50' (unpub. D.Phil. thesis, University of Oxford, 1961).

30 See above, p. 120.

31 For 'printing' see Lipset, *et al.*, *op. cit.*, and I. C. Cannon, 'Ideology and Occupational Community', *Sociology*, 1967, pp. 165–87; for 'electrical contracting' D. R. Lewis, 'The Electrical Trades Union and the Growth of the Electrical Industry to 1926' (unpub. D.Phil. thesis, University of Oxford, 1970).

32 S. and B. Webb, *Industrial Democracy* (London: Longmans, 1894), p. 97.

33 For 'instructing' see H. A. Turner, *Trade Union Growth, Structure and Policy* (London: George Allen & Unwin, 1961), p. 228; see also J. D. Edelstein and M. Warner, *Comparative Union Democracy: Organization and Opposition in British and American Unions* (London: George Allen & Unwin, 1975), chap. 9.

34 H. A. Clegg, *The System of Industrial Relations in Great Britain* (Oxford: Basil Blackwell, 1970), pp. 80–2.

35 W. E. J. Macarthy, *The Closed Shop in Britain* (Oxford: Basil Blackwell, 1964).

10 Élite theory: relations between economy and polity within capitalism

1 R. Dahrendorf, *Class and Class Conflict in Industrial Society* (Palo Alto: Stanford University Press, 1959), p. 268.

2 R. Miliband, *Parliamentary Socialism: A Study in the Politics of Labour* (London: George Allen & Unwin, 1961), pp. 265–6.

3 The relationship between élite theory and class theory is complex. Some élite theorists have opposed class theorists (Pareto), some class theorists have been very critical of élite theorists (Zeitlin), and some theorists have incorporated both élite and class elements (Djilas, Burnham and Wright Mills). Historically, élite theory developed as a reaction against Marxist class theory, as Pareto made clear in *Mind and Society*: for Pareto the division of society into élite/mass was a product of politics and personality, not economics. However, more recent élite theorists have viewed Marxism more sympathetically, frequently interpreting the dichotomy between élite and mass as the result of economic developments (as in Burnham's *The Managerial Revolution*). For this reason, and for expository convenience, I have subsumed some contemporary forms of class theory under élite theory, namely those forms of élite/class theory which stress the economic foundations of minority rule.

4 For a brief discussion of 'middle-men' (or 'leg-men', to use R. V. Presthus's expressive term) see C. Wright Mills, *The Power Élite*, pp. 267–8. (See also R. V. Presthus, *Men at the Top*, New York: Oxford University Press, 1964, pp. 116–17.) For a recent 'hegemonic' statement see J. Westergaard and H. Resler, *Class in a Capitalist Society: a Study of Contemporary Britain* (London: Heinemann, 1975), discussed further below, p. 165.

5 For a convenient if limited survey of a vast body of literature see C. J. Hewitt, 'Élites and the Distribution of Power', in P. Stanworth and A. Giddens, *Élites and Power in British Society* (Cambridge University Press, 1974) and the bibliography in I. Crewe, *British Political Sociology Yearbook*, vol. 1, *Élites in Western Democracy* (London: Croom Helm, 1974), pp. 337–50.

6 Stanworth and Giddens, *op. cit.*; Crewe, *op. cit.*; Wright Mills, *op. cit.*; G. W. Domhoff, *Who Rules America?* (Englewood Cliffs: Prentice-Hall, 1967); J. Porter, *The Vertical Mosaic: an analysis of social class and power in Canada* (University of Toronto Press, 1965); R. V. Presthus, *Élite Accommodation in Canadian Politics* (Cambridge University Press, 1973); S. Encel, *Equality and Authority: a Study of Class, Status and Power in Australia* (London: Tavistock, 1970).

7 S. Haxey, *Tory M.P.* (London: Victor Gollancz, 1939), table facing p. 124.

8 P. Stanworth and A. Giddens, 'An Economic Élite: a Demographic Profile of Company Chairmen', in Stanworth and Giddens, *op. cit.*, p. 83.

9 R. K. Kelsall, 'Recruitment to the Civil Service: How Has the Pattern Changed?', in Stanworth and Giddens, *op. cit.*, p. 174.

10 The figures are obviously not directly comparable, owing to the contrasting treatment of direct-grant schools, which are neither public

schools nor local authority schools: the figures quoted effectively understate the extent to which company chairmen were educated at élite schools, for some of the non-public school company chairmen were probably educated at élite direct-grant schools. The figures for company chairmen cover the whole period 1900–72, for higher civil servants only 1966–7. This is only one indication of the problems created by the non-comparability of available evidence, in this instance probably avoidable.

11 Miliband, *op. cit.*, p. 125.

12 I. Crewe, 'Introduction: Studying Élites in Britain', in Crewe (ed.), *op. cit.*, pp. 20–1.

13 L. J. Edinger and D. D. Searing, 'Social Background in Élite Analysis: a Methodological Inquiry', *APSR*, vol. 61, 1967, pp. 428–45; D. Farlie and I. Budge, 'Élite Background and Issue Preferences: A Comparison of British and Foreign Data using a New Technique', in Crewe (ed.), *op. cit.*, pp. 199–240, p. 233.

14 Farlie and Budge, *op. cit.*, p. 236.

15 For one selection from this enormous literature see A. H. Halsey, J. Floud and C. A. Anderson, *Education, Economy, and Society* (New York: Free Press of Glencoe, 1961).

16 Quoted in Crewe, *op. cit.*, pp. 25–6.

17 M. Kohn, *Class and Conformity* (Homewood, Ill.: Dorsey Press, 1969); for a convenient review see M. Rush and P. Althoff, *An Introduction to Political Sociology* (London: Nelson, 1971), chap. 2.

18 H. A. McCloskey, 'Consensus and Ideology in American Politics', 1964, pp. 361–82.

19 Domhoff, *op. cit.*, p. 156.

20 Miliband, *op. cit.*, pp. 47–8, 265.

21 Hewitt, *op. cit.*, p. 53.

22 *Ibid.*, p. 59.

23 A. M. Rose, *The Power Structure* (New York: Oxford University Press, 1967); S. Keller, *Beyond the Ruling Class* (New York: Random House, 1963); G. McConnell, *Private Power and American Democracy* (New York: Knopf, 1966); E. M. Epstein, *The Corporation in American Politics* (Englewood Cliffs: Prentice-Hall, 1969). The quotation is from McConnell, *op. cit.*, p. 339.

24 Epstein, *op. cit.*, p. 240.

25 This is based largely upon their ability to prevent political groups from successfully carrying out hostile policies where their interests are directly involved, as in the difficulties the British Labour government experienced when it attempted to carry out steel nationalization in 1950–1. For a full, early statement of 'veto-group' theory in general terms see D. Riesman, *The Lonely Crowd* (New York: Doubleday Anchor, 1950), pp. 246–59, and 'evaluation' in W. Kornhauser, '"Power Élite" or "Veto Groups"', in R. Bendix and S. M. Lipset (eds), *Class, Status and Power* (2nd ed.) (London: Routledge & Kegan Paul, 1967), pp. 210–18.

26 R. McKenzie and A. Silver, *Angels in Marble: Working Class Conservatives in Urban England* (London: Heinemann, 1968), esp. chap. 5;

R. D. Jessop, *Traditionalism, Conservatism and British Political Culture* (London: George Allen & Unwin, 1974), esp. chap. 2.

27 R. Martin and R. H. Fryer, 'The Deferential Worker?', in Martin Bulmer (ed.), *Working Class Images of Society* (London: Routledge & Kegan Paul, 1975), p. 100.

28 For American business and tariffs see R. A. Bauer, I. de S. Pool and L. A. Dexter, *American Business and Public Policy* (New York: Atherton Press, 1964).

29 For the Industrial Relations Act, 1971, see B. Weekes, M. Mellish, L. Dickens, J. Lloyd, *Industrial Relations and the Limits of the Law* (Oxford: Basil Blackwell, 1975); for a comprehensive analysis of recent changes leading to the breakdown of the traditional boundaries of 'free collective bargaining' in Britain see C. J. Crouch, 'Class Conflict and the Industrial Relations Crisis' (unpub. D.Phil. thesis, University of Oxford, 1975).

30 D. E. Butler and M. Pinto-Duchinski, *The British General Election of 1970* (London: Macmillan, 1971), pp. 102, 55 n. l.

31 H. E. Alexander, *Financing the 1968 Election* (Lexington, Mass.: Heath Lexington, 1971), pp. 117–19; 326–8.

32 For a useful comparative review of the factors influencing voting see S. M. Lipset and S. Rokkan, *Party Systems and Voter Alignments: cross national perspectives* (New York: Free Press, 1967); R. R. Alford, *Party and Society* (Chicago: Rand-McNally, 1963); for Britain see R. Rose, 'Class and Party Divisions: Britain as a Test Case', *Sociology*, vol. 2, 1968, pp. 129–62.

33 D. E. Butler and D. Stokes, *Political Change in Britain* (1st ed.) (London: Macmillan, 1969), pp. 155, 162.

34 *Ibid.*, p. 169; D. E. Butler and D. Stokes, *Political Change in Britain* (2nd ed.) (London: Macmillan, 1974), p. 199.

35 Quoted in Miliband, *op. cit.*, p. 76.

36 For business and the British government see N. Harris, *Competition and the Corporate Society: British Conservatives, The State, and Industry 1945–64*; for American business see Epstein, *op. cit.*, esp. chap. 5; for Canada see Presthus, *op. cit.*, for Australia see Encel, *op. cit.*, part 4. For labour and the British government see I. Richter, *The Political Purpose of Trade Unions* (London: George Allen & Unwin, 1974); for the United States see C. M. Rhemus and D. B. McLaughlin, *Labour and American Politics* (Ann Arbor: University of Michigan Press, 1967); for Canada see Porter, *op. cit.*, chaps 10 and 11; for Australia see R. M. Martin, *Trade Unions in Australia* (Ringwood, Victoria: Penguin Books, 1975).

37 W. C. Mitchell, *Sociological Analysis and Politics: the Theories of Talcott Parsons* (Englewood Cliffs: Prentice-Hall, 1967), p. 78; cf. T. Parsons and N. J. Smelser, *Economy and Society* (New York: Free Press of Glencoe, 1956).

38 Cf. Mitchell, *op. cit.*, pp. 80–1.

39 C. Kerr, J. T. Dunlop, F. H. Herbison, C. A. Myers, *Industrialism and Industrial Man* (London: Heinemann, 1962); P. Halmos (ed.),

The Development of Industrial Societies, Sociological Review Monograph, no. 8.
40 Kerr, *et al.*, *op. cit.*, p. 125.
41 Cf. K. de Schweinitz, *Industrialization and Democracy* (New York: Free Press, 1964).
42 Cf. D. Lane, *The End of Inequality: Stratification under State Socialism* (Harmondsworth: Penguin Books, 1971).
43 Cf. A. Giddens, *The Class Structure of Advanced Societies* (London: Hutchinson, 1973), p. 253.
44 W. L. Baldwin, *The Structure of the Defence Market, 1955–64* (Durham, N.C.: Duke University Press, 1967), p. 196.
45 H. Hutchinson, *Tariff Making and Industrial Reconstruction* (London: Harrap, 1965).
46 D. Schoenbaum, *Hitler's Social Revolution* (London: Weidenfeld & Nicolson, 1967).
47 A. Schweitzer, *Big Business in the Third Reich* (London: Eyre & Spottiswoode, 1964), esp. chap. 11.
48 Miliband, *op. cit.*, pp. 117–18.

11 Conclusion: the sociology of power

1 See entry under 'Slavery' in C. D. Kernig (ed.), *Marxism, Communism and Western Society: a Comparative Encyclopaedia* (New York: Herder & Herder, 1972), vol. 7, p. 337.
2 D. Dickson, *Alternative Technology* (London: Fontana, 1974).
3 G. E. Lenski, *Power and Privilege: A Theory of Social Stratification* (New York: McGraw-Hill, 1966); see review symposium by R. Dahrendorf, L. A. Fallers, S. Thernstrom in *ASR*, 1966, pp. 714–20.
4 See the discussion on feedback in W. J. Buckley, *Sociology and Modern Systems Theory* (Englewood Cliffs: Prentice-Hall, 1967), pp. 52–8.
5 For an interesting debate within the Marxist circle see N. Poulantzas, 'The Problem of the Capitalist State', and R. Miliband, 'The Capitalist State: Reply to Nicol Poulantzas', in J. Urry and J. Wakeford, *Power in Britain: Sociological Readings* (London: Heinemann Educational, 1973), pp. 291–314.
6 J. Westergaard and H. Resler, *Class in a Capitalist Society* (London: Heinemann Educational, 1975), p. 147; see also R. Hyman, *Industrial Relations, a Marxist Introduction* (London: Macmillan, 1974), p. 26.
7 C. Mueller, *The Politics of Communication: a Study in the Political Sociology of Language, Socialization, and Legitimation* (New York: Oxford University Press, 1973), p. 55; see B. Bernstein, *Class, Codes, and Control* (London: Paladin, 1973). For a different approach to the language of power see S. Clegg, *Power, Rule and Domination* (London: Routledge & Kegan Paul, 1975).
8 P. Bachrach and M. S. Baratz, *Power and Poverty: Theory and Practice* (New York: Oxford University Press, 1970), part 2.
9 There is of course an enormous literature on hegemonic culture in capitalist society: see especially H. Marcuse, *One-Dimensional Man* (Routledge & Kegan Paul, 1964).

10 F. Parkin, *Class Inequality and Political Order* (London: MacGibbon & Kee, 1971), pp. 92–4. See also R. M. Blackburn and M. Mann, 'Ideology in the Non-Skilled Working Class', in M. Bulmer (ed.), *Working Class Images of Society* (London: Routledge & Kegan Paul, 1975), pp. 131–60.
11 S. M. Lukes, *Power: A Radical View* (London: Macmillan, 1974), pp. 34–5; cf. p. 34n.
12 Westergaard and Resler, *op. cit.*, p. 248, n. 4.
13 G. Lukács, 'Reification and the Consciousness of the Proletariat', in G. Lukács, *History and Class Consciousness* (New York: Merlin Press, 1971), pp. 149–222.
14 Westergaard and Resler, *op. cit.*, p. 220, n. 23.
15 M. Glucksmann, *Structural Analysis in Contemporary Social Thought: a Comparison of the Theories of Claude Lévi-Strauss and Lois Althusser* (London: Routledge & Kegan Paul, 1974), pp. 112–13.
16 L. Althusser, J. Ranrière and P. Mancherey, *Lire le Capital*, vol. 1 (Paris: François Maspero, 1965), p. 66.
17 F. Engels, *Socialism: Utopian and Scientific*, in L. Feuer (ed.), *Marx and Engels: Basic Writings on Politics and Philosophy* (London: Fontana, 1969), p. 131.
18 Lukács, *op. cit.*, p. 208.
19 A marginal comment by Marx, quoted in K. Marx and F. Engels (ed., C. J. Arthur), *The German Ideology, Part 1* (London: Lawrence & Wishart, 1970), p. 60.
20 Lukács, *op. cit.*, p. 186.
21 *Ibid.*, pp. 208–9.
22 Quoted in R. Bendix, *Max Weber: an Intellectual Portrait* (London: Heinemann, 1960), p. 69.
23 A detailed discussion of Weber's relation to Marxism is inappropriate here. In general, I agree with C. Wright Mills, who commented, 'With Marx, Weber shares an attempt to bring "ideological" phenomena into some correlation with the material interests of the economic and political orders' (ed., C. Wright Mills, *From Max Weber: Essays in Sociology*, London: Routledge & Kegan Paul, 1948, p. 48). Weber in no sense 'disproved' Marx. See also N. Birnbaum, 'Conflicting interpretations of the rise of capitalism: Marx and Weber', *British Journal of Sociology*, 1953, pp. 125–41.

Index

197

Routledge Social Science Series

Routledge & Kegan Paul   London, Henley and Boston

39 Store Street, London WC1E 7DD
Broadway House, Newtown Road, Henley-on-Thames,
Oxon RG9 1EN
9 Park Street, Boston, Mass. 02108

Contents

*Authors wishing to submit manuscripts for any series in
this catalogue should send them to the Social Science Editor,
Routledge & Kegan Paul Ltd, 39 Store Street,
London WC1E 7DD*

●*Books so marked are available in paperback
All books are in Metric Demy 8vo format (216 × 138mm approx.)*

International Library of Sociology

General Editor John Rex

GENERAL SOCIOLOGY

Barnsley, J. H. The Social Reality of Ethics. *464 pp.*
Belshaw, Cyril. The Conditions of Social Performance. *An Exploratory Theory. 144 pp.*
Brown, Robert. Explanation in Social Science. *208 pp.*
● Rules and Laws in Sociology. *192 pp.*
Bruford, W. H. Chekhov and His Russia. *A Sociological Study. 244 pp.*
Cain, Maureen E. Society and the Policeman's Role. *326 pp.*
●**Fletcher, Colin.** Beneath the Surface. *An Account of Three Styles of Sociological Research. 221 pp.*
Gibson, Quentin. The Logic of Social Enquiry. *240 pp.*
Glucksmann, M. Structuralist Analysis in Contemporary Social Thought. *212 pp.*
Gurvitch, Georges. Sociology of Law. *Preface by Roscoe Pound. 264 pp.*
Hodge, H. A. Wilhelm Dilthey. *An Introduction. 184 pp.*
Homans, George C. Sentiments and Activities. *336 pp.*
Johnson, Harry M. Sociology: *a Systematic Introduction. Foreword by Robert K. Merton. 710 pp.*
●**Keat, Russell,** and **Urry, John.** Social Theory as Science. *278 pp.*
Mannheim, Karl. Essays on Sociology and Social Psychology. *Edited by Paul Keckskemeti. With Editorial Note by Adolph Lowe. 344 pp.*
Systematic Sociology: *An Introduction to the Study of Society. Edited by J. S. Erös and Professor W. A. C. Stewart. 220 pp.*
Martindale, Don. The Nature and Types of Sociological Theory. *292 pp.*
●**Maus, Heinz.** A Short History of Sociology. *234 pp.*
Mey, Harald. Field-Theory. *A Study of its Application in the Social Sciences. 352 pp.*
Myrdal, Gunnar. Value in Social Theory: *A Collection of Essays on Methodology. Edited by Paul Streeten. 332 pp.*
Ogburn, William F., and **Nimkoff, Meyer F.** A Handbook of Sociology. *Preface by Karl Mannheim. 656 pp. 46 figures. 35 tables.*
Parsons, Talcott, and **Smelser, Neil J.** Economy and Society: *A Study in the Integration of Economic and Social Theory. 362 pp.*
Podgórecki, Adam. Practical Social Sciences. *About 200 pp.*
●**Rex, John.** Key Problems of Sociological Theory. *220 pp.*
Sociology and the Demystification of the Modern World. *282 pp.*
●**Rex, John** (Ed.) Approaches to Sociology. *Contributions by Peter Abell, Frank Bechhofer, Basil Bernstein, Ronald Fletcher, David Frisby, Miriam Glucksmann, Peter Lassman, Herminio Martins, John Rex, Roland Robertson, John Westergaard and Jock Young. 302 pp.*
Rigby, A. Alternative Realities. *352 pp.*
Roche, M. Phenomenology, Language and the Social Sciences. *374 pp.*

Sahay, A. Sociological Analysis. *220 pp.*
Simirenko, Alex (Ed.) Soviet Sociology. *Historical Antecedents and Current Appraisals. Introduction by Alex Simirenko. 376 pp.*
Strasser, Hermann. The Normative Structure of Sociology. *Conservative and Emancipatory Themes in Social Thought. About 340 pp.*
Urry, John. Reference Groups and the Theory of Revolution. *244 pp.*
Weinberg, E. Development of Sociology in the Soviet Union. *173 pp.*

FOREIGN CLASSICS OF SOCIOLOGY

●**Durkheim, Emile.** Suicide. *A Study in Sociology. Edited and with an Introduction by George Simpson. 404 pp.*
●**Gerth, H. H.,** and **Mills, C. Wright.** From Max Weber: *Essays in Sociology. 502 pp.*
●**Tönnies, Ferdinand.** Community and Association. *(Gemeinschaft und Gesellschaft.) Translated and Supplemented by Charles P. Loomis. Foreword by Pitirim A. Sorokin. 334 pp.*

SOCIAL STRUCTURE

Andreski, Stanislav. Military Organization and Society. *Foreword by Professor A. R. Radcliffe-Brown. 226 pp. 1 folder.*
Carlton, Eric. Ideology and Social Order. *Preface by Professor Philip Abrahams. About 320 pp.*
Coontz, Sydney H. Population Theories and the Economic Interpretation. *202 pp.*
Coser, Lewis. The Functions of Social Conflict. *204 pp.*
Dickie-Clark, H. F. Marginal Situation: *A Sociological Study of a Coloured Group. 240 pp. 11 tables.*
Glaser, Barney, and **Strauss, Anselm L.** Status Passage. *A Formal Theory. 208 pp.*
Glass, D. V. (Ed.) Social Mobility in Britain. *Contributions by J. Berent, T. Bottomore, R. C. Chambers, J. Floud, D. V. Glass, J. R. Hall, H. T. Himmelweit, R. K. Kelsall, F. M. Martin, C. A. Moser, R. Mukherjee, and W. Ziegel. 420 pp.*
Johnstone, Frederick A. Class, Race and Gold. *A Study of Class Relations and Racial Discrimination in South Africa. 312 pp.*
Jones, Garth N. Planned Organizational Change: *An Exploratory Study Using an Empirical Approach. 268 pp.*
Kelsall, R. K. Higher Civil Servants in Britain: *From 1870 to the Present Day. 268 pp. 31 tables.*
König, René. The Community. *232 pp. Illustrated.*
●**Lawton, Denis.** Social Class, Language and Education. *192 pp.*
McLeish, John. The Theory of Social Change: *Four Views Considered. 128 pp.*
Marsh, David C. The Changing Social Structure of England and Wales, *1871-1961. 288 pp.*
Menzies, Ken. Talcott Parsons and the Social Image of Man. *About 208 pp.*

●**Mouzelis, Nicos.** Organization and Bureaucracy. *An Analysis of Modern Theories. 240 pp.*

Mulkay, M. J. Functionalism, Exchange and Theoretical Strategy. *272 pp.*

Ossowski, Stanislaw. Class Structure in the Social Consciousness. *210 pp.*

●**Podgórecki, Adam.** Law and Society. *302 pp.*

Renner, Karl. Institutions of Private Law and Their Social Functions. *Edited, with an Introduction and Notes, by O. Kahn-Freud. Translated by Agnes Schwarzschild. 316 pp.*

SOCIOLOGY AND POLITICS

Acton, T. A. Gypsy Politics and Social Change. *316 pp.*

Clegg, Stuart. Power, Rule and Domination. *A Critical and Empirical Understanding of Power in Sociological Theory and Organisational Life. About 300 pp.*

Hechter, Michael. Internal Colonialism. *The Celtic Fringe in British National Development, 1536–1966. 361 pp.*

Hertz, Frederick. Nationality in History and Politics: *A Psychology and Sociology of National Sentiment and Nationalism. 432 pp.*

Kornhauser, William. The Politics of Mass Society. *272 pp. 20 tables.*

●**Kroes, R.** Soldiers and Students. *A Study of Right- and Left-wing Students. 174 pp.*

Laidler, Harry W. History of Socialism. *Social-Economic Movements: An Historical and Comparative Survey of Socialism, Communism, Co-operation, Utopianism; and other Systems of Reform and Reconstruction. 992 pp.*

Lasswell, H. D. Analysis of Political Behaviour. *324 pp.*

Martin, David A. Pacifism: *an Historical and Sociological Study. 262 pp.*

Martin, Roderick. Sociology of Power. *About 272 pp.*

Myrdal, Gunnar. The Political Element in the Development of Economic Theory. *Translated from the German by Paul Streeten. 282 pp.*

Wilson, H. T. The American Ideology. *Science, Technology and Organization of Modes of Rationality. About 280 pp.*

Wootton, Graham. Workers, Unions and the State. *188 pp.*

CRIMINOLOGY

Ancel, Marc. Social Defence: *A Modern Approach to Criminal Problems. Foreword by Leon Radzinowicz. 240 pp.*

Cain, Maureen E. Society and the Policeman's Role. *326 pp.*

Cloward, Richard A., and **Ohlin, Lloyd E.** Delinquency and Opportunity: *A Theory of Delinquent Gangs. 248 pp.*

Downes, David M. The Delinquent Solution. *A Study in Subcultural Theory. 296 pp.*

Dunlop, A. B., and **McCabe, S.** Young Men in Detention Centres. *192 pp.*

Friedlander, Kate. The Psycho-Analytical Approach to Juvenile Delinquency: *Theory, Case Studies, Treatment. 320 pp.*

Glueck, Sheldon, and **Eleanor.** Family Environment and Delinquency. *With the statistical assistance of Rose W. Kneznek. 340 pp.*

Lopez-Rey, Manuel. Crime. *An Analytical Appraisal. 288 pp.*
Mannheim, Hermann. Comparative Criminology: *a Text Book. Two volumes. 442 pp. and 380 pp.*
Morris, Terence. The Criminal Area: *A Study in Social Ecology. Foreword by Hermann Mannheim. 232 pp. 25 tables. 4 maps.*
Rock, Paul. Making People Pay. *338 pp.*
●**Taylor, Ian, Walton, Paul,** and **Young, Jock.** The New Criminology. *For a Social Theory of Deviance. 325 pp.*
●**Taylor, Ian, Walton, Paul,** and **Young, Jock** (Eds). Critical Criminology. *268 pp.*

SOCIAL PSYCHOLOGY

Bagley, Christopher. The Social Psychology of the Epileptic Child. *320 pp.*
Barbu, Zevedei. Problems of Historical Psychology. *248 pp.*
Blackburn, Julian. Psychology and the Social Pattern. *184 pp.*
●**Brittan, Arthur.** Meanings and Situations. *224 pp.*
Carroll, J. Break-Out from the Crystal Palace. *200 pp.*
●**Fleming, C. M.** Adolescence: Its Social Psychology. *With an Introduction to recent findings from the fields of Anthropology, Physiology, Medicine, Psychometrics and Sociometry. 288 pp.*
● The Social Psychology of Education: *An Introduction and Guide to Its Study. 136 pp.*
●**Homans, George C.** The Human Group. *Foreword by Bernard DeVoto. Introduction by Robert K. Merton. 526 pp.*
● Social Behaviour: *its Elementary Forms. 416 pp.*
●**Klein, Josephine.** The Study of Groups. *226 pp. 31 figures. 5 tables.*
Linton, Ralph. The Cultural Background of Personality. *132 pp.*
●**Mayo, Elton.** The Social Problems of an Industrial Civilization. *With an appendix on the Political Problem. 180 pp.*
Ottaway, A. K. C. Learning Through Group Experience. *176 pp.*
Plummer, Ken. Sexual Stigma. *An Interactionist Account. 254 pp.*
●**Rose, Arnold M.** (Ed.) Human Behaviour and Social Processes: *an Interactionist Approach. Contributions by Arnold M. Rose, Ralph H. Turner, Anselm Strauss, Everett C. Hughes, E. Franklin Frazier, Howard S. Becker, et al. 696 pp.*
Smelser, Neil J. Theory of Collective Behaviour. *448 pp.*
Stephenson, Geoffrey M. The Development of Conscience. *128 pp.*
Young, Kimball. Handbook of Social Psychology. *658 pp. 16 figures. 10 tables.*

SOCIOLOGY OF THE FAMILY

Banks, J. A. Prosperity and Parenthood: *A Study of Family Planning among The Victorian Middle Classes. 262 pp.*
Bell, Colin R. Middle Class Families: *Social and Geographical Mobility. 224 pp.*

Burton, Lindy. Vulnerable Children. *272 pp.*
Gavron, Hannah. The Captive Wife: *Conflicts of Household Mothers.*
 190 pp.
George, Victor, and **Wilding, Paul.** Motherless Families. *248 pp.*
Klein, Josephine. Samples from English Cultures.
 1. Three Preliminary Studies and Aspects of Adult Life in England.
 447 pp.
 2. Child-Rearing Practices and Index. *247 pp.*
Klein, Viola. The Feminine Character. *History of an Ideology. 244 pp.*
McWhinnie, Alexina M. Adopted Children. *How They Grow Up. 304 pp.*
● **Morgan, D. H. J.** Social Theory and the Family. *About 320 pp.*
● **Myrdal, Alva,** and **Klein, Viola.** Women's Two Roles: *Home and Work.*
 238 pp. 27 tables.
Parsons, Talcott, and **Bales, Robert F.** Family: Socialization and Inter-
 action Process. *In collaboration with James Olds, Morris Zelditch and*
 Philip E. Slater. 456 pp. 50 figures and tables.

SOCIAL SERVICES

Bastide, Roger. The Sociology of Mental Disorder. *Translated from the*
 French by Jean McNeil. 260 pp.
Carlebach, Julius. Caring For Children in Trouble. *266 pp.*
George, Victor. Foster Care. *Theory and Practice. 234 pp.*
 Social Security: *Beveridge and After. 258 pp.*
George, V., and **Wilding, P.** Motherless Families. *248 pp.*
●**Goetschius, George W.** Working with Community Groups. *256 pp.*
Goetschius, George W., and **Tash, Joan.** Working with Unattached Youth.
 416 pp.
Hall, M. P., and **Howes, I. V.** The Church in Social Work. *A Study of*
 Moral Welfare Work undertaken by the Church of England. 320 pp.
Heywood, Jean S. Children in Care: *the Development of the Service for the*
 Deprived Child. 264 pp.
Hoenig, J., and **Hamilton, Marian W.** The De-Segregation of the Mentally
 Ill. *284 pp.*
Jones, Kathleen. Mental Health and Social Policy, 1845-1959. *264 pp.*
King, Roy D., Raynes, Norma V., and **Tizard, Jack.** Patterns of Residential
 Care. *356 pp.*
Leigh, John. Young People and Leisure. *256 pp.*
●**Mays, John.** (Ed.) Penelope Hall's Social Services of England and Wales.
 About 324 pp.
Morris, Mary. Voluntary Work and the Welfare State. *300 pp.*
Nokes, P. L. The Professional Task in Welfare Practice. *152 pp.*
Timms, Noel. Psychiatric Social Work in Great Britain (1939-1962).
 280 pp.
● Social Casework: *Principles and Practice. 256 pp.*
Young, A. F. Social Services in British Industry. *272 pp.*

SOCIOLOGY OF EDUCATION

Banks, Olive. Parity and Prestige in English Secondary Education: a Study in Educational Sociology. *272 pp.*

Bentwich, Joseph. Education in Israel. *224 pp. 8 pp. plates.*

●**Blyth, W. A. L.** English Primary Education. *A Sociological Description.*
  1. Schools. *232 pp.*
  2. Background. *168 pp.*

Collier, K. G. The Social Purposes of Education: *Personal and Social Values in Education. 268 pp.*

Dale, R. R., and **Griffith, S.** Down Stream: *Failure in the Grammar School. 108 pp.*

Evans, K. M. Sociometry and Education. *158 pp.*

●**Ford, Julienne.** Social Class and the Comprehensive School. *192 pp.*

Foster, P. J. Education and Social Change in Ghana. *336 pp. 3 maps.*

Fraser, W. R. Education and Society in Modern France. *150 pp.*

Grace, Gerald R. Role Conflict and the Teacher. *150 pp.*

Hans, Nicholas. New Trends in Education in the Eighteenth Century. *278 pp. 19 tables.*

● Comparative Education: *A Study of Educational Factors and Traditions. 360 pp.*

●**Hargreaves, David.** Interpersonal Relations and Education. *432 pp.*

● Social Relations in a Secondary School. *240 pp.*

Holmes, Brian. Problems in Education. *A Comparative Approach. 336 pp.*

King, Ronald. Values and Involvement in a Grammar School. *164 pp.*
  School Organization and Pupil Involvement. *A Study of Secondary Schools.*

●**Mannheim, Karl,** and **Stewart, W. A. C.** An Introduction to the Sociology of Education. *206 pp.*

Morris, Raymond N. The Sixth Form and College Entrance. *231 pp.*

●**Musgrove, F.** Youth and the Social Order. *176 pp.*

●**Ottaway, A. K. C.** Education and Society: An Introduction to the Sociology of Education. *With an Introduction by W. O. Lester Smith. 212 pp.*

Peers, Robert. Adult Education: *A Comparative Study. 398 pp.*

Pritchard, D. G. Education and the Handicapped: *1760 to 1960. 258 pp.*

Stratta, Erica. The Education of Borstal Boys. *A Study of their Educational Experiences prior to, and during, Borstal Training. 256 pp.*

Taylor, P. H., Reid, W. A., and **Holley, B. J.** The English Sixth Form. *A Case Study in Curriculum Research. 200 pp.*

SOCIOLOGY OF CULTURE

Eppel, E. M., and **M.** Adolescents and Morality: *A Study of some Moral Values and Dilemmas of Working Adolescents in the Context of a changing Climate of Opinion. Foreword by W. J. H. Sprott. 268 pp. 39 tables.*

●**Fromm, Erich.** The Fear of Freedom. *286 pp.*

● The Sane Society. *400 pp.*

Mannheim, Karl. Essays on the Sociology of Culture. *Edited by Ernst Mannheim in co-operation with Paul Kecskemeti. Editorial Note by Adolph Lowe. 280 pp.*

Weber, Alfred. Farewell to European History: *or The Conquest of Nihilism. Translated from the German by R. F. C. Hull. 224 pp.*

SOCIOLOGY OF RELIGION

Argyle, Michael and **Beit-Hallahmi, Benjamin.** The Social Psychology of Religion. *About 256 pp.*

Glasner, Peter E. The Sociology of Secularisation. *A Critique of a Concept. About 180 pp.*

Nelson, G. K. Spiritualism and Society. *313 pp.*

Stark, Werner. The Sociology of Religion. *A Study of Christendom.*
  Volume I. *Established Religion. 248 pp.*
  Volume II. *Sectarian Religion. 368 pp.*
  Volume III. *The Universal Church. 464 pp.*
  Volume IV. *Types of Religious Man. 352 pp.*
  Volume V. *Types of Religious Culture. 464 pp.*

Turner, B. S. Weber and Islam. *216 pp.*

Watt, W. Montgomery. Islam and the Integration of Society. *320 pp.*

SOCIOLOGY OF ART AND LITERATURE

Jarvie, Ian C. Towards a Sociology of the Cinema. *A Comparative Essay on the Structure and Functioning of a Major Entertainment Industry. 405 pp.*

Rust, Frances S. Dance in Society. *An Analysis of the Relationships between the Social Dance and Society in England from the Middle Ages to the Present Day. 256 pp. 8 pp. of plates.*

Schücking, L. L. The Sociology of Literary Taste. *112 pp.*

Wolff, Janet. Hermeneutic Philosophy and the Sociology of Art. *150 pp.*

SOCIOLOGY OF KNOWLEDGE

Diesing, P. Patterns of Discovery in the Social Sciences. *262 pp.*

● **Douglas, J. D.** (Ed.) Understanding Everyday Life. *370 pp.*

● **Hamilton, P.** Knowledge and Social Structure. *174 pp.*

Jarvie, I. C. Concepts and Society. *232 pp.*

Mannheim, Karl. Essays on the Sociology of Knowledge. *Edited by Paul Kecskemeti. Editorial Note by Adolph Lowe. 353 pp.*

Remmling, Gunter W. The Sociology cf Karl Mannheim. *With a Bibliographical Guide to the Sociology of Knowledge, Ideological Analysis, and Social Planning. 255 pp.*

Remmling, Gunter W. (Ed.) Towards the Sociology of Knowledge. *Origin and Development of a Sociological Thought Style. 463 pp.*

Stark, Werner. The Sociology of Knowledge: *An Essay in Aid of a Deeper Understanding of the History of Ideas. 384 pp.*

URBAN SOCIOLOGY

Ashworth, William. The Genesis of Modern British Town Planning: *A Study in Economic and Social History of the Nineteenth and Twentieth Centuries. 288 pp.*

Cullingworth, J. B. Housing Needs and Planning Policy: *A Restatement of the Problems of Housing Need and 'Overspill' in England and Wales. 232 pp. 44 tables. 8 maps.*

Dickinson, Robert E. City and Region: *A Geographical Interpretation 608 pp. 125 figures.*

The West European City: *A Geographical Interpretation. 600 pp. 129 maps. 29 plates.*

● The City Region in Western Europe. *320 pp. Maps.*

Humphreys, Alexander J. New Dubliners: *Urbanization and the Irish Family. Foreword by George C. Homans. 304 pp.*

Jackson, Brian. Working Class Community: *Some General Notions raised by a Series of Studies in Northern England. 192 pp.*

Jennings, Hilda. Societies in the Making: *a Study of Development and Redevelopment within a County Borough. Foreword by D. A. Clark. 286 pp.*

●**Mann, P. H.** An Approach to Urban Sociology. *240 pp.*

Morris, R. N., and **Mogey, J.** The Sociology of Housing. *Studies at Berinsfield. 232 pp. 4 pp. plates.*

Rosser, C., and **Harris, C.** The Family and Social Change. *A Study of Family and Kinship in a South Wales Town. 352 pp. 8 maps.*

●**Stacey, Margaret, Batsone, Eric, Bell, Colin,** and **Thurcott, Anne.** Power, Persistence and Change. *A Second Study of Banbury. 196 pp.*

RURAL SOCIOLOGY

Haswell, M. R. The Economics of Development in Village India. *120 pp.*

Littlejohn, James. Westrigg: *the Sociology of a Cheviot Parish. 172 pp. 5 figures.*

Mayer, Adrian C. Peasants in the Pacific. *A Study of Fiji Indian Rural Society. 248 pp. 20 plates.*

Williams, W. M. The Sociology of an English Village: *Gosforth. 272 pp. 12 figures. 13 tables.*

SOCIOLOGY OF INDUSTRY AND DISTRIBUTION

Anderson, Nels. Work and Leisure. *280 pp.*

●**Blau, Peter M.**, and **Scott, W. Richard.** Formal Organizations: *a Comparative approach. Introduction and Additional Bibliography by J. H. Smith. 326 pp.*

Dunkerley, David. The Foreman. *Aspects of Task and Structure. 192 pp.*

Eldridge, J. E. T. Industrial Disputes. *Essays in the Sociology of Industrial Relations. 288 pp.*

Hetzler, Stanley. Applied Measures for Promoting Technological Growth. *352 pp.*

Technological Growth and Social Change. *Achieving Modernization. 269 pp.*

Hollowell, Peter G. The Lorry Driver. *272 pp.*

●**Oxaal, I., Barnett, T.,** and **Booth, D.** (Eds). Beyond the Sociology of Development. *Economy and Society in Latin America and Africa. 295 pp.*

Smelser, Neil J. Social Change in the Industrial Revolution: *An Application of Theory to the Lancashire Cotton Industry, 1770–1840. 468 pp. 12 figures. 14 tables.*

ANTHROPOLOGY

Ammar, Hamed. Growing up in an Egyptian Village: *Silwa, Province of Aswan. 336 pp.*

Brandel-Syrier, Mia. Reeftown Elite. *A Study of Social Mobility in a Modern African Community on the Reef. 376 pp.*

Dickie-Clark, H. F. The Marginal Situation. *A Sociological Study of a Coloured Group. 236 pp.*

Dube, S. C. Indian Village. *Foreword by Morris Edward Opler. 276 pp. 4 plates.*

India's Changing Villages: *Human Factors in Community Development. 260 pp. 8 plates. 1 map.*

Firth, Raymond. Malay Fishermen. *Their Peasant Economy. 420 pp. 17 pp. plates.*

Gulliver, P. H. Social Control in an African Society: a Study of the Arusha, Agricultural Masai of Northern Tanganyika. *320 pp. 8 plates. 10 figures.*

Family Herds. *288 pp.*

Ishwaran, K. Tradition and Economy in Village India: *An Interactionist Approach.*

Foreword by Conrad Arensburg. 176 pp.

Jarvie, Ian C. The Revolution in Anthropology. *268 pp.*

Little, Kenneth L. Mende of Sierra Leone. *308 pp. and folder.*

Negroes in Britain. *With a New Introduction and Contemporary Study by Leonard Bloom. 320 pp.*

Lowie, Robert H. Social Organization. *494 pp.*

Mayer, A. C. Peasants in the Pacific. *A Study of Fiji Indian Rural Society. 248 pp.*

Meer, Fatima. Race and Suicide in South Africa. *325 pp.*

Smith, Raymond T. The Negro Family in British Guiana: *Family Structure and Social Status in the Villages. With a Foreword by Meyer Fortes. 314 pp. 8 plates. 1 figure. 4 maps.*
Smooha, Sammy. Israel: Pluralism and Conflict. *About 320 pp.*

SOCIOLOGY AND PHILOSOPHY

Barnsley, John H. The Social Reality of Ethics. *A Comparative Analysis of Moral Codes. 448 pp.*
Diesing, Paul. Patterns of Discovery in the Social Sciences. *362 pp.*
●**Douglas, Jack D.** (Ed.) Understanding Everyday Life. *Toward the Reconstruction of Sociological Knowledge. Contributions by Alan F. Blum. Aaron W. Cicourel, Norman K. Denzin, Jack D. Douglas, John Heeren, Peter McHugh, Peter K. Manning, Melvin Power, Matthew Speier, Roy Turner, D. Lawrence Wieder, Thomas P. Wilson and Don H. Zimmerman. 370 pp.*
Gorman, Robert A. The Dual Vision. *Alfred Schutz and the Myth of Phenomenological Social Science. About 300 pp.*
Jarvie, Ian C. Concepts and Society. *216 pp.*
●**Pelz, Werner.** The Scope of Understanding in Sociology. *Towards a more radical reorientation in the social humanistic sciences. 283 pp.*
Roche, Maurice. Phenomenology, Language and the Social Sciences. *371 pp.*
Sahay, Arun. Sociological Analysis. *212 pp.*
Sklair, Leslie. The Sociology of Progress. *320 pp.*
Slater, P. Origin and Significance of the Frankfurt School. *A Marxist Perspective. About 192 pp.*
Smart, Barry. Sociology, Phenomenology and Marxian Analysis. *A Critical Discussion of the Theory and Practice of a Science of Society. 220 pp.*

International Library of Anthropology

General Editor Adam Kuper

Ahmed, A. S. Millenium and Charisma Among Pathans. *A Critical Essay in Social Anthropology. 192 pp.*
Brown, Paula. The Chimbu. *A Study of Change in the New Guinea Highlands. 151 pp.*
Gudeman, Stephen. Relationships, Residence and the Individual. *A Rural Panamanian Community. 288 pp. 11 Plates, 5 Figures, 2 Maps, 10 Tables.*
Hamnett, Ian. Chieftainship and Legitimacy. *An Anthropological Study of Executive Law in Lesotho. 163 pp.*
Hanson, F. Allan. Meaning in Culture. *127 pp.*
Lloyd, P. C. Power and Independence. *Urban Africans' Perception of Social Inequality. 264 pp.*

Pettigrew, Joyce. Robber Noblemen. *A Study of the Political System of the Sikh Jats. 284 pp.*
Street, Brian V. The Savage in Literature. *Representations of 'Primitive' Society in English Fiction, 1858–1920. 207 pp.*
Van Den Berghe, Pierre L. Power and Privilege at an African University. *278 pp.*

International Library of Social Policy

General Editor Kathleen Jones

Bayley, M. Mental Handicap and Community Care. *426 pp.*
Bottoms, A. E., and **McClean, J. D.** Defendants in the Criminal Process. *284 pp.*
Butler, J. R. Family Doctors and Public Policy. *208 pp.*
Davies, Martin. Prisoners of Society. *Attitudes and Aftercare. 204 pp.*
Gittus, Elizabeth. Flats, Families and the Under-Fives. *285 pp.*
Holman, Robert. Trading in Children. *A Study of Private Fostering. 355 pp.*
Jones, Howard, and **Cornes, Paul.** Open Prisons. *About 248 pp.*
Jones, Kathleen. History of the Mental Health Service. *428 pp.*
Jones, Kathleen, with **Brown, John, Cunningham, W. J., Roberts, Julian,** and **Williams, Peter.** Opening the Door. *A Study of New Policies for the Mentally Handicapped. 278 pp.*
Karn, Valerie. Retiring to the Seaside. *About 280 pp. 2 maps. Numerous tables.*
Thomas, J. E. The English Prison Officer since 1850: *A Study in Conflict. 258 pp.*
Walton, R. G. Women in Social Work. *303 pp.*
Woodward, J. To Do the Sick No Harm. *A Study of the British Voluntary Hospital System to 1875. 221 pp.*

International Library of Welfare and Philosophy

General Editors Noel Timms and David Watson

● **Plant, Raymond.** Community and Ideology. *104 pp.*
● **McDermott, F. E.** (Ed.) Self-Determination in Social Work. *A Collection of Essays on Self-determination and Related Concepts by Philosophers and Social Work Theorists. Contributors: F. P. Biestek, S. Bernstein, A. Keith-Lucas, D. Sayer, H. H. Perelman, C. Whittington, R. F. Stalley, F. E. McDermott, I. Berlin, H. J. McCloskey, H. L. A. Hart, J. Wilson, A. I. Melden, S. I. Benn. 254 pp.*
Ragg, Nicholas M. People Not Cases. *A Philosophical Approach to Social Work. About 250 pp.*

● **Timms, Noel,** and **Watson, David** (Eds). Talking About Welfare. *Readings in Philosophy and Social Policy. Contributors: T. H. Marshall, R. B. Brandt, G. H. von Wright, K. Nielsen, M. Cranston, R. M. Titmuss, R. S. Downie, E. Telfer, D. Donnison, J. Benson, P. Leonard, A. Keith-Lucas, D. Walsh, I. T. Ramsey. 320 pp.*

Primary Socialization, Language and Education

General Editor Basil Bernstein

Adlam, Diana S., *with the assistance of Geoffrey Turner and Lesley Lineker.* Code in Context. *About 272 pp.*

Bernstein, Basil. Class, Codes and Control. *3 volumes.*
   1. *Theoretical Studies Towards a Sociology of Language. 254 pp.*
   2. *Applied Studies Towards a Sociology of Language. 377 pp.*
● 3. *Towards a Theory of Educatiomal Transmission. 167 pp.*

Brandis, W., and **Bernstein, B.** Selection and Control. *176 pp.*

Brandis, Walter, and **Henderson, Dorothy.** Social Class, Language and Communication. *288 pp.*

Cook-Gumperz, Jenny. Social Control and Socialization. *A Study of Class Differences in the Language of Maternal Control. 290 pp.*

●**Gahagan, D. M.,** and **G. A.** Talk Reform. *Exploration in Language for Infant School Children. 160 pp.*

Hawkins, P. R. Social Class, the Nominal Group and Verbal Strategies. *About 220 pp.*

Robinson, W. P., and **Rackstraw, Susan D. A.** A Question of Answers. *2 volumes. 192 pp. and 180 pp.*

Turner, Geoffrey J., and **Mohan, Bernard A.** A Linguistic Description and Computer Programme for Children's Speech. *208 pp.*

Reports of the Institute of Community Studies

●**Cartwright, Ann.** Parents and Family Planning Services. *306 pp.*
   Patients and their Doctors. *A Study of General Practice. 304 pp.*

Dench, Geoff. Maltese in London. *A Case-study in the Erosion of Ethnic Consciousness. 302 pp.*

●**Jackson, Brian.** Streaming: *an Education System in Miniature. 168 pp.*

Jackson, Brian, and **Marsden, Dennis.** Education and the Working Class: *Some General Themes raised by a Study of 88 Working-class Children in a Northern Industrial City. 268 pp. 2 folders.*

Marris, Peter. The Experience of Higher Education. *232 pp. 27 tables.*
   Loss and Change. *192 pp.*

Marris, Peter, and **Rein, Martin.** Dilemmas of Social Reform. *Poverty and Community Action in the United States. 256 pp.*

Marris, Peter, and Somerset, Anthony. African Businessmen. *A Study of Entrepreneurship and Development in Kenya. 256 pp.*
Mills, Richard. Young Outsiders: *a Study in Alternative Communities. 216 pp.*
Runciman, W. G. Relative Deprivation and Social Justice. *A Study of Attitudes to Social Inequality in Twentieth-Century England. 352 pp.*
Willmott, Peter. Adolescent Boys in East London. *230 pp.*
Willmott, Peter, and Young, Michael. Family and Class in a London Suburb. *202 pp. 47 tables.*
Young, Michael. Innovation and Research in Education. *192 pp.*
●Young, Michael, and McGeeney, Patrick. Learning Begins at Home. *A Study of a Junior School and its Parents. 128 pp.*
Young, Michael, and Willmott, Peter. Family and Kinship in East London. *Foreword by Richard M. Titmuss. 252 pp. 39 tables.*
The Symmetrical Family. *410 pp.*

Reports of the Institute for Social Studies in Medical Care

Cartwright, Ann, Hockey, Lisbeth, and Anderson, John L. Life Before Death. *310 pp.*
Dunnell, Karen, and Cartwright, Ann. Medicine Takers, Prescribers and Hoarders. *190 pp.*

Medicine, Illness and Society

General Editor W. M. Williams

Robinson, David. The Process of Becoming Ill. *142 pp.*
Stacey, Margaret, *et al.* Hospitals, Children and Their Families. *The Report of a Pilot Study. 202 pp.*
Stimson, G. V., and Webb, B. Going to See the Doctor. *The Consultation Process in General Practice. 155 pp.*

Monographs in Social Theory

General Editor Arthur Brittan

●Barnes, B. Scientific Knowledge and Sociological Theory. *192 pp.*
Bauman, Zygmunt. Culture as Praxis. *204 pp.*
●Dixon, Keith. Sociological Theory. *Pretence and Possibility. 142 pp.*
Meltzer, B. N., Petras, J. W., and Reynolds, L. T. Symbolic Interactionism. *Genesis, Varieties and Criticisms. 144 pp.*
●Smith, Anthony D. The Concept of Social Change. *A Critique of the Functionalist Theory of Social Change. 208 pp.*

Routledge Social Science Journals

The British Journal of Sociology. *Editor – Angus Stewart; Associate Editor – Leslie Sklair. Vol. 1, No. 1 – March 1950 and Quarterly. Roy. 8vo. All back issues available. An international journal publishing original papers in the field of sociology and related areas.*

Community Work. *Edited by David Jones and Marjorie Mayo. 1973. Published annually.*

Economy and Society. *Vol. 1, No. 1. February 1972 and Quarterly. Metric Roy. 8vo. A journal for all social scientists covering sociology, philosophy, anthropology, economics and history. All back numbers available.*

Religion. Journal of Religion and Religions. *Chairman of Editorial Board, Ninian Smart. Vol. 1, No. 1, Spring 1971. A journal with an interdisciplinary approach to the study of the phenomena of religion. All back numbers available.*

Year Book of Social Policy in Britain, The. *Edited by Kathleen Jones. 1971. Published annually.*

Social and Psychological Aspects of Medical Practice

Editor   Trevor Silverstone

Lader, Malcolm. Psychophysiology of Mental Illness. *280 pp.*

● **Silverstone, Trevor,** and **Turner, Paul.** Drug Treatment in Psychiatry. *232 pp.*

Printed in Great Britain by Unwin Brothers Limited
The Gresham Press Old Woking Surrey
A member of the Staples Printing Group